Contesting Publics

Anthropology, Culture and Society

Series Editors:
Professor Vered Amit, Concordia University
and
Dr Jon P. Mitchell, University of Sussex

Recent titles:

CONTESTING PUBLICS
Feminism, Activism, Ethnography

Lynne Phillips and Sally Cole
with Marie-Eve Carrier-Moisan and Erica Lagalisse

PlutoPress
www.plutobooks.com

First published 2013 by Pluto Press
345 Archway Road, London N6 5AA

www.plutobooks.com

Distributed in the United States of America exclusively by
Palgrave Macmillan, a division of St. Martin's Press LLC,
175 Fifth Avenue, New York, NY 10010

British Library Cataloguing in Publication Data
A catalogue record for this book is available from the British Library

ISBN   978 0 7453 3284 0   Hardback
ISBN   978 1 8496 4812 7   PDF eBook

Library of Congress Cataloging in Publication Data applied for

This book is printed on paper suitable for recycling and made from fully managed
and sustained forest sources. Logging, pulping and manufacturing processes are
expected to conform to the environmental standards of the country of origin.

10   9   8   7   6   5   4   3   2   1

Designed and produced for Pluto Press by Chase Publishing Services Ltd
Typeset from disk by Stanford DTP Services, Northampton, England
Simultaneously printed digitally by CPI Antony Rowe, Chippenham, UK and
Edwards Bros in the United States of America

Contents

Illustrations

Acknowledgements

We would like to thank women and men working for social change every day in diverse ways and challenging contexts across Latin America. Maria Rosa Achundia, Andrea Aguirre, Faviola Arias, Auxiliadora Dias Cabral, Mary Cabrera, Maria de Conceição Dantas de Moura, Isolde Dantas, Liliana Duran, Nalu Faria, Gladys Fuentes, Luz Haro, Maria Hernandez, Gioconda Herrera, Emma Illescas, Magdalena León, Neylar Lins, Rosa Lopez, Monica Munõz, Suely de Oliveira, Soldedad Puente, Junia Puglia, Rocio Rosero, Lucia Salamea, Neli Shewan, Analba Brazão Teixeira, Silvia Vega and Marina Vera especially gave us their time, shared their passion, energy and commitment and led us to the new theoretical insights we present in *Contesting Publics*. It has been an inspiring journey, one that renewed our own hopes for the future. We would like to thank the Social Sciences and Humanities Research Council of Canada for funding. We also warmly thank Pluto Press's anonymous readers who gave such strong support for the project and its re-visiting of old debates on the 'public' and the 'private', its questioning of the meaning of 'civil society' and its effort to clear theoretical space for imagining alternative futures.

LP and SC, July 2012

Preface: Contesting Publics

Sally Cole and Lynne Phillips

Between 2006 and 2009 we interviewed feminist activists working in a variety of transnational networks and national democracy-building projects in Latin America. We started by interviewing feminist officers of the United Nations Development Fund for Women, UNIFEM (now UN Women) in Brazil and Ecuador. Despite differences in language, colonial history and physical size between these countries, we found the comparison fruitful as both countries are tied to the 'machinery' of the UN (Phillips and Cole 2009), yet both are also experimenting with new modes of participatory democracy in which women's movements are actively engaged. We 'followed' (Marcus 1998; Tsing 2005) the roots and routes of feminists' activities in both countries and found ourselves entering increasingly diverse spaces and scales of political action. We interviewed activists working in the national state agencies that are conceived as part of democracy-building in both Ecuador and Brazil: CONAMU (Consejo Nacional de las Mujeres, National Council of Women) in Ecuador and SPM (Secretaria Especial de Políticas para as Mulheres, Special Secretariat for Policy for Women) in Brazil. And, in both countries, we interviewed activists in unions, in transnational networks and in small non-governmental organizations (NGOs) in rural settings.

We saw that activists at all scales are continually making decisions about when and how to bring women's concerns to public arenas – a process we describe as a feminist 'politics of presence' (see Phillips and Cole 2009; see also A. Phillips 1996; Pinto 2007). We also saw Latin American feminists creating new public spaces such as the regional network, REMTE (Red Latinoamericana Mujeres Transformando la Economía/Latin American Network of Women Transforming the Economy). And, we saw them producing what we call *publics-in-formation* such as Mujeres de Frente (Women's Front) working with women in prison in Ecuador. The excitement of creating new feminist spaces through public activism was palpable in Latin America. For us, this energy contrasted sharply with our experience in Canada – in our classrooms, where our own students typically disclaim any association with feminism, and in broader public discourse where we find feminism largely absent. However, in Ecuador and Brazil, we also became aware of how gender inequalities not only persisted but were being inscribed in new ways – something we also see in Canada (see, for example, Beaman 2012). Specifically, we found a significant relationship between the *meaning* of the public and the ways in which some matters – the 'private' – were left outside of public parameters. We began to track the differential access some feminists (and some women who may not define themselves as feminist) have to spaces of power. *Contesting Publics: Feminism, Activism, Ethnography* addresses this contradiction of dramatic public changes in Latin America and yet continuing re-inscriptions of gender inequalities in the new political spaces that are being produced despite (and at times through) feminist activism.

Feminists in Latin America are bringing to public attention issues such as security and women's rights in contexts of increasing violence and the hypersexualization and commodification of women's bodies through global consumerism and the beauty industry. They are contesting the increasing inequality, poverty and privatization that have accompanied neoliberal globalization. And they are mobilizing in support of projects for food sovereignty, pluri-nationalism and fairer trade. The women activists we met took us into a variety of publics. *Their* point of view on – and their experience in – these political spaces have shaped our views on publics. Latin American feminists' theorizing of gender equality challenged and reframed ours. For, like Fregoso and Bejarano (2010: 4–5), we engage with Latin America as a 'place where theory is produced' rather than as a 'field of study'. Latin America has been a place of collective thinking and praxis for social change for us; it has never been only a 'field site'. Thus, in *Contesting Publics* the voices of Latin American activists 'speak nearby' (Chen 1992; Trinh 1992: 96) ours.

As our research unfolded, we observed the gap between some public feminist activists and women of the *base* (grassroots) but we began to conceive of it less as a divide between women than as a reflection of the continuing salience and dynamic production of 'common-sense' ideas about public and private. And, as we began to theorize and work with our concept of publics, we soon saw its relationship to a set of more conventionally recognized discourses: the debates on the Habermasian public sphere; the deliberations on participatory democracy in Latin America and feminism's role in building new democracies; and the public–private dichotomy in feminist theoretical discussions. We found our work informed by, yet in tension with, the ways in which the public is discussed in these different discourses. We began to appreciate that one of the main contributions of our idea of publics was its foundation in ethnographic observation and research. In *Contesting Publics*, we explore this trajectory of thinking about publics in chapter 1, 'Towards an Ethnography of Publics'.

As we were developing our ideas about publics as contested and 'contesting', we found Melissa Wright's (2010) term 'public:private women' provocative – 'good to think with' (Lévi-Strauss 1962). She writes about the Mujeres de Negro (Women in Black) activists who organize public protest against the Mexican government's failure to respond to the torture and murders of women that have escalated since the 1990s. Dressed in black clothing to signify mourning, domesticity and modesty, Mujeres de Negro deliberately place the 'private woman' in public. They perform the role of mothers whose reason to enter public space is the sanctioned maternal one that they are 'looking for their children'. As Wright puts it, they 'stand in the public sphere to represent the private sphere'. Their attempt to humanize the victims as 'daughters' calls attention to the murders. Paradoxically, however, it also re-inscribes the victims as 'matter out of place' (Douglas 1966). For, the victims are not only 'family girls'; they are also students, workers, prostitutes and migrants, and as such they are also 'public women'. In a cultural context where women's 'proper' place continues to be in the home, the discourse on the public woman as 'whore' is readily at hand and is quickly mobilized by both media and the state, effectively to blame victims for their own murders.

We think of the women who organized Toronto's recent SlutWalk, for example, also as public:private women. On 3 April 2011, women university students organized SlutWalk in response to remarks made by a Toronto police officer who had been invited to speak at York University Law School about safety on campus. The meeting was part of the university's efforts to encourage students to report cases of sexual assault. Instead, the officer had shocked women students by advising them to 'not dress like a slut' in order to avoid assault. The officer turned the discussion away from the problem of violence against women and instead he took the opportunity to reinforce dominant sexual norms by dividing women – according to their dress – into respectable women who are deserving of police protection and rape-able women who apparently incite violence by their dress. Enraged, the students launched SlutWalk; more than

2,000 people marched on the streets of Toronto (Church 2011). SlutWalk sought to 'refunction' (Taussig 1992 [1989]: 49) the whore discourse and urged women to reclaim control over their sexuality: 'It's my hot body. I do what I want', placards read. SlutWalk has since 'gone viral' and similar marches have been organized around the globe (www.slutwalktoronto.com). Meanwhile, social media also empowered some men who moved quickly to discipline and re-sexualize women in their terms by posting comments such as 'on the bright side, very few of these women are in any danger of getting raped... i guess that's one benefit of being ugly ...'.[1]

In their decision to politicize the private – in their refusal to 'bracket the private' (Warner 2002) – 'public:private women' inhabit public space in new ways, thereby contesting publics and producing possibilities for the development of more egalitarian publics. In our view, then, feminisms' publics are a contradictory terrain shared by both feminist activists (including ourselves), who may bracket our private lives in diverse ways, and women of the *base* (grassroots), whose private lives we see as increasingly monitored and made public in contexts of globalization and social and economic inequality.

Understanding the meanings of publics and privates has guided our research interests in anthropology since the beginning of our careers. In the current context, we are finding that the research of many graduate students and emerging scholars is also located on the terrain of the public:private as they explore topics such as: women and the Pill; women and poverty; food activism; the public world of childhood where child labour is an economic necessity; the public–private lives of youth on the internet; and the queering of public spaces. To reflect this emergent scholarship, in 2009 we invited two new scholars, Marie-Eve Carrier-Moisan and Erica Lagalisse to our discussion. The resulting intergenerational dialogue is reflected in the different tones and styles of writing that are an important feature of *Contesting Publics*. Cole and Phillips were trained in the early 1980s, when feminism engaged with such topics as 'the household' and 'women and the state'. Here, they return to apply a feminist lens to these social spaces in the twenty-first century. Carrier-Moisan and Lagalisse are young scholars who have been trained in what many call a post-feminist era, when feminists are seen as '*las viejas*', when the question of the public and the private is seen as long past being of interest, and when 'patriarchy' and 'women's oppression' are seen as master narratives that need not be revisited. Against this tide, Carrier-Moisan and Lagalisse describe how their experiences and observations of gender inequality during their ethnographic field research led them to reconsider the insights of a feminist analysis that remembers the private. In so doing, their research helps us move into new analytical terrain where old master narratives come into view again for re-consideration. Cross-generational dialogue among feminists is rare but it is essential to the creation of new social spaces that might actively work against the reproduction of gender and other inequalities. In chapter 6, 'A Pedagogical Conversation', *Contesting Publics* concludes with thoughts on what we have learned from this dialogue and the implications for public scholarship.

Contesting Publics documents how feminist efforts, on the one hand, produce new spaces for women's participation and, on the other, may produce new silences, exclusions and re-inscriptions of inequalities. The ethnographic cases presented here, taken together with the experiences of Latin American feminist activists, speak to the larger theoretical question: what is the meaning of 'public' in contemporary Latin America? Despite state and social movement discourses of 'participation', it remains difficult for feminist proposals to be 'heard' and to be taken up as public issues. Many of women's concerns continue to be viewed as private and as secondary; social change, it is presumed, will simply 'trickle down' to positively affect women's lives. In this book, we argue against these assumptions. We make the claim that gender inequality persists and is being inscribed in the new public spaces of democratization because the everyday gendered concerns of women and men in households and other 'mixed' (women and men) spaces are bracketed as private concerns and remain off public political agendas.

The research presented in *Contesting Publics* demonstrates that the tensions and diversity among public feminist and democracy-building agendas are the result of bracketing private matters differently in different ethnographic contexts. What is considered private is found to shift with context and to contribute to the persistence of class and race inequalities alongside gender inequalities. We find that publics are seldom homogeneous; they involve different opinions and sensibilities – including *ideas* about difference – which form the basis of debate, deliberation and collaboration. Publics are mobile, contingent and contested – and the collaborations and alliances associated with them are contradictory and awkward. We hope readers see in this volume an opportunity: to recognize the diverse and contradictory ways feminism enters and creates publics; to engage critically with other ways that public space is being represented; and to imagine and invent publics for alternative feminist futures.

1
Towards an Ethnography of Publics

Sally Cole and Lynne Phillips

What is meant by the term 'public'? What are 'publics'? Who do they include (and exclude)? How should we engage them? In this introductory chapter, we explore the meaning of public in light of three conceptual frames: the public as a sphere; the public as a scale; and the public as a cultural space. We then highlight the extent to which the market and the state may re-inscribe publics, and we document the various ways in which publics are being created, governed and contested in Latin America and beyond.

We undertake this review to develop theoretical clarity on publics. In a time of constant talk of the impact of privatization on the public good, appropriate public behaviour and assaults on the public domain, the meaning of the public is often ambiguous and confusing. Our approach in *Contesting Publics: Feminism, Activism, Ethnography* is to engage in what Ratna Kapur (2012) calls 'space-clearing' – analysis that seeks to open up space for new and 'eclectic' political possibilities. In this book, we clear analytical space by examining publics, and what we call 'publics-in-formation', as contests over meaning. Our hope is that this analytical frame may enable – may bring to light – new openings, new meanings, new political possibilities for citizen-scholars, students and activists to reflect on and initiate social change.

In this chapter we make three arguments. First, we propose that the public be recognized as a shifting domain of power that reflects and produces inequalities and that these are inequalities in which social scientists are also embedded. Second, we claim that the *public* is contingent on the *private* and that this co-constitutive relationship shifts and is critical to analyse in context. We use the term 'public:private' (Wright 2010) to reflect that contingent relationship. Third, we argue and illustrate in this volume that investigating publics ethnographically – as sites for theorizing action – both brings new, emergent and overlooked publics into view and offers the opportunity to re-examine conventional publics through

1

new lenses. Our purpose here is to explore publics in ways that illustrate their critical importance for equality projects that may contribute to the development of alternative feminist visions for the future.

PUBLICS IN PERSPECTIVE

What is a public and what are its parameters? This may seem like an old question. For example, early feminist debates focused on the public but largely defined it negatively, as a space where politics, economics and men dominate – that is, as all that is not private, familial or domestic (Fraser 1990).[1] This view, however, does not help us to address the persistent *reformulation* and the *varied* ways in which public:private relations are reworked, recruited and deployed over time and space. And this is our concern in *Contesting Publics*.

The Public Sphere

Critical debates in democratic theory offer a useful starting point to theorize publics. In this literature, the public historically has been seen in its relationship to the nation-state through Jürgen Habermas's concept of the *public sphere*. The public sphere, as Habermas sees it, is the political space within which citizens of liberal nations deliberate issues of 'common concern' (1989 [1962]: 36). In the eighteenth century, with the shift in authority of the church and the state in Western Europe, the public sphere was viewed as essential for challenging and monitoring the monopoly of these authorities over the interpretation of 'matters of concern'. The idea of the public sphere coincided historically with the emergence of independent spaces of communication, such as newspapers and coffee houses – and a reading public – which Habermas views as essential for informed public debate. For Habermas, the public sphere today has essentially been annihilated, developing instead – with the dramatic expansion of capitalism and corporate media – 'into an arena infiltrated by power' (1992: 437).

Habermas's conception of the public sphere as a unitary forum for reasoned deliberation has fuelled debate within democratic theory. Critics argue that *if* Habermas's public sphere exists somewhere, it is the product of an elite prerogative to exclude certain populations and points of view (see Benhabib, Eley, Fraser, Ryan and Warner in Calhoun 1992). Informed also by feminist and queer perspectives, critique has generated interest in exploring the existence of not just one public but multiple publics competing for a hearing on uneven ground that is *always* 'infiltrated by power'.

In order to construct the public sphere as unitary, Habermas 'brackets' inequalities and private matters (Fraser 1990; Warner 2002). This creates exclusions. Those excluded – the politically, economically and sexually disenfranchised – may form their own counterpublics or what John Guidry (2003) calls 'popular publics'. These are alternative publics that work to redraw the boundaries of dominant public spheres, a perspective that highlights the potential dynamic interplay among popular or alternative publics. For example, Nancy Fraser (1990) explains how – through the sustained efforts of feminist movements – issues can move out of what she calls a 'subaltern counterpublic' to become a recognized public matter of concern, as has happened in the case of the issue of violence against women. But, clearly, matters of concern can also travel in the reverse direction, as when we hear public appeals to sanctify the nuclear family – leading Wendy Brown (2009) and others to refer to the 'holy' family.

Thus, we cannot assume in advance that counterpublics denote particular political positions. The extent to which counterpublics are a kind of mirror image of the dominant public sphere or have 'their own dynamics of emergence and peculiar forms of internal life' (Eley 1992: 304) is a matter for ethnographic investigation. Moreover, some spaces blur the boundaries between the two, as is the case for what Susan Dewey (2009) calls the 'parallel public sphere'. Dewey analyses the national advice column in a women's magazine in India. She argues that, when a dominant, masculinist public sphere views conjugal abuse as 'domestic' – as 'private' – and presents no options for women to present grievances, a parallel public sphere – such as the national advice column – assists individual women to navigate the power which shapes their lives (2009: 137). Such a parallel public does not threaten to change the dominant public sphere; indeed, as long as women seek individual solutions to their grievances, in some ways it permits the reproduction and maintenance of the dominant public. Nonetheless, this parallel public should not be overlooked as a critical site for public discussion about female sexuality and violence against women. As Kapur (2012), writing on the Pink Chaddis (panties) campaign in India reminds us, there is always the possibility that alternative publics are in the making (see also Enke 2007).

Thus, to conceive of the public as a uniform, stable, politically consensual 'sphere' is not only theoretically inadequate but also politically misleading. Theorizing the public as a dynamic domain of power requires taking into account the inequalities that underlie any construction of a public consensus or a public good. In *Contesting Publics* the reader will find this critical position evident in the ways the ethnographic chapters of this volume engage with notions of the public. It is a position that demands reflexivity on the part of researchers about *their* own location within dynamic and conflicting publics, and how that location complicates a public engagement or sensibility. This critical perspective challenges the idea that the public is somehow 'out there' – a bounded object of study with a discernible point of entry by a neutral observer.

Scales of the Public

The idea of multiple publics, counterpublics, popular publics or parallel publics sets the stage for recognizing *scales* of publics and for de-linking publics from the nation-state (as Habermas saw it), a nation-state that has in any case been considerably realigned in the current phase of globalization. Transnational processes including social media have made it possible to create new border-crossing publics – such as the alter-globalization movements, the 'Arab Spring' or the 'Occupy' movements – often with dramatic political effects. For many scholars, the new transnational spaces produced through the intensification of international migration and the rapid spread of electronic communication systems, require a reappraisal of the public sphere if it is, as Fraser (2007: 24) puts it, to 'keep faith with its original promise to contribute to struggles for emancipation' (see also Lara 2003; McLaughlin 2004). It has not taken long at all for the concept of 'transnational publics' to be explored for its political potential. The related literature on transnational feminism represents heterogeneous and divergent points of view (see, for example, Dufour et al. 2010; Eschle 2001; Ferree and Tripp 2006; Grewal 2005; Grewal and Kaplan 1994; Hawkesworth 2006; Hertel 2006; Moghadam 2005; Thayer 2010).

It is now well documented that the global changes associated with transnationalism have permitted feminisms to travel – to translate and to be translated – in new ways, horizontally and vertically (Davis 2007; Gal 2003; Phillips and Cole 2009; Walby 2002). This literature clarifies that, while feminism is by no means only a movement from the 'north' (there are indeed many feminisms), transnational feminisms remain fraught with contradictions. Moreover, new transnational public spaces are not celebratory for everyone. Nicole Doerr (2007), in a study of deliberative decision-making in the transnational space of the European Social Forum, cautions that the development of what activist organizers called 'another public sphere' might have negative consequences for some women. For example, immigrant women may lack financial resources or women from Eastern European countries ('peripheral Europe') may encounter border and visa restrictions that prevent their participation (see also Bickham Mendez 2008).

A focus on scale raises questions about the interface of feminisms and a transnational public:private. Has the emergence of transnational spaces created new publics at the expense of privatizing some matters as 'personal' problems? When is it seen by women to be advantageous to 'jump scale' – to move from engagement with their local community to the transnational context (or vice versa) – and when is it not? How does the realignment of Latin America – with its new focus on regional integration and nation-based democratic experiments, on the one hand, and its extra-territorial resonance around the world, on the other – complicate the terrain of a transnational public sphere?

Some scholars have argued that, with the overwhelming fluidity of ideas and practices associated with emergence of the scales of the transnational and the global, the distinction between public and private should 'be dispensed with since nothing much of contemporary social life remains on one side or other of the divide' (Sheller and Urry 2003: 122). Our observation – as the research presented in *Contesting Publics* documents – is that, despite (or perhaps because of) cultural flows, on the one hand, and the privatization of public space, on the other hand, the idea of the private (and the public) still stands strong in both Latin American and North American imaginaries. Only by ignoring the long-standing feminist literature on the topic can one fail to appreciate that the distinction between the public and private has always been a construction of power. Dismissing this power only reinforces the notion that poverty, race, sexual orientation, reproductive health, care-giving and violence are secondary 'social' issues rather than public sites for political work.

The chapters in *Contesting Publics* illustrate the significance of scale for understanding how feminisms shape publics and how publics shape feminisms. In chapter 2, the scale of the household offers fresh insights into the changing dynamics of the relations between the state and poor women's activism in Brazil. In chapter 3, we see how a contested transnational–regional public – concerned to take on sex tourism – excludes the points of view of the women (known as *garotas de programa*) involved. Chapter 4 shows how a constitutional project to build a nation in the current transnational context permits new inclusions of ideas and people but also produces new ways to marginalize. The scale of transnationalism is also central to the analysis of anarchist politics in chapter 5, yet the power that male activists can wield in this context helps to keep the private apolitical. In the testimonies of activists, Mariza, Susana, Luísa and Cecilia, we hear how decisions about the scale of political engagement pose constant, though varied, dilemmas for feminists in Latin America. Precisely how transnationalism may buoy, realign or even challenge women's struggles to create alternative, 'equality-building' (Brown 2006: 88–89) publics is shown to be a significant ethnographic question.

Publics as Cultural Spaces

Publics, then, are political spaces with unwritten rules about who is included and who is not, and why. Being accepted as a member may be viewed as entailing a kind of 'civilizing process' (Elias 1978), where bodily comportment and speech – what Pierre Bourdieu calls *habitus* – are subject to micro-surveillance practices that determine who is heard and seen in public and who can make decisions on behalf of others. Publics, in this sense, are cultural spaces.

John Guidry, in his analysis of the strategies of activists in 'popular' neighbourhoods in Belém, Brazil, describes how they 'struggle to be seen'. Pressing the government for basic services such as garbage collection, drinking water, electricity and education, activists told Guidry that it is the 'educated' and those who 'know how to speak' (2003: 497) who engage most successfully with the public sphere. Guidry's work is part of a larger literature on groups that dispute the way their concerns are represented in the dominant public sphere (de la Dehesa 2007, 2010; Klein 2002).

Cultural exclusions can occur even in venues such as the World Social Forum (WSF) that are explicitly formed to bring together diverse concerns and voices in an alternative public. Michal Osterweil (2004) reflects on criticisms that the WSF excluded many voices and points of view, despite its rhetoric of creating 'another world'. Osterweil recognizes the difficulty of 'being seen' in this counterpublic but argues that, rather than using such criticisms to dismiss the WSF, they should be understood productively, as part of the struggle to reconstitute the political in everyday life. Her argument is a useful reminder that power is confronted culturally in the 'micro-political and quotidian elements' (2004: 185) of publics – even those constructed as oppositional.

Describing feminism as a 'revolution in habits and culture', Maria Pia Lara (1998) analyses the productive relationship between feminism and the public sphere. She elaborates what she calls *emancipatory narratives* – 'communicative tools that provide new meanings and contest earlier ones' (1998: 4) – proposing that 'women's success in attaining recognition has been intimately linked with how they have drawn a new meaning of the public' (1998: 7). Lara argues that feminism's emancipatory narratives 'have reordered understandings of what the public sphere is, by casting doubt on previous views of the reasons for cultural, social and political marginalisation' (1998: 3). That is, feminism's success in de-naturalizing women's position has changed the terms of debate in the public sphere. Lara reveals how feminist storytelling in publics is cultural and political and has the power to effect change; Cole employs this approach to analyse the public work of Brazilian women's personal narratives in chapter 2 of this volume.

James Holston (2008), writing on the challenges to 'civility' posed by 'insurgent citizens' in São Paulo's *favelas*, also analyses the cultural dimensions of publics. He describes how national myths of inclusion in Brazil, such as Carnaval and the Lusotropicalist idea of 'racial democracy', work to maintain entrenched class relations and their accompanying ideas of civility. In the context of such powerful national discourses, to contest publics is often constructed as 'uncivil'. In the new Brazil, for example, the discomfort of having to take the same elevator as your domestic help – in the private space of your own apartment building – is a contradiction in democratizing publics that cannot be ignored (Holston 2008). Such elite discomfort was also expressed in Ecuador when the Constitutional Assembly was restructured to include indigenous, afro-descendant and female voices (see Phillips, chapter 4 this volume); for some, this transformation was a sign of being led by the 'ignorant' or by 'people who don't matter' (*gente que no pesa*). These examples of how publics are the products of quotidian judgements – often reserved for expression in private – indicate how difficult, and essential, it is to re-work the cultural meanings of publics.

The activist testimonies woven throughout *Contesting Publics* all indicate how publics are cultural spaces that shape the work they do. Mariza, an activist leader in the rural women workers' movement in Northeast Brazil (MMTR-NE), speaks of how 'timidity' can make it hard for rural women to get their concerns onto the agendas of the National Conferences for Women in ways in which they will be paid attention to; and, she speaks of how difficult it often is for rural women to 'shine' (*brilhar*) in transnational feminist spaces like the World March of Women. Activists Susana and Luísa, recount the challenges of presenting women's concerns in the masculine cultural contexts of Brazil's agro-ecology and solidarity economy movements – challenges echoed in the words of Zapatista women activists recorded by Lagalisse in chapter 5. And Ecuadorian activist Cecilia, a member of REMTE (the Latin American Network of Women Transforming the Economy), describes the network's struggle to change dominant cultural perceptions that gender equality is a secondary 'social' or 'women's' issue. She works to ensure that debating gender equality is central to economic and political visions for 'another world' as put forward, for example, by the World Social Forum.

Our theorizing of the concept of the public thus far – calling attention to the exclusionary, scalar and cultural dimensions of publics – has illustrated the extent to which publics are *contested* sites. Moving forward, we now suggest that publics are not only dynamic and contested but are *in formation* all around us. Historian Anne Enke (2007), who set out to 'find' the women's movement in the United States, offers ethnographic insight on this point. She locates feminism at the margins of the American public sphere in innovative places such as commercial spaces (bookstores and cafes), in self-proclaimed feminist institutions (shelters and health clinics), and in contested civic spaces (such as parks). In *Contesting Publics* we, like Enke, find publics-in-formation being crafted in kitchens and households, forged on the street, debated in prisons and negotiated in spaces as diverse as NGOs, conferences and constitutional assemblies.

The question then is not so much about the *parameters* of the public. Rather, we need to ask: what are the ways in which publics are created, and how might they be re-invented (or invented) in ways that germinate, circulate and buoy equality projects rather than re-entrenching inequalities?

PUBLICS, MARKETS, STATES

Publics are made, and they can be unmade. Economic relations (the market) and regimes of rule (the state) can determine whether or not public arenas permit deliberative debate and diverse interaction. That is, the market and the state – and the powerful elites and institutions that support them – can determine whether or not publics remain robust.

People everywhere living in cities today have likely experienced how the invasion and protection of private interests in urban spaces has made it more difficult to meet and converse with people, that is, to retain the social and cultural dimensions of publics. Many of the struggles within the city are about 'saving' public spaces – community gardens, dog runs, pools, arenas, libraries, parks and even universities – from market privatization. The literature on these processes has indicated how the expansion and securitization of commodified spaces, such as shopping malls and gated communities, reflect and strengthen an ever-increasingly consumer-oriented public for whom social relations and cultural behaviour become directly mediated by the market (Caldeira 2000; Harvey 2003; Lofland 1998; Low and Smith 2006; Radice et al. 2011). This literature highlights the deepening fault-lines of economic and racialized inequality in the Américas, and reveals how the proliferation of violence, security issues and fear can feed into the manufacture and protection of some – exclusionary – publics and the stigmatization of other publics. It is in contrast to this vision of the ever-expanding commodification of space – and its reservation for the wealthy – that some scholars and activists are retrieving and mobilizing the idea of 'the commons' as a way to challenge the market's hold on public life (Gibson-Graham 2006; Ostrom 1990).

What is imagined (and experienced) as the state can also play a powerful role in diminishing the cultural vitality of publics. Recall that Habermas positions the public sphere as a foil to the state: the public sphere, in his view, makes the state accountable to the people. With this kind of argument in mind, some scholars have pinned hopes on the revival and mobilization of civil society to ensure 'healthier' states that are not corrupt or repressive (Oxhorn 1995, 2009; Feinberg et al. 2006). Yet, the broad way in which the concept of civil society has been adopted in international development circles raises questions about its utility. Who and what is being tamed in the name of civil society? Our interrogation of publics in *Contesting Publics* challenges the current uncritical acceptance of the concept of civil society and queries the lack of interest in the internal dynamics of this 'black box'.

As we will see below, there has been lively debate in the 'new' Latin America about the possibilities and pitfalls of engaging with the state. To speak of the new Latin America is to refer to the shift in many Latin American countries (Argentina, Bolivia, Brazil, Chile, Ecuador, Uruguay and Venezuela) from an authoritarian state (or dictatorship) to an electoral preference for left-leaning government, what some refer to as the 'pink tide' (Moraña 2008; Spronk 2008). Many of these countries have been significantly transformed by social movements of various kinds pressing for greater democracy in response to political repression and decades of debilitating neoliberal policy. The various projects of what has been called 'deepening democracy' have included invitations from government to participate in democratic social change at municipal, national and regional levels. While these projects signal a new era of collaboration and hope, feminist activists have moved forward cautiously. It is apparent that not everyone is 'heard' in these new spaces, and many governments seem able to accommodate demands for inclusion and greater democracy and still keep inequalities intact. Thus, although engaging with new democracies may appear to be an ideal opportunity finally to be heard or 'seen', such engagement can also involve high costs for individuals who do not 'fit' (Silber 2008) and for social movements trying to advance indigenous, labour, queer, environmental and/or women's issues. Powerful indigenous movements in Ecuador, for example, have engaged with the state with quite contradictory results (de la Torre 2006, 2007; Zamosc 2007).

Aradhana Sharma and Akhil Gupta (2006) have called for ethnographic studies of how the state comes into being in particular contexts. They make the case that 'states need to be seen as cultural artifacts and effects' (2006: 20). This perspective not only reveals that the separation of state from 'non-state' realms is an effect of power (see Scott 2009), it also identifies how everyday practices, mundane bureaucratic encounters and cultural representations of the state play significant roles in producing and maintaining the state as a regime of rule. This perspective is politically important because '[h]ow states are portrayed and imagined by people located in different social positions affects both scholarly and activist engagements with the state' (Sharma and Gupta 2006: 27; see also Jimeno 2008; Mitchell 2006 [1999]). This point alerts us to the need to think in terms of different questions concerning representations of the state and their role in shaping publics. If, for example, states are said to have 'shrunk' with the advance of neoliberal policies, we are prompted to ask how regimes of rule are being dispersed or reassembled and what new social and cultural landscapes are thereby implicated.

Wendy Brown, reworking Foucault's concept of governmentality, argues that, despite neoliberal globalization, the state and its institutions have been able to maintain legitimacy by other means. She focuses specifically on the state's current call for 'tolerance', which she views as 'both a subject-regulating and state-legitimating discourse' (2006: 84) that enables the state to accommodate demands for 'inclusion' and 'participation' at the same time that it keeps inequalities intact. A discourse of tolerance buries alternative solutions to demands. For example, Brown asks why the term 'tolerance' is privileged over 'emancipation', 'equality', 'autonomy' or 'sovereignty' (2006: 86). For her, a discourse of tolerance promotes a passive view of citizenship and undermines the vitality of public life:

> [T]he call for tolerance aims to reduce encounters with difference in the public sphere – that is, to reduce public engagement with difference and, by this means, to reduce the very problem of difference as an expressly political problem, referring it instead to 'culture' or 'nature' and thereby depoliticizing its sources and solutions ... In short, tolerance as a dominant political ethos and ideal abandons not only equality projects but also the project of connection across differences, let alone solidarity or community in a world of difference. (2006: 88–89)

Brown's critique of tolerance resonates with Charles Hale's (2006) discussion of 'neoliberal multiculturalism' in Guatemala, where the marginalization of Maya is 'solved' through the management of difference rather than through a politics of equality. In *Contesting Publics*, we see cultural practices of civility – that can dismiss equality projects as 'uncivil' or unnecessary – as further ways to manage difference, making it difficult to build alternative futures.

There are also cases where publics are simply destroyed by the actions of undemocratic regimes. Catherine Conaghan's (2005) scathing critique of Fujimori's 'democratic' authoritarian rule in Peru (1990–2000) shows how his success was rooted in a cynical dismantling of the public sphere – including both the media and public institutions – until there were few spaces left in which debate, let alone grievances, could be communicated.

The governing capacities of a nation-state can also be deeply compromised by the brute accumulation of wealth and the rapid expansion of privatization. In these circumstances, a shadow state – what Segato (2010) calls 'the second state' – may operate as a surrogate state, often controlled by an elite, with little accountability and often more brutality. This is the case in Mexico, where the decline of the state has opened spaces for drug cartels to torture and publicly display, with impunity, the bodies of hundreds of murdered women (Fregoso and Bejarano 2010). It is difficult to be optimistic about the possibilities for either gender equality or healthy publics in these kinds of contexts, though we should never assume that women and men who live in deeply fractured democracies – no matter what their citizenship – are paralysed and not imagining and acting on alternatives.

If public debate is to have a transformative edge, we need to develop a clearer understanding of how the triumvirate of the market, the state and civil society – including the academy (see chapter 6) – produces particular *meanings* of public. This requires looking at what underlies constructions of a public consensus, a 'public good' or a public spectacle. In *Contesting Publics* we argue that ethnographic investigation of publics as contested sites of culture reveals these underlying constructions. And this is a necessary step toward building transformative feminist futures.

There is a final point that sometimes remains hidden in discussions of the public which we want to make explicit: how publics are constructed – and the debates, manipulations, or silences they produce – have material effects on people's lives. Publics make a difference to whether (and how) women's poverty or youth employment or sexual rights or feminicide are addressed as issues of *common* concern. When they are not, people are left to deal with their situations as private individuals. When common responsibilities are defined as individual problems, individuals usually lose, especially if they do not have a lot of resources. And recognizing common responsibilities always requires vigilance as the public:private dialectic is continually being redrawn, takes new forms and enters new domains.

PUBLIC SPACES AND THE DEMOCRACY DEBATE IN THE NEW LATIN AMERICA

The above discussion indicates why the current state of democracy in the Américas continues to be hotly debated. In these debates the question of the public has become a crucial one. Latin American scholars in particular have pointed to the possibility of concentrating political energy on – of 'working' (Laurie and Bondi 2005) – strategic spaces to make nation-states more responsive to democratic and public participation.

A broad literature takes the view that certain kinds of citizen participation can undermine the conventional mechanisms of governance, effecting greater accountability and transparency on the part of those in power on the one hand, and offering greater decision-making power for citizens on the other (Ackerman 2003; Cornwall and Coelho 2007; Dryzek 2000; Fung and Wright 2003; Kabeer 2005). The success of such public participation requires a different way of doing politics: as Guidry (2003: 494) puts it, 'pushing contention beyond the politics of opposition toward a process of deepening democracy'. Most studies on democracy-building in the new Latin America have focused on the relative success of negotiating with municipal spaces (Abers 2000; Avritzer 2002, 2009; Baiocchi 2005; Cameron 2010). For example, Baiocchi (2005) argues that the municipal participatory budgets in Porto Alegre, Brazil, are an 'emergent' public sphere that, while facilitated by the state, expands ways of being a citizen – being a spirited decision-maker rather than a dependent client of the state.

However, other studies on the project of deepening democracy in Latin America appeal for caution. Dennis Rodgers (2007), following Cornwall (2004), focuses on what he calls 'invited' spaces of the state, that is, state invitations for the public to participate in municipal and national decision-making, through conferences, forums and town halls. Considering the case of municipal budgets in Buenos Aires, Argentina, Rogers warns that such participatory spaces do not automatically lead to 'better decision-making, better outcomes, and the creation of better citizens' (2007: 182). Invitational spaces, he reminds us, must be understood to be embedded in specific political configurations that will shape the range of meanings and potential outcomes of participation in those spaces. As the following chapters illustrate, this kind of undertaking calls for ethnographic inquiry if we are to gauge the different meanings and practices people bring to these public spaces and their potential for transforming publics.

This argument directly confronts the noted lack of interest in things private in the participatory democracy literature. In our view, this lack of interest is a key to explaining why, despite the dramatic legal and political accomplishments of women's movements in Latin America, gender inequalities persist and are being inscribed in new ways. It is also why we argue that the public:private is a necessary and ongoing site of political work. As long as some issues continue to be defined and settled as private problems, there needs to be an investigation of the ways this bracketing of the private shapes the production of publics. Although the struggle for women's citizenship in Latin America is well documented (see Caldwell 2007; Lebon and Maier 2006; Maier and Lebon 2010; Rosero Garcés et al. 2000, among others), the literature that analyses projects to deepen democracy seldom places gender equality at the centre of analytical attention. And scholars and policy-makers analyse experiments in 'gender-responsive budgets' as an international development initiative in a literature that remains quite apart from the deepening democracy literature (Cooper and Sharp 2007; UNIFEM 2002, 2004). Gender equality has become a criterion for allocating international aid, an export of western democracies and a measure of economic development. Instead of debating this version of gender equality, much of the literature on democracy debates in Latin America remains silent. This raises concern that democratic experiments may be putting 'unruly' feminist issues on hold. Thus, the space of civil society cannot be *assumed* to be a counterpublic that is good for women. To avoid deepening the production of what post-socialist European feminists have called 'masculine democracy' (Watson 1997), civil society spaces – publics – always need to be recognized and theorized as contested spaces.

Contesting Publics reveals how feminism in liberal democracies is not immune to taking on civilizing projects in the name of what is 'good' for women. Carrier-Moisan, in chapter 3, offers an important lesson about the potential costs to women when feminism is empowered in a particular kind of regional/transnational public, in her case sex tourism.

In this chapter we have reviewed conceptual approaches to the public, calling attention to publics as emergent sites of power with dialectical relationships to the private, to the uncivil and to those who don't '*pesa*' (matter). We have indicated that public scholars and activists need to be asking theoretical questions not only about how publics are made but also how they might be re-invented. The critical, reflexive approach to publics that we envision not only challenges the re-inscription and eclipsing of inequalities in publics; it also assumes that 'uncivilized' public orientations need to survive. A public engagement that takes heed of the mobilities, erasures and insurgent possibilities in publics is more likely to make an effective political difference.

Under current conditions of inequality the public:private distinction is no longer only about distinguishing between domestic concerns and the formal public sphere. It is also mobilized to make further distinctions between civil and uncivil behaviour, between what is considered to be 'respectable' and what is treated as 'matter out of place', and between good citizens and unruly citizens. *Contesting Publics* proposes an ethnographically informed theoretical focus on publics as a way to analyse the dynamic, contradictory and contested spaces of contemporary activism. It is our hope that theorizing publics in this way will help support the political work that is needed to open up and interrogate public spaces in order for equality projects to move forward.

ORGANIZATION OF THE BOOK

Contesting Publics: Feminism, Activism, Ethnography traces the complicated ground that troubles public efforts to confront gender inequality. Activist narratives and ethnographic analyses present the challenges equality projects encounter as they engage publics to dispute gender, race and class-based exclusions and representations.

Three activist testimonies weave between four ethnographic chapters. The testimonies were selected from among Cole and Phillips' conversations with activists in Brazil and Ecuador in 2007 and 2008. Mariza, Susana, Luísa and Cecilia work in a variety of types of organizations, at different scales and with diverse political agendas and strategies. As activists and public intellectuals, they speak here of the dilemmas they face in bringing feminist visions and practices into the complicated terrain of 'mixed spaces' in the new Latin America.

Chapters 2 to 5 consider the implications for gender (in)equality of women's engagement with publics in different kinds of political configurations. These chapters employ an ethnographic sensibility that makes power visible by attending to the details of how people engage with the world. Ethnography and activism illuminate the costs and compromises involved in working between and within a range of publics and privates.

Against the grain of the current focus on global spaces, Sally Cole turns her lens on the conventional space of the household in chapter 2 to explore the changing public:private interface in contemporary Brazil. She describes women's household management strategies in a Brazilian town and analyses the household as an 'autoconstructed feminist public' – a space of 'unorganized' activism where women's public narratives work to transform 'habits and culture' that define gender relations. In chapter 3, Marie-Eve Carrier-Moisan analyses the contradictory impacts for women of economic development based on tourism in the Brazilian Northeast. She describes the politics of campaigns against sex tourism – a new transnational public space – and documents the tensions between feminist activists, young women sex workers and state and local economic interests. In chapter 4, Lynne Phillips assesses feminist participation in the public space of the 'inviting state', focusing on the innovative strategies and conceptual work of women activists in recent constitutional change in Ecuador. She illustrates how President Correa's 'post-neoliberal' model presents activists with new challenges and possibilities for negotiating gender equality. In chapter 5, Erica Lagalisse analyses the masculinist gender dynamics that define the public:private in a transnational activist network of young self-defined anarchists working in solidarity with the Mexican Zapatista movement.

Contesting Publics: Feminism, Activism, Ethnography begins with the assumption that 'working' (Laurie and Bondi 2005) publics is an effective strategy for achieving social transformation. In our above review of the literature we define publics as spaces within which ideas about 'matters of concern' – and the resources associated with them – are negotiated. The publics explored in the ethnographic cases presented in the following chapters are mobile, contingent and contested, and the collaborations and alliances associated with them are often contradictory and awkward. To 'work' such spaces effectively is found to require contesting cultural ideas about the 'proper' way to engage them – to require transforming ideas of civility, respectability and appropriate conduct.

2
Auto-constructed Feminist Publics: Household Matters in Northeast Brazil

Sally Cole

Transnational feminism has, since the 1990s, moved attention – scholarly and activist – away from the scale of the household, which was the key site feminists had targeted for change in the 1970s and 1980s (Harris 1981; Luxton 1980; Young et al. 1981). And 'NGO-ization' (Alvarez 1998, 2009) has, at the same time, professionalized much of the work of defining women's political issues. In twenty-first-century Brazil, feminist activists are focusing public attention on: legal changes to criminalize violence against women and protect women's rights within an international human rights framework; critique of the 'beauty industry' and of media images that cultivate women as consumers; developing alliances with anti-ALCA (Free Trade Area of the Americas) campaigns through transnational networks to highlight the impacts on women; and, participation in government forums such as the Brazilian National Women's Conferences in 2004 and 2007 (Cole and Phillips 2008; Faria and Nobre 2003, 2005; Phillips and Cole 2009; Pinto 2007).

In her testimony following this chapter Mariza, a member of the Brazilian women agricultural workers' union MMTR-NE, speaks of how difficult it is to get rural women's economic needs onto the public political agendas of both national 'mixed' labour unions and transnational feminist organizations. Describing rural women like herself as 'empowered in their knowledge and awareness but, economically ... poorer every day', she relates how difficult it is for rural women to be 'heard' in these professionalized political contexts: 'When we do go to the conferences and forums, our [rural women's] participation is still very timid ... When we're there, [the issues of] others take up all the space ... we aren't seen.'

In fact, most women in Brazil's populous Northeast live outside of formal activist organization and work on their own to respond to everyday opportunities and challenges. In interviews Marie-Eve

Carrier-Moisan and I conducted during ethnographic field research in 2004 and 2005 in the town of Cascavel in Northeast Brazil, women workers made it clear that the household was the site they targeted for change (Cole and Carrier-Moisan 2005).[1] We found that the primary way women in Cascavel seek to transform their lives is by innovating new household forms and new gender discourses. 'Unorganized' by NGOs or social movements, these women individually work to re-make their daily lives to achieve greater economic autonomy, remove themselves from the control of abusive partners and offer alternative futures to their children. For these women, migration, wage work and restructuring the household are the means. 'I do not need a husband, I need a job' was the mantra of many. 'There is no husband who is worth more than a job', said one 54-year-old woman who has worked more than 30 years in the local cashew factory (I-40). 'Work is everything in life', said another (I-42). Indeed, many of the women we met in Cascavel had made decisions not to re-marry after divorce or separation or not to marry at all: 'I don't need a husband to look after, a husband who goes out, drinks, has other women', the women say. '*É melhor sozinha que mal acompanhada*' (lit. 'It's better [to be] alone than [to be] badly accompanied') (I-36). The political action of these women is to move from private worlds of isolated dependence on men to public worlds engaged with state and market.

Envisioning feminist futures from the point of view of women in households involves not only a change of scale. Silence on the household also hides class differences between households, and gender and generational conflict within households (Benería and Roldán 1987; Branco 2000; Hoodfar 1996; Wolf 1992). Class differences between urban activists and women in low-income households – 'grassroots' women on whose behalf feminist activists seek to speak – are highlighted in the person of the domestic worker. Activists who work to ensure that women's concerns are on the public agendas of governments and social movements rarely profile the issues of domestic workers who comprise 19 per cent of the Brazilian female labour force – and their own presence in public arenas is often facilitated by the domestic work of a poorer woman in their homes (Goldstein 2003; Melo 1998). As it is off the public agenda, who does domestic work is presumed to be a private issue. More than maintaining class and gendered privilege, taboos on speaking about inequalities within and between households maintain the public perception that the household is a private space.

In this chapter, I focus analysis on the scale of the household and treat the low-income households of migrant women workers as public spaces. I view the household as an 'auto-constructed' (Holston 2008) feminist public, meaning a site of work to transform 'habits and culture' (Lara 1998) in order to reduce gender inequality. The term *auto-constructed feminist public* recognizes that the women workers of Cascavel are innovating household structures at the intersections of state and market and inscribing the everyday realities of these new social spaces in emancipatory narratives of *liberdade* (in its dual sense of both freedom and rights). I describe the internal dynamics of three Cascavalense households and the attending narratives that women create to authorize these new household forms. I present these material and discursive spaces as women's organic activism to transform their lives and the lives of those around them.

CASCAVEL: NEW OPPORTUNITIES, INEQUALITIES AND DIVERSITIES

Located on the North Atlantic coast of the state of Ceará, 60 km east of the state capital, Fortaleza, the town of Cascavel (pop. 36,000) has for more than two centuries been known for its weekly market, the second largest in the state. Here, vendors come from the surrounding coastal and riverine communities and interior farming hamlets to sell local produce: fish, sugar, *aguardente*, manioc flour, beans, corn, mangos, bananas, coconut and pineapple, and palm straw hats, baskets and brooms as well as lace and embroidery work. Vendors at the lively market sell these regional products along with clothing, housewares, bicycle parts and electronics. The town is also the service and administrative centre for the surrounding municipality.

The town grew rapidly in the last decades of the twentieth century due to in-migration from the surrounding impoverished and drought-ridden rural areas to take wage employment in newly established garment, leather and cashew-packing factories. In 1970, the town's population was 14,827; by 2004, it had more than doubled to 36,000. In the 1960s, 77 per cent of the population of the municipality lived in rural areas; by 2000, 83 per cent lived in town. In 1970, more than two-thirds of the active population worked in agriculture. By 2004, agriculture contributed only 8.4 per cent of the GDP of the municipality; industry contributed 56 per cent (Governo do Estado do Ceará 1980, 2004a, 2004b, 2004c). In 2004–5, during the fieldwork period, Cascavel's wage labour force comprised: 1,600 workers (mostly women) in cashew-processing; 1,300 workers (approximately equal numbers of women and men) in leather furniture manufacture; 350 workers (mostly women) in shoe manufacturing; 300 workers (mostly men) in a ceramic tile factory; and 1,300 workers (mostly women) in 34 garment factories ranging in size from those employing fewer than 30 workers to two factories that each employ approximately 250 workers. Other employment is found in the municipal government, in social services, in shops, and in an expanding informal economy.

Economic inequality increased over the 1990s and continues to increase. Average annual per capita income in Cascavel in 2004 was R$2,400 (US$736), one-third the national average. Although the official minimum monthly wage has quadrupled since 1994 from R$64 to R$260 in 2004, real income after inflation has not. Formally employed workers are paid the legal minimum wage; in Cascavel this is 40 per cent of the earnings of the average industrial worker in southern Brazil. In the 2000 census, 35 per cent of Cascavel's economically active population (defined as those over 10 years of age) earned one minimum monthly wage or less; 47 per cent of the population was recorded as having no income at all. Meanwhile 4 per cent were earning more than three minimum salaries (Governo do Estado do Ceará 2002). And income inequality has increased: the income share of the richest 20 per cent of households rose from 55 per cent in 1991 to 67 per cent in 2001; in 2004, two-thirds of Cascavel households are categorized as *baixa renda* (low-income), eligible for assistance under the federal government's Bolsa Família programme.[2]

Despite an initial period of growth in formal sector employment, the informal sector has expanded far more rapidly. Downturns and lay-offs in the formal sector have occurred throughout and since the 1990s. At the same time, educational requirements have increased for formal sector jobs. Re-hiring after lay-off is determined by education level and performance on a sequence of tests rather than seniority. Middle-aged women – who have held a factory job since they were teenagers and are often the primary wage earners in their households – typically have little formal education. Many try to find time to attend night school in a bid to improve their chances of being re-hired; nonetheless, once laid off, they are encountering more and more difficulty being taken on again in the formal sector. Increasingly, they take up work in the informal sector often in home-based food vending or garment manufacturing. The threat of loss of guaranteed minimum wage jobs (and the pensions and other benefits that come with formal employment) requires that households manage a diversity of sources of income to reduce economic precarity.

In the discussion that follows I illustrate how Cascavel households seek to bring in a spectrum of sources of income by incorporating in their membership individuals who are formally employed, individuals who work in the informal sector and individuals who capture social assistance from state programmes. Women's employment – often as the primary wage earner – positions them as managers or co-managers in households. Multiple-income strategies deployed by 'working' (Laurie and Bondi 2005) the public spaces of state and market – spaces that are shifting – reconfigure household dynamics with women often becoming heads of households with or without men. Radically transformed from the rural male-headed households they left behind, the household – this auto-constructed feminist public – is the primary site for Cascavel women's activism to change their lives.

LEAVING THE RURAL

In 2004, we conducted interviews with 95 women workers, 90 per cent of whom had migrated into town from the small hamlets of tenant farmers in the interior semi-arid *sertão* or from the coastal and riverine fishing communities in the wider municipality of Cascavel. We conducted follow-up interviews in 2005 with ten of these women (along with other members of their households) to record detailed household histories and itemized household budgets, documenting sources of income and basic expenses. More than half of the women we interviewed were over 40 years of age and had migrated as young women to work in the cashew factory, Cascaju. They had spent their entire working lives in the factory. The younger women (ages 18–39) we interviewed had also initially been formally employed in the cashew factory; the majority of women in this age group, however, were now working as seamstresses in small garment factories without benefits or job security – often paid by the day (*avulso*) – or in various forms of informal employment in the service sector.[3]

Cascaju opened in the town of Cascavel in 1970 and by the end of its first year employed 400 people, 70 per cent of them women. Four years later the plant employed 1,100 workers, the majority women (Grupo Edson Queiroz 1986). And in 2004 the plant had 1,600 employees, mostly women. Here workers receive the *carteira assinada* (document of formal employment) entitling them to the minimum wage and to pension benefits. Cascaju was the first major wage employer in the town and the main magnet drawing women into town; women's wages and benefits became the mainstay of migrant households in Cascavel.

As important as the draw of wage employment at the cashew factory were the strong 'push' factors driving women out of rural areas. The women we interviewed were the daughters of tenant farmers or sharecroppers; they grew up in nuclear family households bound in contractual arrangements with particular landowners. Their fathers worked in agriculture (*na roça*) and, in some cases, in fishing; the women described their mothers as housewives (*donas de casa*). Typically, the landowner (*patrão*) provided a plot of land on which to build a straw hut, tend a few domestic animals (chickens, goats, pigs) and harvest a few banana, mango, coconut and cashew trees. In exchange, tenants cleared land, tended cattle and cultivated crops of sugarcane, manioc, cotton, beans and corn for the *patrão*. Men were primarily responsible for the work in the fields; women worked around the house, processing manioc, collecting water and firewood, cooking, and caring for children. Women also did lace and embroidery work and wove straw (from the carnaúba palm) hats, bags and baskets for sale.

The women remembered hardship growing up. Recurrent droughts (*secas*) destroyed crops and killed animals. Even in years when agricultural production was good, the tenant household's share was often not enough to feed the large families. The women recalled that deaths of babies and young children were common. As Angélica, age 47, told us:

> My mother had 15 children, 7 died of malnutrition. I was one of the youngest. My mother only had my sister, Inês, and another baby boy after me. I remember watching that little thing die of hunger. It was enormous misery. (I-43)

Another woman, Julia, age 47, recalled that she decided at age 11 to help (*ajudar*) her parents. The *patrão* arranged work for her as a *doméstica* (domestic, servant) for a family he knew in Fortaleza. She is the second of seven children:

> The whole family worked. I started as a child doing lacework. I left the house at 11 years old to help my father and mother because I saw them struggling, struggling. I saw my father try to

survive the drought by hunting. I saw my mother, crying, all of us on the floor, dying of hunger. I wanted to help. (I-45)

Another woman, Eugenia, age 41, who grew up along the Choró River in the municipality of Cascavel, and has worked 25 years in the cashew factory recalls:

> When I was small, when I was 7 years old, I went to work in a firm processing manioc. We left the house at dawn and returned at night. We went fishing at night. We suffered a lot when I was little. I was the third of nine children. I helped my mother with the younger children and also did lacework. When I was 12 years old I moved to Cascavel. I wanted to leave to have a better life, to see if it was possible to have a better life. There, in the Choró, it was very difficult. (I-67)

Eugenia's godmother took her to a family with whom she lived and worked as a nanny for three years in exchange for room, board and clothes. When Eugenia was 15, she entered the cashew factory and has worked there ever since. Another woman who migrated to Cascavel in 1974 to work in the cashew-packing plant – where she still works – recalls growing up along the Choró River:

> I was the fourth of 11 children. My mother had 14 children but three died as babies. From when I was small, as far as I can remember, I helped my mother. Washing clothes. Caring for the younger children. Making manioc flour. Doing embroidery. Making brooms and rope from the carnaúba palm. Often because we had nothing to eat, I went fishing with a net, harvesting shellfish, crabs, shrimp. I liked to fish … (I-69)

Many of the women we interviewed said that the misery of their childhoods was compounded by observing the hard lives of their mothers. Tied to the domestic work of sustaining the house and children on a daily basis, they depended on their husbands to sell the household's produce and crafts at the Saturday market and to bring home the cash. Many women instead recalled that their fathers spent the earnings on their own entertainment in town and returned home Monday morning surly and empty-handed. The women remembered not only material hardship but also male control and violence.[4] Almost half of the women we interviewed said they moved to town to escape the violence their mothers endured in their marriages and to seek egalitarian marriages or to choose not to marry at all.[5] In town, the women are no longer confined to marriage and nuclear family households. They live in a diversity of types of households.

AUTO-CONSTRUCTED FEMINIST PUBLICS: CASCAVEL'S NEW HOUSEHOLDS

Auto-construction (*autoconstrução*) is the term James Holston (2008) uses to refer to architectural improvisation in the 'peripheries' (*periferias*), the shantytowns and *favelas* that have grown throughout Brazil in its process of rapid urbanization. I am adapting it here to refer to the social innovations that urban migrants also make as they inhabit these material structures. Viewing households as publics breaks down continuing assumptions of a private–public 'divide'. It directs attention instead to the ways that the public:private interface changes as the public spheres of market and state increasingly permeate households, and as household members engage this shifting terrain in pursuit of their own goals. That I refer to these households as 'feminist publics' acknowledges both my analysis that these are projects of social transformation for gender equality *and* the women's own narratives of *liberdade*. For the women frame their perceptions of the need to change relations within their households as a necessary and integrated part of their personal projects for better lives as women and to 'be human' (*ser humana*).

Households in Cascavel are malleable units with fluid boundaries reflecting their dynamic engagement with fluctuating market conditions, access to state social programmes and reliance on diverse social networks. Three broad patterns of household organization, however, can be identified: conjugal; extended, multi-generational; and women-and-children-only. As previously noted, conjugal households were the historical pattern and cultural norm in the rural communities from which Cascavalense have migrated. However, only 32 per cent of the women we interviewed lived in conjugal households in town while 33 per cent lived in women-and-children-only households and 28 per cent lived in extended, multi-generational households; the remaining 7 per cent lived in reconstituted conjugal households based on subsequent unions and blended families.

The highest proportion of conjugal households (48 per cent) was found in the youngest cohort (ages 18–29). This may be expected as this is the age group that is beginning child rearing. However, only 32 per cent of women over the age of 40 remained in their first conjugal union and only 22 per cent of the women in the middle cohort (aged 30–39) lived in households based on a first conjugal union. The average size of conjugal households was 5.2 members. Seventy per cent of these households had at least one member formally employed; 70 per cent also had one member working in the informal sector.

Extended, multi-generational households were represented in the greatest proportion (40 per cent) among the oldest cohort, in part reflecting that these households incorporate adult children who remain unmarried (including an increasing number of women who are choosing not to marry) and that these households re-absorb adult children whose marriages dissolve (and also absorb the children of these marriages). Average size was seven members. Eighty per cent of these households have at least one member formally employed; 88 per cent have at least one member informally employed and more than two-thirds of these households have at least one member receiving some form of state support, usually a pension.[6]

Women-and-children-only households were represented in the greatest proportion (40 per cent) of households in the middle cohort (aged 30–39) and in 36 per cent of households among the oldest cohort of women (those over 40 years of age). These are the most economically fragile and often socially marginal households with the smallest social networks and thus fewest ties of support (*ajuda*). The average size of these households is 4.4 members. Forty-five per cent of these households have no member formally employed (no member earning a guaranteed monthly salary) and only 30 per cent of these households have one adult member receiving a pension.

Household members seek to incorporate a mix of individuals within the household who together will bring: the security of the minimum monthly wage and other benefits of formal employment; the flexibility of informal employment; eligibility to tap state social security programmes such as rural retirement pensions and the Bolsa Família; a dense social network of reciprocal exchanges (*ajuda*); and, in some cases, a clientelist relationship with a local patron or politician. Typically a decision-making co-management team (husband–wife; sister–sister; mother–daughter) emerges within the household – what Agarwal refers to as 'intrahousehold bargaining coalitions' (1997: 58) – to coordinate the tasks of 'working' the diversity of spaces necessary to capture the widest possible spectrum of resources. To manage this complexity, one woman member is designated the household administrator responsible for: balancing resources and expenses; identifying new sources of income; directing the activities of other household members; and, increasingly important, navigating government bureaucracy. In low-income households in Cascavel, designating a woman member as household administrator is a strategic measure to ensure the economic security of the household.[7] In Cascavel, as the cases discussed below illustrate, household administrators also view their managerial roles as complementary to the realization of personal goals.

In the next section I present three households that illustrate common forms of household management: a conjugal partnership practising a flexible division of labour; a mother-daughter team managing an extended household engaged in a project of social mobility; and, the dynamics of decision-making in a women-and-children-only household. Tables 1 and 2 present the sources of income and expenses for each household. Figures 2.1–2.3 revise classical anthropological kinship charts to illustrate resource flows within and among households.

Table 2.1   Sources of household (HH) income (R$/yr)

	1 Conjugal HH	2 Extended HH	3 Women-and-children-only HH
HH members	4	6	8
Average age (yrs)	27.5	44.5	19.1
Formal wage employment (R$/yr)[1]	3,380	3,380	0
Informal sector	1,860[2]	480[3]	5,580[5]
State (pensions, Bolsa Família)	540	9,450[4]	1,230[6]
Total annual income	5,780	13,310	6,810
State assistance as % of total household income	9.3%	70.2%	18.0%
Per capita income	1,445	2,216	851

Notes
1. R$1 = US$0.30. Calculations are based on the minimum monthly salary of R$260 in 2005. The monthly salary is doubled for the month of December so that the annual salary of a formally employed worker (with *carteira assinada*) was R$3,380.
2. This is José's estimated annual contribution to the household. He purchases and pays for all fresh foods, an average of R$120/month, and is responsible for paying the monthly electricity bill of R$15. He also gives occasional money to his daughters for their personal spending estimated at R$10 per child/month. His estimated income from net-making averaged over the year is about R$200/month, indicating that he keeps an estimated R45/month for his own spending, mainly alcohol.
3. This is the estimated annual contribution of João, an unmarried adult male household member, who is employed irregularly as a construction worker and gives Cláudia a portion of his earnings, keeping the remainder for his own personal consumption, mainly alcohol.

4. This figure is the combined retirement pensions of Cláudia's parents. Monthly pension payments, like the minimum wage, are also doubled in the month of December. Her mother receives a rural pension equivalent to the minimum monthly wage. Her father's monthly pension is equivalent to slightly more than 1.5 minimum monthly salaries. According to Cláudia he is not receiving all that he is entitled to and she is actively working through bureaucratic channels to try to reclaim unpaid pension benefits.
5. This figure includes: the estimated income from the sewing Aura does for private clients at home; Margarida's estimated annual income working as a seamstress on an irregular basis for a subcontractor in the clothing industry; and her daughter Marina's earnings: during the period (May 2004–May 2005) Marina worked for a few months as a sales clerk and then as a gas station attendant.
6. This amount combines the payments of R$45 every second month that Margarida receives under the national Fome Zero programme and the R$80/month that Aura receives for her three children from the federal government's Bolsa Família programme.

Table 2.2 Essential household expenses (R$/yr)[1]

	1 Conjugal HH	2 Extended HH	3 Women-and-children-only HH
Food (R$/yr)	3,000	7,260	4,224
Utilities (water, gas, electricity, phone)	648	1,572	936
House (furnishings, repairs)	300	1,560	0
Rent, loans	0	0	600[2]
Transportation	0	0	480
Education	84	0	240
Social insurance	576	420	228
Drugs, vision care	0	480	0
Annual expenses	4,608	11,292	6,708
Expenditure per person per year	1,152	1,882	838

Notes
1. R$1 = US$0.30. This table records the costs that interviewees reported were essential for their households to pay each month. It does not include: clothing; toiletries; foods for special occasions; unforeseen travel or health costs; or allowances given to or retained by household members, for example, Cláudia gives her father an allowance of R$50/month; Margarida recently needed to buy eyeglasses for her granddaughter.
2. This amount is a monthly payment on a loan taken out to buy the land on which they are building their house. Often Margarida's niece, who has built an adjoining house on the same plot of land, will make this monthly payment for Margarida. Margarida's electricity line is also attached to her niece's and her niece usually makes these payments as well.

THREE HOUSEHOLDS

Household 1: Conjugal Partnership

Somos iguais. Somos companheiros. (We're equal. We're partners.)

Household 1 is a couple, Maria, age 44, and José, age 39, married for almost 20 years. They have two teenage daughters. Maria has worked for 20 years in the cashew factory; José has held various jobs, including seasonal fishing. As Table 1 shows, the foundation of the household's income is Maria's wage; José's net-making brings in additional income from the informal sector. As Table 2 reveals, approximately 80 per cent of household income goes to basic necessities, most to food. The state contributes 9.3 per cent of the household's income through the Bolsa Família programme.

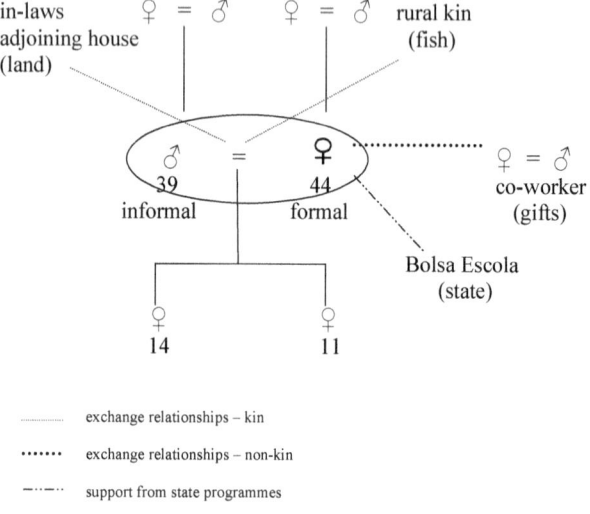

Figure 2.1   Conjugal partnership

Maria is one of many women we interviewed who said she migrated to leave behind the violence she had seen in her parents' marriage and that she feared would soon be her fate. On her own, at age 24, she left the rural fishing community she grew up in to move to Cascavel, 20 km away. At her first job in the cashew factory, she met José, the son of a woman who also worked at the factory (who had herself escaped an abusive marriage in the countryside by moving into town). Maria has found, with José, the conjugal partnership she was seeking. He is caring and non-violent. And, since the birth of their second child, he has stayed at home and assumed the primary responsibility for childcare, food shopping and meal preparation. Maria overlooks his occasional *vícios* of drinking and infidelity in a bid to maintain stability and security for her household.

Maria and José both describe the relationship as equal: 'Somos iguais. Somos companheiros', they say, discursively representing and solidifying their work as a co-management team. Maria carries the burden (*preoccupação*) of administration and responsibility for the household, but she also assumes a level of personal autonomy and mobility equal to José's: he frequents bars, she goes to night school – something many husbands prevent their wives from doing. Maria makes visible and normalizes her role as primary earner and household administrator through her creation of a personal proverb: '*A mulher tem [que ter] a cabeça mais controlada*', she says. 'The woman has to have the head [sense] to be more disciplined [than a man does].'

Maria's work for the household also includes maintaining a set of ties of *ajuda* (support) that insert her household in a widening diversity of public spaces (see Figure 2.1). In addition to her formal employment that will provide her with a retirement pension, Maria navigates the state bureaucracy to maintain her household's categorization as *baixa renda* (low-income) in order to be eligible to receive the monthly Bolsa Família subsidy; she has informed herself about the new pension plan programme for fishermen and ensured that her husband, a former fisherman, applied for it; she supports her husband in domestic tasks and assists him in net-making when she can; she maintains ties and exchanges gifts with members of her rural natal household from whom she regularly receives fish; and she maintains reciprocal daily exchanges with her in-laws whose house adjoins hers (and who gave José and Maria the land on which to build their house). And, of great importance to her, she maintains her friendship with a former co-worker, Lúcia: '*Lúcia é tudo p'ra mim*' (Lúcia is everything to me), she says.

Maria worked side by side with Lúcia at the cashew factory for 20 years. They confide in each other when they have troubles; consult one another about their children; discuss pension plans and other job-related decisions; and share information about prices of food and consumer goods. Lúcia recently retired and is receiving her pension. She and her husband have opened a small bar in the neighbourhood that has quickly become successful. Lúcia has had surgery that has left her with little physical strength and Maria helps with many of the hard domestic tasks in Lúcia's household, especially laundry, an almost daily chore. In return, Lúcia gives Maria food and small sums of money. Maria describes this as 'Just a help [*só uma ajuda*]. I help her. She helps me. She is very good to me. Sometimes she gives me money. Other times, no. But it is little. *É só uma ajuda*.' This reciprocal relation of *ajuda* is critical to the economic security of Maria's household, to Maria's sense of personal well-being and to her assessment of the success of her migration strategy. Despite its objective economic vulnerability (Table 1), Maria emphasizes her household's 'wealth' (cf. Guyer 1997) found in: her daughters' plans to complete high school; her own employment and future pension; her caring partner; her deep friendship with a co-worker; and her ability to attend night school.

Household 1's ties to market and state make it a site of public as much as private relations and have created household dynamics very different from those her mother faced in a rural conjugal household.

Household 2: Mother and Daughter

> *Eu me sinto como estou administrando um país na minha cabeça. Eu me 'tou sentindo Lula.* (I feel like I am administering a country in my head. I feel like Lula.)

Household 2, a large extended and multi-generational household, has a strong diversified income base including numerous adult contributors and substantial state support. The household is co-managed by the mother, Eva, age 61, and eldest daughter, Cláudia, age 42. Cláudia earns a minimum monthly wage through formal employment in the cashew factory. Her mother and father, as retired agricultural workers, collect monthly rural pensions from the state. Two unmarried adult children make irregular contributions, one in the form of cash earnings from informal work in construction and the other gives occasional gifts such as shoes for the parents or a household appliance. More than 80 per cent of the household's income goes to meet basic necessities, including notable expenditures such as household consumer goods and utilities; state programmes contribute 70 per cent of household income (see Tables 1 and 2).

The mother–daughter management team emerged as a result of migration. The family had owned a small *engenho* (sugar mill) in the countryside less than 20 km from Cascavel, but the income from sugar and *aguardente* could not support the growing family of nine children. In the first years in town, Eva worked at the cashew factory and Cláudia looked after her younger siblings. When Eva left the factory because the acid cashew juice burned her hands, Cláudia tried several different jobs, including migrating to the state capital, Fortaleza, to work. She soon settled back in Cascavel in 1986 to take a job at the cashew factory herself and has worked there ever since. Her wage is the stable foundation of the household, along with her parents' pensions; a diversity of additional material and social resources also support the household.

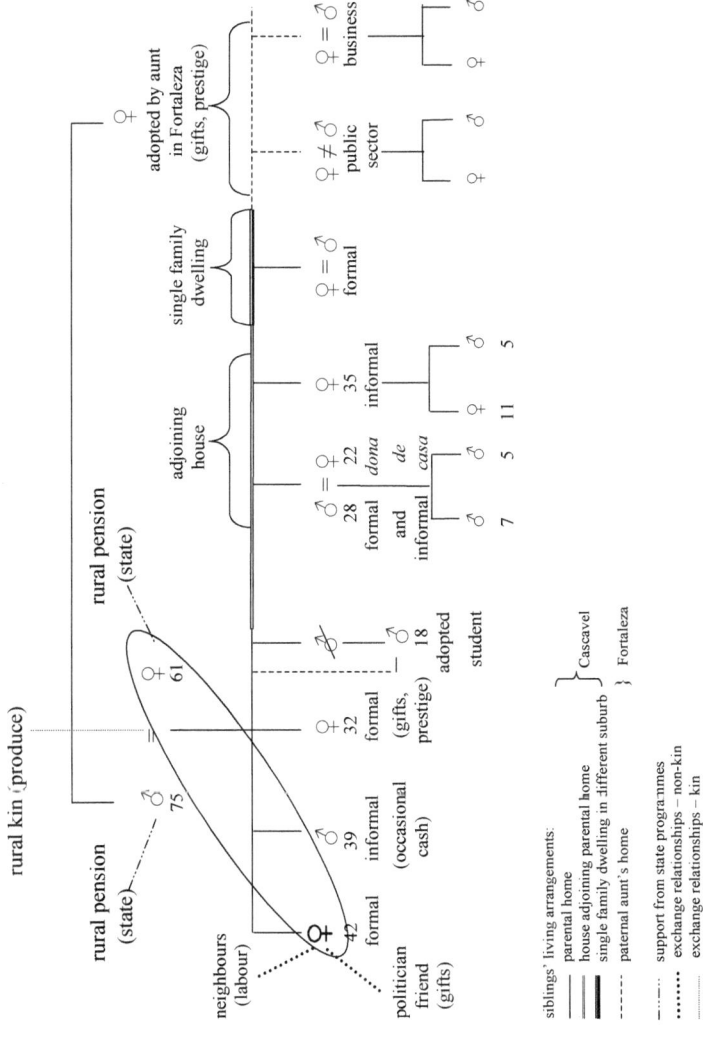

Figure 2.2 Mother and daughter co-management

siblings' living arrangements:
——— parental home
━━━ house adjoining parental home
- - - single family dwelling in different suburb
- - - paternal aunt's home

·-·-· support from state programmes
·········· exchange relationships – non-kin
——— exchange relationships – kin

Eva describes Cláudia as the administrator of the household: 'She has the better head [*cabeça*] for managing money. She administrates. She orients me. Her head is better than mine. Cláudia is better at managing money.' Eva describes herself as the *dona de casa*, taking care of most of the cooking, laundry and food shopping. She developed this partnership with her daughter in part to redress her husband's financial mismanagement: he had a habit of loaning money to his friends and not collecting repayment. Mother and daughter now control his spending by centralizing all monies coming into the household – including his pension – and doling out an allowance to him. It is Cláudia who keeps informed of government policies and handles the paperwork to maintain her parents' eligibility to receive pensions as retired agricultural workers. Cláudia describes her work as household administrator as like Lula's job as president administering the country: '*Eu me sinto como estou administrando um país na minha cabeça. Eu me 'tou sentindo Lula*' (I feel like I am administering a country in my head. I feel like Lula.) For Cláudia, taking on the role of household administrator also enables her personal projects of social mobility and consumption. She invests in home furnishings and renovation and speaks of the house as hers and the other household members almost as guests. '*A minha casa é uma pousada*' (My house is a hotel), she says.

Cláudia was 14 when she moved with her parents and siblings into Cascavel. She has chosen not to marry saying: 'I don't think about marrying. Better to stay single. A rich husband is never going to appear, only poor men.' She has also chosen not to have children. She is so determined not to have children that, in a town where almost half of households – 46 per cent of households of interviewees – have an adopted member, Cláudia says, 'I would be the first woman in Cascavel *not* to accept a baby left on my doorstep to raise [*crear*, to adopt].'

The mother–daughter team nurtures a dense and extensive set of ties with kin, friends and neighbours (Figure 2.2). These networks provide economic and social resources that assist the household in a collective project not only of daily maintenance but of social mobility – a project shared with two other siblings who have built houses attached to Cláudia's: a married brother who works as a bus driver and owns a small restaurant in the bus station and a divorced sister who returned from Fortaleza with her two children and operates a food kiosk in the centre of town. These two households are semi-autonomous; they manage their earned income separately but obtain unpaid domestic labour from Cláudia's household.

The women of household 2 maintain exchange relationships with rural kin from whom they receive agricultural produce and to whom they bring small gifts from town. They also have ties with urban kin: two of Cláudia's younger sisters were 'given' (*dar*) for adoption as children to their father's sister living in Fortaleza. They are now employed in the city: one has a government job; the other operates a small business with her husband. They regularly come to Cascavel to visit, bearing gifts, information and social status. Cláudia and Eva also perform domestic tasks for two unmarried, childless adult members: one male who gives a portion of his wage earnings from irregular employment as a construction worker and one adult female who also does not pay rent but who gives occasional gifts such as appliances to the household. The mother and daughter co-managers accommodate this adult woman as a member of the household, doing laundry and preparing meals for her; in exchange, through her status as the office manager at one of the larger clothing factories, this member lends symbolic support to the household's social mobility aspirations.

Cláudia and Eva also give food and clothing to poor women neighbours who are raising children on their own, and they often give the daily noon meal to single or widowed men in the neighbourhood. These relations with neighbours have their roots in the horizontal ties of mutual support that rural migrants developed in their early years in town when they did not have kin nearby. In the current context of the growing economic inequality in Cascavel, however, they increasingly take on characteristics of patron–client relations as this large co-managed household appears to be achieving greater economic security than many others. The neighbour women reciprocate by providing unpaid labour when Cláudia needs help to prepare a *festa*, which she does several times a year. At these BBQs in the courtyard of the house, Cláudia entertains town councillors from whom she extracts favours and who she hopes will help her run for political office one day – a role she sees less as participation in democracy than as a pragmatic route to material betterment, especially her goal of one day owning a car. She also draws on her ties with local politicians to help family members and neighbours find jobs or medical assistance. In exchange, she delivers the neighbourhood's votes to her favoured town councillor.

As administrator of household 2, Cláudia manages a complex set of relations with market, state, kin and neighbours, not only in order to carry out the work of household reproduction but also to achieve her goals for personal advancement. As in the case of household 1, the reconfiguration of public:private boundaries through a combination of socio-economic changes and women's own actions has transformed household dynamics.

Household 3: Women and Children Only

> *É precisa ter coragem.* (It's necessary to have courage.)

Household 3 comprises four adult women: a mother, Margarida, aged 50, her three adult daughters and their four children all under the age of 7. This household is the most impoverished and vulnerable. Half of household members are dependent children. No member of the household has secure formal employment. The household depends on Margarida's informal sector earnings as a seamstress and the earnings of her second daughter, Marina, who works in various forms of informal employment – currently as a gas station attendant. The national Bolsa Família and Fome Zero government programmes contribute 18 per cent of household income. Essential household expenses are not met by income.

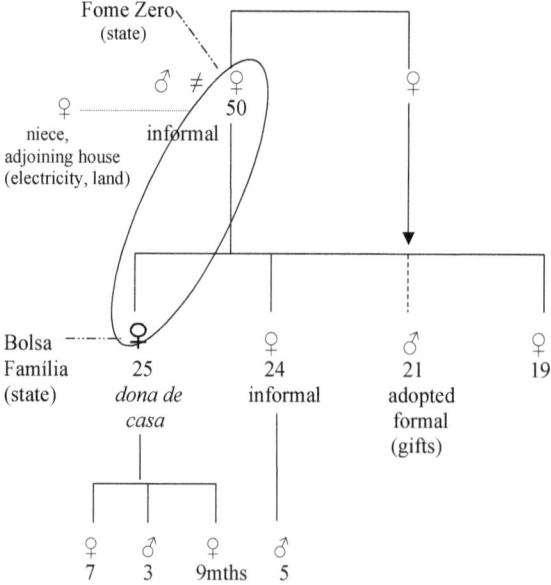

Figure 2.3   Women-and-children-only household

When her third daughter was born, Margarida's husband had moved permanently to Fortaleza to live with a second wife and family. Left on her own to raise her daughters, Margarida then formed a household with her unmarried sister, Francisca, and formally adopted Francisca's 2-year-old son. As the primary wage earner at the time, Margarida worked in the cashew factory while her sister, as the *dona de casa*, managed the household and cared for the children. These children are now adults and Margarida and Francisca live in separate households but near each other. Margarida now co-manages a household with her eldest daughter, Aura. Margarida is still the primary earner; Aura is the *dona de casa*. Margarida says, '*Aura tem a cabeça* [Aura has the head]' to manage money and to make ends meet. Aura keeps track of expenses in a notebook and does all shopping for the household.

This household is organized around the tasks and responsibilities of raising Margarida's grandchildren: Aura's three children and the son of her second daughter, Marina. None of the four fathers of the four children provides any form of child support (*ajuda*) (this was also the case for Margarida, who received no *ajuda* from the father of her children). The household receives some help from a niece who lives next door and has extended her electricity line to Margarida's house; her niece also helps Margarida make the payments on the loan they took out to purchase the land on which they are building their homes. Margarida's adopted son helps occasionally with school supplies or shoes for the children (see Figure 2.3).

A few years ago, Margarida lost her job at the cashew factory due to her frequent absences when she was caring for her dying mother; as a result, at the same time, she lost her rights to receive a retirement pension from her employer in the future. Now, with four young children in the household, she chooses to work informally as a seamstress, paid by the day (*avulso*), in order to maintain the flexibility to be available for childcare as needed. The lack of a secure income prohibits any planning or saving. It also makes it difficult for Margarida's household to maintain regular gift and labour exchange relationships, with the result that the household is also increasingly becoming socially isolated, which adds to its economic precarity. Margarida and her adult daughters respond to economic insecurity by making private adjustments that will have long-term consequences. In order to feed the children (and to buy milk formula and diapers), the adults often go without eating. And, more and more frequently, one of her daughters is going into

Fortaleza for the weekends to 'party' with Brazilian and European tourists who offer gifts of clothing, meals and consumer goods in exchange for fun, companionship and sex.

Yet Margarida maintains personal goals, pride in her accomplishments and hope for the future. She has ensured that her daughters have completed high school – she recalls that she used to break a pencil in half to make pencils for two daughters.[8] She dreams of opening a sewing school 'to pass on what I know to others'. And she treasures her personal autonomy. This she sees as her greatest achievement: 'I don't need a husband', she says. 'I need a job.' Thus, despite the mounting evidence of her household's increasing economic insecurity, Margarida remains calmly certain that her well-being is better than it would be with intermittent and unreliable *ajuda* from her husband. She focuses on the project at hand: feeding and raising her grandchildren. Paradoxically, Margarida's feelings of responsibility for her young grandchildren and her worries about her adult daughters also give her strength of purpose, strength that she affirms discursively when she describes herself as both provider and caregiver: 'I am father and mother [*pai e mãe*].'

Like Maria in household 1, Margarida has created a narrative that generalizes her own experience to the 'lot' (*luta*; struggle) of women: 'A woman's responsibility is a heavy burden, right? To look after these children, this large family, to keep everything going, you have to have courage' (*A responsibilidade duma mulher é carga pesada, viu? É manter essas crianças, essa família grande, numerosa. Manter tudo certo. Precisa ter coragem.*) The case of household 3 presents the challenges that women-and-children-only households face: childcare remains the 'private' responsibility of women and household income is increasingly insecure as formal employment contracts and the informal sector expands. Margarida, however, chooses to engage with and locate herself within the vibrant discourse of Cascavel women that emphasizes opportunity, choice and change – a contradictory discourse reflecting women's awareness of necessary *compromissos* (compromises).

These three households are rich sites of innovation to transform women's lives. The visibly diverse roles for women in the town in a variety of public settings – in factories, in the informal economy, in neighbourhoods – and the networks these roles make possible are also the stages on which women, through everyday storytelling, articulate new cultural norms and actively manage local gender discourses.

NARRATIVES OF *LIBERDADE*

These three households illustrate the range and complexity of spaces women inhabit and 'work' in Cascavel. From these diverse locations, Cascavel women have converged on a shared discourse of *liberdade* that they explore and embellish at the end of each day as they sit together outside their houses to catch the evening breeze and analyse the day's events and decisions. Through this routine of public storytelling the women recognize the critical role that emancipatory narratives play in transforming gender norms – 'habits and culture' (Lara 1998) – and changing the terms of debate in the public sphere (see also chapter 1, this volume).

First and foremost, to Cascavel women, *liberdade* means earning a wage:

> The woman who does not work [for wages outside the home] does not have *liberdade*. When a woman has her own money in her hands, she has *liberdade*. (I-16)

Liberdade is independence and having choice:

> In the past, there was only agriculture or domestic work. Now women can work outside the home. (I-33)

> Today a woman is independent, she can lead the life she wants. Before, she had to marry. She could not stay single in the past. There are more work opportunities. In the past, women were domestic workers only. (I-36)

> With work, a woman is not dependent on a man; she becomes independent and has more rights [*liberdades*]. In the past, it was the father or husband who decided. Now a woman doesn't have to beg; she has the freedom [*liberdade*] to buy things. (I-20)

> Nowadays women's lives are freer [*mais liberada*]. A woman doesn't stay at home. Now she can go where she wants, do what she wants. (I- 67)

Women's *liberdade* also enables a woman to choose to leave a bad marriage or send an errant husband away:

> A woman has rights [*direitos*] and if a husband is not satisfactory, the woman has the possibility to decide to ask him to leave.

Formerly, a woman did not have the courage to do this ... or the circumstances ... In the past, women suffered a lot at the hands of men. Nowadays, a woman does not put up with it [*não aguenta mais*]. (I-21)

The biggest change is women's *liberdade*. She works. She wants to do what men do. She is leading her own life. Nowadays many couples separate because a woman no longer will put up with [*não aguenta*] what women used to have to endure. They are independent. (I-67)

Women who have male partners who contribute fully to the household consider themselves lucky and recognize the support it provides. Octavia, a 51-year-old woman who sells cooked food in the market proclaims that women's lives have changed for the better:

because today a woman is liberated [*libertar-se*]. She is accountable to herself. In the past, she could only live with the support of a husband. She depended on a husband for everything. She stayed only in the house and in the kitchen. The work in the home was very humiliating.

She described her husband as:

the husband I prayed to God for. He never goes out without me; he doesn't drink; he doesn't leave me alone to go to a *festa*. He never beats me. Therefore, he is great [*ótimo*]. He is friend, father, husband, companion. He is everything. (I-31)

Her portrait of her husband recognizes and strengthens her relationship with him at the same time that it publicly affirms views of the ideal husband that are widely shared among women.

Liberdade, for Cascavel women, is also the choice to have few or no children.

Things have gotten a lot better for women. In the past a woman could not work. She was obligated to stay at home. In the past, a woman had five or six children – or more. Today a woman has one or two children. She has more freedom [*liberdade*] to work. (I-31)[9]

Women emphasized that ideas are also changing – if slowly – to support *liberdade*:

> A lot has changed for women. Even our ideas [*pensamentos*]. The greatest change is the freedom of expression [*a liberdade de expressão*]. Nowadays life is more open, a woman has freedom to go out ... a woman is more independent. (I-61)

Women celebrated their *liberdade* in contrast to the constraints their mothers faced, but they also pointed to new challenges that they and their daughters are confronting: childcare; personal security; and rising consumer needs and costs in the face of increasingly insecure employment. Their everyday narration of *liberdade* works to recognize what were once private household dynamics and decisions as public, shared experiences – thereby laying the groundwork for collective social transformation. However, narratives of *liberdade* may hide other private constraints, contradictions and compromises.

THE CONTRADICTORY SHIFTING TERRAIN OF HOUSEHOLDS

Childcare remains the responsibility of households, and primarily of women within households, and affects many women's ability to hold employment. When couples separate, fathers typically do not provide economic support for their children. There is no public (state) or employer provided or subsidized childcare in Cascavel. Arranging care for a child shapes the composition of households. For example, a working mother might live with an aunt, mother or sister, or build a house next door to kin who will assist with childcare. Local practices of informal adoption, fostering and child circulation continue to be common ways women manage childcare in town. Lapses in childcare lead to frequent changes in employers, women often forsaking formal employment (giving up the *carteira assinada* and future pensions) for more flexible informal work that offers a daily wage but without benefits or regulated working conditions.

Women's new autonomy in public spaces contests old gender norms. But entrenched ideas about women's 'respectability' and male prerogative are slow to change. Choosing to leave a marriage or to live without a man thus brings risks of stigma and harassment. Juliana told us that, because she lives alone, men simply show up at her door bringing food they expect to exchange for sex. And, Margarida explained that she decided to move out of one neighbourhood because she and her daughters were frequent objects of men's insults and stalking. She has relocated her women-and-children-only household to a new neighbourhood of young families where she is building a small house adjoining the house of her married niece and her family.

If many women told us how they had been able to extricate themselves from abusive partners and to sustain households through their own earnings and networks, others explained their decisions to remain living with drinking or violent partners. One woman said that she chose to live with a male partner even though she did not like him because he provided protection from her ex-husband – who had been worse. New divisions are emerging among women: women who have managed to remove themselves from situations of domestic violence and to work to raise their children on their own may criticize other women who feel compelled to remain in abusive situations. Eufrosina is a 45-year-old woman who has worked since she was 7 years old, when her mother ran away from her father leaving the six children for him to raise. After many changes of employment, Eufrosina currently operates a small snack bar from her home. She says:

> I have never put up with a bad man. For this reason, I have worked all my life. I am so against a woman who stays suffering because she doesn't have the courage to confront her life. There are women who are afraid of dying of hunger, who do not have the courage to work. Not me. If things don't work out with a man, I send him right away. I have two arms, two hands to work. (I-77)

She is silent about her own steady relationship with a married man who comes to spend each Saturday night with her, bringing with him meat, gifts and, one time, a refrigerator.[10]

Women describe themselves as 'like [former President] Lula', burdened (*supercarregada*) in multiple spheres of responsibility and navigating necessary *compromissos* as they construct and negotiate their *liberdade*. As we have seen, they often take on more than one form of employment, combining wage work with small home-based businesses such as selling snacks or sewing clothes. They exchange goods and services with kin, neighbours and co-workers. They persevere with bureaucracy to access changing state programmes. They manage households of complex and fluid membership. And, they construct and publicly circulate transformative narratives that both support their personal projects and work to change gender norms and relations.

Households are conventionally thought of as private, domestic spaces where the work of social and biological reproduction takes place. This chapter highlights how Cascavel women's daily efforts to disentangle their lives from economic and emotional dependence on men have transformed relations within the household and enmeshed households in diverse scales of social networks and in new webs of relations with state and market. Cascavel households are profoundly moulded by market forces, and state policies and women's engagement with these publics draws them out of private, dyadic relations to see their lives in broader terms.

As both the state and the market are sites of flux and change, however, the repertoire of choices and the contexts within which women must make decisions are continually changing. Just as the lives of Cascavel's first generation of women migrants, as described in this chapter, are radically different from their mothers', so are the opportunities and constraints different for their own daughters. The first generation of women migrants was the first to earn a guaranteed minimum monthly wage and to receive benefits from state programmes. Their daughters, however, are facing the contraction rather than the expansion of formal employment, increasingly finding themselves in precarious spaces of informal work. The women who speak here so passionately about their own *liberdade* also speak of worries for their daughters who, with their higher levels of education and consumer expectations, often cannot find commensurate employment. Future studies focused on this younger generation are needed; preliminary indications from our research in Cascavel suggest that, accompanying their economic precarity, some are entering new relations (*compromissos*) with men based on material exchanges for sex – whether these be public as in sex work or unspoken and 'private' as in marriage. Carrier-Moisan (chapter 3, this volume) is one young scholar who has undertaken recent ethnographic research with this next generation of women, who have moved from the scale of the household to the contradictory transnational public sphere of sex tourism seeking to transform their lives.

In this chapter, ethnographic research has revisited the scale of the household – a once-classical site of feminist research. The analytical focus is shifted from viewing the household as a private sphere of kinship and domestic work to recognizing the household as deeply embedded in state and market forces and as a key locus of women's political activism: an auto-constructed feminist public. For, through their renovations of the household in response to everyday exigencies and perceived possibilities – and independent of any organization or social movement – Cascavel women are undertaking a revolution in 'habits and culture'. Feminist activists seeking to do the work of accompaniment with women like the women of Cascavel need to re-examine the role and dynamics of the household if they are to put forward political agendas for social transformation that engage these women's visions, accomplishments and compromises.

Activist Testimonial: Mariza

'Today, one of the greatest priorities is the economic position of women.'

Mariza has worked in the rural women workers' movement (the MMTR, Movimento de Mulheres Trabalhadoras Rurais) in Northeast Brazil for more than 20 years. She tells us of the political challenges rural women face as they seek to have their economic issues adopted on the agendas of the 'mixed spaces' of the male-dominated rural union movement, the national spaces of the Brazilian feminist movement and transnational spaces such as the World Social Forum. At the same time, Mariza describes the 'beauty' of public participation in the Women's Marches and the transformative political work of recording rural women's life stories. The following is from our conversation with her in Recife, Brazil, on 23 April 2008.

I am a rural worker, nothing more. I am an *educadora*, a popular educator. I have been in social movements my entire life. More than 30 years. I've been in the women's movement since the 1980s. I have worked with the MMTR for 21 years. My role has been to collaborate and to help rural women workers to understand questions. And this occurs mainly through organization. MMTR has five programmes: training leaders; training educators; income generation; communication; and documentation, which we call the citizenship [*cidadania*] programme.[1]

Today, within the movement, one of the greatest priorities is the economic position of women. We have more than 20 years of the movement, of organizational work and articulation, and the women are empowered in their knowledge and awareness. But, economically, they are poorer every day. So we have a responsibility as a movement to intervene in this. For us, a great challenge is to work with this question of the economy, as much as with the women as with the organization. It's *very* difficult. And it also involves questions of agriculture, solidarity economy [*economia solidária*] and the environment. Mixed spaces. It all has to be worked on systematically. And all this goes through a collective process. It won't work otherwise. Won't be worth it.

We do try working with the federal government; it is very difficult. A lot of bureaucracy. The government offers, offers, offers. But when the money arrives, so come a lot of demands in order to acquire the funds and they come late. It's very complicated. I don't have the knowledge for this. I am not an economic manager.

We work with partnerships. Historically, this movement [of rural women] constructed itself within alliances with social movements. What movements? The first movement was the rural union movement, the union of rural workers. This was the first. And along with this, some NGOs that were interested specifically in working with women – like SOS-CORPO, which is a feminist organization here in Recife and CENTRA in Ceará [a neighbouring state]. In each state rural women workers made different alliances. With pastoral organizations, and with various NGOs, from feminist NGOs to those working with agro-ecology.

Before the World March of Women – the 'Marcha' (Marcha Mundial das Mulheres) – SOF (Sempreviva Organização Feminista)[2] was our partner for a long time. For us, it's interesting that the MMTR played an important role in the history of the World March of Women in Brazil; people recognize this. We were the ones who organized the Marcha das Margaridas[3] who took the first position paper to Brasilia. We can't forget this. Here in Brazil it was us who took it. But, who gets the credit now? The World March of Women took it over – the feminists. Even so, the Marcha das Margaridas is really beautiful. Today the Marcha is a huge movement: 20,000 women marched to Brasilia in 2000 and 50,000 in 2003 and 2007. The goal is to present the demands of women. The big agenda of the Marcha combines the issues that have been defined on the global stage – for example at the UN conferences – with goals and priorities defined in local contexts concerning: (1) land, water and ecology; (2) nutritional security and food sovereignty; (3) work, revenue and solidarity economy; (4) guaranteed employment and better conditions of life and work for the employed; (5) minimum salary; (6) public, mutual social welfare; (7) public health; (8) non-sexist education; (9) combating violence against women.

As far as the World Social Forum goes, it's been very difficult to participate. Very difficult. Because it's for social movements as a whole. And when women's movements arrive it's about global policy. When it gets to specifics, it's specifics according to the big organizations. And when we participate in the Social Forums at the state level, it's the state that pushes the agenda. The Social Forum sets the agendas and organizes the people to participate. And now, there's the forum on food sovereignty in Brasilia. For sure we want to participate. But it's all very difficult. And it's difficult for us economically.

In my view, the movement [MMTR] participates in spaces [*campos*] in order to be strengthened – and to shine [*brilhar*]. But you can only shine if you can open your mouth – and be heard. It's a challenge. This movement – this question of the autonomous organization of rural women – is an incredible experience. Most are mixed [women and men] organizations. Or, women's secretariats and councils within mixed organizations [like the unions]. We have to participate [in these mixed spaces]. But we lack the technical capacity and financial resources. And when we're there, the [issues of] others take up all the space … we aren't seen.

Of course, we try to act within mixed spaces. But we work with specific issues. We try to take our message there. We make a certain contribution. But let's just say that when we go there – when women arrive there – the participation of women with equality with men is very difficult. Very difficult. It's difficult because the discrimination is very great. The inequality is tremendous. It is women who have a mixed sensibility [*cabeça*]. But a woman has difficulty to advance this. Often when she gets to the mixed space, she forgets the specific struggle of women. It's very complicated …

I would say that still one of the greatest challenges is for women to be able to actualize themselves … because women who work also have the reality of the space of the family. It's very important to construct just and equal relations between women and men; and you have to first work in the space of the family. Another challenge is to change self-conception, isn't it? In this *machista* world, this patriarchal world in which we live. To change this … You say something – you defend a theory – and, many times, you know that the practice is completely different from this. I would say one of the greatest challenges is to close the gap between theory and practice. It's one thing in the space of women. But in society as a whole, in social movements as a whole, we have all this work of partnership with mixed NGOs, with the unions, with the government, so today it's a big challenge … Because sometimes you say something but when you look at the practice you will see enormous difficulty, sometimes it's a problem of violence, of discrimination. It's complicated. You put one thing out but you are living something else inside. So I would say this is a great challenge.

I don't believe the [mixed] rural workers' union is really interested in MMTR. It's just a strategic interest for them. So this is an obstacle for MMTR. But we have to try. The union has different priorities.

But we can't spend the time involved in their public forums if we can't shine [*brilhar*]. It's not worth it. We can spend days preparing and days participating and then, when the report is published, our ideas are not even there. So these alliances are hard to maintain. Very difficult. A huge challenge.

We participate in the National Conferences for Women and on various councils at the municipal level, and not just women's councils but others on the solidarity economy and the environment. But I would say that our [rural women's] participation is still very timid. But in some states rural women can participate more readily than others. It depends on the relation the state has with rural women. There's a bureaucracy. To go to the National Conferences you have to first participate in conferences at the municipal level and then at the state forums. The power of rural women to make an intervention is still very small. I think what we have contributed most to is the discussion of the question of documentation. But for the question of documentation to get on the agenda of the National Conferences it has to first pass through a process of discussion at municipal and state levels. And as we get to the state level, the number of rural women participating is even smaller and it's harder to get our issues on the agenda. Some municipalities have greater participation and political power … but when you arrive at the state conference there is lots of fighting [*brigas*] and much confusion, much conflict. And the rural women stay quiet, are shy.

Look, I think the conferences are a good idea for the movement but I have a more critical perspective on this question. I am a very critical person. I think that, on the whole, there are too many conferences. I don't like it. There's a conference for everything today. Conferences are in fashion in Brazil. You can pass your whole life in conferences. And when you look at the result, it's very small, very small. So there's lots of propaganda, lots of noise. It's good to discuss policy and to hold it up to the mirror. Very good. But when you get inside … There is some good – but the bureaucracy is enormous. If you look at the history of documentation [to receive a pension], for example, it's a government programme very tied to the history of citizenship. But today it's a big bureaucracy. Many women remain without documents; men still have more ease in getting them. Some states are better organized, but in some municipalities the whole question of documentation has not even been opened up and it's not a priority. For the government the priority is the new INCRA settlements.[4] But we work with rural women, not with women in the settlements. So, here was another shock. It's another challenge to get the government programmes to be equally available to all women.

The movement of rural women is an activity of feminism. And that's good. Feminism has made an important contribution. It gave the opportunity for us to discuss policy for women in a general way. But, look, we did not see the rural world in feminism. There was nothing for rural women. But feminism wasn't pushed on us. It was us. We looked inside. And we saw that feminism offered a great opportunity. And we took it to rural women. It's a good thing.

We have worked to develop a life-history methodology specifically for working with rural women … something I'm impassioned about. It helps women a lot. Because, on the one hand, it's a methodology but, at the same time, it's very political. It produces much conflict. Many conflicts, because it works with the question of mentality. Many times when I work, I encounter fights, in organizations, in groups. To change social relations is to encounter fights, to encounter fights between women themselves. Because it destroys preconceptions. We worked more than two years to develop this approach to education within the movement. And it's not easy to do this. I have worked to call attention to this – for its value to be recognized. I am a fighter. I am a person who has had to fight for professional qualifications. I am a person who knows how to fight. Many women like to fight. But, really, my life is a conflict. But this does not bother me in the least. It's necessary to know how to manage conflict, but it's difficult.

3
Saving Women? Awkward Alliances in the Public Spaces of Sex Tourism

Marie-Eve Carrier-Moisan

On 10 November 2006, the newspaper headline in the *Diário de Natal,* read: 'In Ponta Negra, a Public Act against Sex Tourism'.[1] This caption was accompanied by a picture of the event: a march in the street of Ponta Negra with a notable symbol of sex tourism: a 2-metre high *papier-mâché* sculpture of a white phallus, adorned with the flags of the United States, France, Germany, Great Britain and Portugal, among other countries (see Figure 3.1). The street protest was provocatively and humorously labelled 'The Big White Penis Act'.[2] Since the early 2000s, Ponta Negra, a tourist district in Natal, the capital of the state of Rio Grande do Norte in Northeast Brazil, has become the centre of several interventions against sex tourism. Among the various agents involved in fighting sex tourism were: the municipality of Natal, the state of Rio Grande do Norte, the federal government, associations of local residents and business owners, and non-governmental organizations (NGOs). While they coalesced in their attempts to fight sex tourism, their understanding of what 'sex tourism' meant differed greatly. These misunderstandings did not stop their joint mobilization; rather, confusions over the meanings of sex tourism created the conditions for different agendas to co-habit and led to awkward alliances across differences.

In *Friction: An Ethnography of Global Connection,* anthropologist Anna Tsing (2005) examines the different interests of various actors managing the rainforest in Indonesia. She documents the timber extraction that began in the 1970s with the complicity of the state and Japanese businesses, and provides ethnographic fragments of the successful halt to massive destruction by nature lovers, village leaders and national activists. While each had a 'different kind of commitment to nature' (2005: 246) they avoided the corporate destruction of the forest – not because they operated on similar premises or shared goals – but due to messy misunderstandings,

Figure 3.1   The Big White Penis Public Act against sex tourism in Natal,
8 November 2006.
Source: http://www.sospontanegra.blogspot.com Photo by Carlos Santo/DN.

or 'productive confusion' (2005: 247). Tsing uses the metaphor of
friction to examine the contingencies that make global connections
possible – friction referring to 'the awkward, unequal, unstable, and
creative qualities of interconnection across difference' (2005: 4).

Tsing's work provides important insights into the complex
articulations – or frictions – that allow collaborative objects to
come into being. In the campaigns against sex tourism in Natal,
activists, local residents and state agents, as well as hotel, bar and
restaurant owners converged to fight sex tourism in a multiplicity of
ways, despite their distinct agendas (Tsing 2005: 246). At times, this
collaboration is manifested in their participation in similar forms
of mobilization, including for instance their participation in 'The
Big White Penis Act'. More often, they coalesce through the myriad
separate sets of discourses and practices in which they engage to
co-manage sex tourism. It is when these various interventions
are juxtaposed that it is possible to grasp the magnitude and the
contradictions of the fight against sex tourism in Natal. In this
chapter, I thus engage with the various frictions that set disparate
agents in motion in a 'common' struggle against sex tourism.

In the spirit of the contributions to this volume, I consider sex
tourism as a new political space – or 'public'. This lens allows

consideration of what remains unaddressed in Tsing's work: the processes whereby difference and exclusion are also inscribed in these awkward alliances. As such, I see sex tourism as a *contested public*, marked by various political interests that re-inscribe exclusions. As Cole and Phillips propose in chapter 1, gender inequalities may persist in spite of, or even through, feminist activities. The various campaigns against sex tourism in Natal bring into sharp relief the negotiations of power that characterize emerging (feminist) publics in newly democratic spaces. As we shall see, these campaigns have the effect of further entrenching the marginalization of the very women they mean to rescue: the predominantly impoverished, black or mixed-race women engaging in commercial sex with foreigners. This chapter thus uncovers how the street march and other campaigns against sex tourism in Natal are entangled within local micro-politics and crisscrossed by a multiplicity of political interests that re-inscribe local hierarchies of race, class, gender, sexuality and civility. In this sense, this chapter seeks to contribute to one of the central claims of this volume: the need to consider, as suggested by Cole and Phillips, the public as a dynamic domain of power and to take into account the inequalities that underlie any construction of a public consensus or a public good. Given the rhetoric of protecting and 'saving' women that motivates various agents to campaign against sex tourism in Natal, I focus here on the contradictory ways in which notions of gender equality, women's interests and/or feminism(s) engage in/with the new political space that sex tourism constitutes in Natal.

The chapter draws on ethnographic research I conducted in Ponta Negra from July 2007 to June 2008. I conducted participant-observation in bars, restaurants and on the beaches, and interviewed male European tourists and Brazilian women. I also interviewed representatives from the city government, NGOs and local associations of residents and business owners, and participated in municipal and regional forums, protests and conferences where sex tourism was on the agenda. The chapter begins with a history of the emergence of Ponta Negra as a tourist district within the city of Natal, and the tensions over class, race, sexuality and civility generated by new spatial configurations. Then, I critically examine the campaigns against sex tourism and the different interests underlying them, considering the following threads: different levels of government; local businesses and residents; NGOs, feminist activists and academics; and women engaging in sex tourism. As their articulations are complex and as they constitute complex agents, I treat them in their myriad of interconnections, rather than as exclusively separated actors with distinct strategies. When possible, I trace their specific interventions to fight sex tourism and underlying interests, but I find that, more often, collusion and collaborative friction aptly describe their practices – collaborations that ultimately inscribe new forms of power, exclusion and (in)civility. By considering sex tourism through the lenses of the 'public', I aim to engage with the salient question of who is included/excluded and why.

SPATIAL TENSIONS IN THE CITY OF PLEASURE

Situated in the state of Rio Grande do Norte, the city of Natal with a population of 803,739 is relatively small when compared to other state capitals in Brazil (IBGE 2010). Natal was long considered a provincial town, dominated by local elites. It played an important role during the Second World War, due to its strategic location as the closest point between South America and Europe. In 1942, a military naval base was built, leading to an increase in the presence of Brazilian military, and the selection of Natal to serve as a base for the U.S. military. Economically, the city, much like the state, was highly reliant on the oil industry, as well as on fishing and agricultural and textile production. Today, tourism (both domestic and international) is the most significant source of revenue and employment for the state (Governo do Estado do Rio Grande do Norte 2010). Like its neighbour states in the region, the state of Rio Grande do Norte began favouring tourism as a strategy of economic development in the 1980s, with a focus on the implementation of infrastructure meant to develop the coastal regions. Natal played a central role in this development, as it came to be promoted as a tourist destination, initially intended as a sort of 'local Copacabana' (Lopes Júnior 2000: 39).

Brazilian sociologist Edmilson Lopes Júnior (2000) analyses the production of Natal as a 'city of pleasure' for the local middle class and documents the main social changes leading to its particular socio-spatial configuration as a tourist city. The district of Ponta Negra played a significant role in this development. Situated about 14 km south from the city centre, Ponta Negra is famous for its beautiful beach and unique sand dune, the Morro do Careca (the Bald Hill), attracting both domestic and international tourists. For most tourists Ponta Negra is defined by its beach and by the nightlife on the hill above the beach known as the Alto de Ponta

Negra. But Ponta Negra is also a divided residential neighbourhood comprised of the Vila (or the village), the oldest and poorest part of Ponta Negra, historically rooted in fishing, and the Convenho, a middle-class residential area comprising a shopping mall and gated, private residences under security surveillance.

For a long time, Ponta Negra was a peripheral area of the city. It was a fishing community that had expanded up into the hills, where fishing families built small houses facing away from the beach view. During the 1960s and 1970s, Ponta Negra became a privileged site for second residences for Natal's elite, who built large houses on the shore. An important change transforming the spatial configurations of the city occurred in the early 1980s when a coastal highway, the Vía Costeira, was constructed to foster tourism development by connecting Ponta Negra to the city centre 14 km away (Lopes Júnior 2000:39). The urbanization of the southern part of the coast soon followed, bringing dramatic changes. Hotels, bars and restaurants replaced the summer residences of the local elite, who then moved to more distant and secluded beaches south of the city, to get away from the hubbub. In the 1980s and 1990s, Ponta Negra was also marketed for tourism as a 'different' place and began to attract the emergent local middle class, who established the residential neighbourhood of the Convenho. With the city expansion and tourism development, Ponta Negra transformed into an urbanized beach. With its sand dunes and protected areas, its fine restaurants, chic nightclubs and fancy bars, and with the development of the Convenho as a new residential area and shopping mall, Ponta Negra became associated with a middle-class lifestyle (Lopes Júnior 2000: 55).

By 2000, Natal had symbolically become a city of pleasure for leisure and local tourism, and Ponta Negra was its 'postcard' (Lopes Júnior 2000: 56). Further significant transformations, however, contributed to even more drastic changes. In 2000, following the construction of a new terminal, the airport of Natal inaugurated its first international flights, connecting Natal to several major European cities. Natal quickly became a major destination of European tourism, given its strategic location as the Brazilian capital city closest to Europe. Between 2002 and 2007, the number of visitors almost doubled, with the number of international tourists increasing 100 per cent, and international flights increasing from 5 a week in 2002 to more than 30 in 2010 (Governo do Estado do Rio Grande do Norte 2010; Infraero 2010).[3] In 2007, Natal was the third most visited city by international tourists in Northeast Brazil, and the sixth most visited city for the whole country, after

São Paulo, Rio de Janeiro, Salvador, Porto Alegre and Fortaleza, an impressive position given its relative small size. Tourism was accompanied by massive foreign investment.[4]

Ponta Negra, as the privileged site of tourism in the city, was transformed by this rapid influx of tourists and foreign investment. In addition to tourists, foreign-owned businesses came to sit next to locally owned businesses and skyscrapers became a common feature. Ponta Negra became a transnational space, marked by the presence of foreigners, mostly Europeans. Furthermore, the site began to attract impoverished migrant workers from the rural interior and workers from the Vila and from poorer parts of the city, especially from the Zona Norte.[5] With this influx, came women looking to find their luck at transnational marriage, or seeking to engage in various forms of commercial sex with foreigners.[6] Once seen as the site of *gente de família* ('respectable' families),[7] the visible presence of *gringos* (foreigners) and Brazilian *garotas*[8] now associates Ponta Negra with sex tourism, generating new spatial tensions. In 2007–2008, when I was conducting fieldwork in Ponta Negra, many local residents complained about the changes brought by tourism; for although these changes have translated into new economic opportunities for many, they have also transformed the social relations and the landscape. These residents, along with business owners, have formed local associations such as the Movement SOS Ponta Negra or Ame Ponta Negra (Love Ponta Negra)[9] to promote sustainable, balanced and responsible development in Ponta Negra (Trigueiro 2005).

Campaigns against sex tourism have further altered the locality by forcing recent bar closings on the beach, with the result that nightlife has moved up the hills into the Alto de Ponta Negra, a space that, until the arrival of mass tourism, had been the exclusive domain of middle-class young professionals and university students. The Alto has become, as one journalist put it, 'infested with this forbidden diversion' (*O POTI–Diário de Natal* 2006) – the forbidden diversion referring to the *gringos* and *garotas* seeking to meet one another in the local bars and restaurants. The presence of *gringos* and *garotas* thus disturbs what the local middle class see as their space. For them, sex tourism is a catalyst for other problems, including criminality, traffic in women and the overall decadence of the neighbourhood.

Here, the work of anthropologist James Holston (2008) on civic participation in Brazil provides an important conceptual framework for thinking about the inscriptions of new silences. Holston documents the historically and ethnographically 'differentiated citizenship' characteristic of Brazil's democracy, a citizenship he describes as 'universally inclusive in membership but massively inegalitarian in the distribution of rights and resources' (2008: 284). He also analyses the exercise of 'insurgent citizenship' by those who occupy the margin and who 'disrupt the differentiated' (2008: 275) through struggles over space. Holston's analysis is particularly useful for thinking about the tension between the middle class in Natal, accustomed to spatial exclusivity, and the *garotas* disrupting these privileges. Furthermore, Holston's analysis, as suggested by Cole in chapter 2 of this volume, provides an entry point to engage spaces of 'unorganized activism' and to recognize the transformative potential of the innovative social practices of *favelados* (inhabitants of shantytowns), migrant workers or *garotas de programa*.

In his work on civic participation in São Paulo, Holston documents how spatial practices in apartment buildings contribute to enforcing a sense of privilege and deference among the middle class and elites, as different entrances and elevators form part of the design of apartment buildings. While this unique spatial practice was intended to differentiate between owners and their domestic workers and service providers, recent shifts have produced new proximities and anxieties as owners and their employees are brought into the same elevators and entrances. These new proximities result in spatial struggle disrupting those who occupy privileged positions. As Holston argues: 'from administration to residence, from infrastructure to consumption, Brazil's insurgent citizens have pushed themselves into urban spaces and even personal spaces elites used to dominate with complete assurance' (2008: 280). The black/mixed-race impoverished women who participate in sex tourism can thus be seen as insurgent citizens, as they disrupt spaces associated with the (white) middle class. These women frequent the same bars, restaurants and nightclubs as the middle class and, through their intimate relationships with foreigners, momentarily enjoy the same economic privileges. These practices disturbed the unwritten rules of civility and thus intensified the 'micro surveillance practices that determine who is heard and seen in public and who can make decisions on behalf of others' (Cole and Phillips, chapter 1 this volume) – an aspect I shall return to later. While this is the broader spatial context in which the campaigns against sex tourism took place in Ponta Negra, key articulations – or frictions – provided the fuel for intricate alliances between residents, business owners, governments, NGOs and feminists, with important consequences for the Brazilian women engaging in sex tourism.

SEX TOURISM AS AN EMERGENT PUBLIC IN NATAL

Since early 2000, sex tourism in Natal has captured wide public attention in the area. The topic has also triggered a boom of research, publications, academic discussions and debates (Lopes Júnior 2005; Pruth 2007; Ribeiro and Sacramento 2006, Teixeira and Batista 2002). In the first few weeks of my fieldwork, I was made aware of some of the tensions present in Natal, as I was warned to be careful with the dissemination of my research due to the potential reactions it could incite, especially given that two of my predecessors – foreign anthropologists who had done research on sex tourism in Natal – had been publicly condemned for their work.

In August 2005, the municipality of Natal and its city council had declared Portuguese anthropologists Fernando Bessa Ribeiro and Octavio Sacramento 'personas non grata' in response to the presentation of their research in one of the local newspapers, the *Diário de Natal* (Azevedo 2005c; Guimarães 2005). One city councillor claimed the anthropologists had 'offended the women of the city' (Guimarães 2005) because they had proposed that sex tourism and family tourism could peacefully co-habit. The condemnation stirred a polemical debate in Natal, with some local academics from the federal university and feminist activists from the NGO Coletivo Leila Diniz using the same local newspaper to voice their critique of the condemnation, which they saw as retrograde and provincial (Azevedo 2005b; Sousa 2005). One of the two anthropologists replied stating that their intentions were not to offend Natal's citizens but to suggest that, like other commercial activities, the sex trade in Natal should be regulated by the state, itself a contentious issue (Azevedo 2005a).

It was not the first time sex tourism had been debated in Natal. Throughout the 2000s, it was a key subject of discussion and policy-making, becoming a new public arena of interventions. As in the rest of Brazil, the concern for sex tourism had begun with preoccupations about the sexual exploitation of children and adolescents in the context of tourism. The city of Natal went further than any other Brazilian city in confronting this problem; it was the first to adopt the 'Code of Conduct for the Tourism Industry against the Sexual Exploitation of Children' hereafter referred to as 'the Code'.[10] One of the most striking moments in the constitution of this emergent public was March 2006, six months after the incident with the two researchers. What triggered this moment was special media coverage from the national news network, Globo, whose journalists went undercover with hidden cameras and revealed the inaction of the city of Natal[11] and the complicity of many local businesses in facilitating prostitution in tourism (*Jornal da Globo* 2006a, 2006b, 2006c, 2006d, 2006e). Such coverage, distributed on national television, in newspapers and on the internet, has had a significant impact on the city of Natal. It has brought the topic into the public arena but on a much larger scale than the polemic over the anthropologists' research. Natal, a *Cidade do Sol* (Sun City) as its nickname goes, had not only been tarnished with images of child exploitation and sex tourism, but the city itself was identified as facilitating this situation. As a result, Natal embarked upon a vigorous crusade to 'save' the women and children involved in sex tourism in an attempt to revamp its image as an attractive sun destination.

In the weeks following this media coverage, the state of Rio Grande do Norte, along with associations of business owners and residents, took various actions to stop sex tourism, leaving its meanings largely undefined. A week after this coverage, the city council of Natal held a public hearing on the issue of sex tourism (Dickson 2006; Régis 2006), and ten days after the coverage, the state of Rio Grande do Norte also held a special meeting to elaborate a plan of action against sex tourism in which different state and non-state actors took part (Oliveira 2006). The goal of the meeting was to coordinate their efforts to fight sex tourism in an attempt to make clear that the state took the problem of sex tourism very seriously. The operation 'Free Ponta Negra' (Ponta Negra Livre) was launched.

As part of this massive operation, the first of a series of raids took place less than a month after the Globo coverage, involving the deployment of 150 military, civil and federal police officers. The main street along the beach in Ponta Negra was blocked at both ends, and a total of 120 foreigners were approached; nine of them (all men) were eventually detained. These arrests were carried out under the guise of fighting 'sex tourism'. However, the term seemed to apply to a panoply of practices, including prostitution (which is not illegal in Brazil, although its incitement and facilitation are). The crimes committed were not related to pimping nor to the sexual exploitation of minors; five Portuguese men were arrested for possession of marijuana, two Spanish men were arrested because they did not carry their passports[12] and, finally, two men, one Italian and one Swede, were arrested for having overstayed their tourist visas (Bezerra 2006; Freire 2006). Similar raids followed, one of which resulted in the interrogation of 323 foreigners; 78 were without their passports and thus arrested (Bezerra and Lopes 2006).

A couple of weeks after these operations, the municipality installed surveillance cameras at the beach to deter illicit activities related to 'sex tourism' (Araújo 2006). Yet these cameras became a tool, in subsequent media reporting (Souza 2007), to discourage prostitution. The municipality also launched the bilingual campaign 'Stop Sex Tourism' at the airport and in the city. Similar to the beach operation, the meaning of sex tourism was left largely undefined, with slogans such as: 'If you have come to enjoy Natal, welcome. If you have come for sex tourism, please go back home' (*Tribuna do Norte* 2006a). The campaign included an ad with the image of a tanned white man with a red face and a condom over his head, with the caption: 'It won't protect you against shame' (see Figure 3.2). The implicit meaning was that even safe sex practices would not protect the sex tourist from either the moral stigma of his acts nor the potential 'embarrassment' if he were to face criminal charges. Indeed, with the condom and the caption 'Stop sex tourism' apparent, this ad is more suggestive of adult prostitution than sex with minors.

Figure 3.2   Ad from the city campaign: 'It won't protect you against shame.'
Source: *Tribuna do Norte* (2006a).

A similar ad appeared on beer coasters in bars. On one side, the image of a young, white, blond man with a red face was accompanied by the caption in English: 'Blushing or tanning? Sex tourism: don't put yourself through this embarrassment', and on the other side, a collage of men's names – mostly evoking foreign nationalities – were written along with the caption 'Don't let sex tourism stain your name' (see Figure 3.3). The emphasis of the slogans was on shame (see also Figure 3.4), and, notably, did not prominently feature the sexual exploitation of children and adolescents. The only indication that 'sex tourism' meant the sexual exploitation of children was written in extremely fine print: 'Child molesting is a grave crime and will be punished with 6 to 10 years in jail' (Figures 3.3 and 3.4).

The message of the city campaign so thoroughly conflated the issues that it led Resposta, the NGO responsible for monitoring the Code, to distance itself from the campaign. The problem, for the NGO, was the city campaign's failure to make it clear that the

Figure 3.3   Ad from the city campaign: 'Blushing or tanning?'.
Source: SECTUR.

Figure 3.4   Ad from the city campaign: 'If you're here after sex tourism, get your bags and go back home.'
Source: SECTUR.

campaign was targeting sexual exploitation of children and adolescents. Resposta does not use the phrase 'sex tourism' because it recognizes that it carries multiple meanings, one of which is sex between consenting adults in a context of tourism. The director of Resposta, Ana Paula Felizardo, explains:

> Our campaign is always with a focus on sexual exploitation … The municipal campaign is completely wrong: that campaign and the guy with a condom [on his head]! Our relationship with the municipality has turned bad because we don't endorse this campaign, because it's wrong!

One of the problems, for her, is the confusing message sent by the campaign: 'The logic is that the condom does not cover the shame on the face. In so doing, it stigmatizes the condom which is a struggle of the AIDS and HIV movement.' For Ana Paula, the campaign subverted the fight against child sex tourism into a crusade against commercial sex between consenting adults, while undermining the efforts of the AIDS movement in Brazil to normalize condom use. In short, the campaign stigmatizes condom use rather than condemning the sexual exploitation of minors.

The state was not alone in this conflation of prostitution and the sexual exploitation of children and adolescents in the aftermath of the Globo media coverage. In November 2006, local residents and activists from different NGOs were involved in the campaign to eradicate sex tourism in Natal, marching in the streets of Ponta Negra with the symbol of sex tourism that introduces this chapter: the 'Big White Penis' sculpture (*Diário de Natal* 2006). The march clearly targeted the bars, nightclubs and restaurants seen as fostering encounters between Brazilian women and foreigners. Yet many of these activists conflated sex tourism with the sexual exploitation of children and adolescents, as this conversation with Danúbio, founder of the NGO Pau e Lata, which co-organized the march, reveals:

D: Our focus was sex tourism, targeting child abuse.
ME: The march was not against prostitution?
D: No, it was [against prostitution] yes. It was two issues. It was against sex tourism. And inside sex tourism, we focused specifically on the involvement of children and adolescents.

This comment reveals the extent to which local actors indiscriminately connect child exploitation with prostitution and sex tourism. The street demonstration thus made strategic use of the repudiation inspired by the sexual exploitation of children and adolescents in tourism to legitimate opposition to 'sex tourism'. In other words, it enabled the attack on adult prostitution, without making this explicit.

By using the symbol of a giant white penis, the street protest reinforced the notion of foreigners as the bad guys exploiting local women and equated sex tourism with sexual violence. The giant white penis – as a racial, gendered, international and sexual symbol – also expressed many anxieties and tensions about the massive presence of white European and North American tourists in Natal. Standing for imperialism, colonialism, globalization and (sex) tourism, the phallic sculpture allowed the inhabitants of Natal to rally against a common, easily identifiable enemy. Thus, the march served as a catalyst to protest against the evils of foreign (mostly western) tourism, seen as form of neo-colonialism.

The fact that sex tourism is the particular concern of this movement here underscores anxieties about sex, power and sovereignty. In effect, during the march, as in other interventions against sex tourism in Natal, the exploitation of the land and nature was connected, even conflated, with the sexual exploitation of Brazilian women. As one street protester, poet and visual artist Pedro Grilo, explains to one local newspaper: 'I'm in solidarity with the common good, refusing the ambitious and insensitive land speculation. I take revenge in my canvas, where Ponta Negra only has palm trees. Previously, Ponta Negra was such a bucolic scenery' (*Diário de Natal* 2006: 8). Thus, under the umbrella of combating the exploitation of children and adolescents, activists also rallied against mass tourism and neo-colonialism and their side effects, including prostitution and environmental degradation. Much of the opposition to sex tourism thus exposes racial, class-based, even territorial tensions specific to Natal. Perhaps even more significantly, the focus on sexuality and respectability deflects attention away from problematic state economic policies that favour tourism and foreign investment above all else.

FIGHTING EXPLOITATION? FEMINISMS AND THE CAMPAIGNS AGAINST SEX TOURISM IN NATAL

Beyond these campaigns, different organizations also gathered together regularly at the municipal, state and regional levels to discuss ways of combating sex tourism. In one such meeting in which I participated during the Forum Social Nordestino[13] held in Salvador in August 2007, a feminist organization based in Recife (Coletivo Mulher Vida) organized a session called, 'Sex Tourism, Traffic and Immigration: What do we have to do with this?'[14] in which several feminist organizations and NGOs from Natal took part. In this session, seamless links between pornography, human trafficking, violence and sex tourism were made, as if all of these were the same phenomena. This further entrenched the assumptions that all paid sex is a form of violence against women, that trafficking is the same as migration (for sex) and that sex tourism is inevitably a form of sexual exploitation.

The question of women's agency was at the centre of the discussion at the meeting. Prostitution, several feminist activists iterated repeatedly, is a form of *vício* (addiction, vice). Thus, if women engage in sex tourism it is because they are enslaved by Brazilian consumer society and driven to make 'easy money' to purchase consumer goods. Furthermore, feminist activists at the meeting described women in sex tourism as dupes, believing that a 'Prince Charming' (the foreign tourist) would eventually save them, and as unable to make informed choices due to their economic position and lack of education. The notion of *vício* was invoked to explain why so many women engaged in commercial sex with foreigners – why else would they, since it necessarily harms them?

These visions are well captured in the writings of organizations in the region that serve as both models and inspiration for other NGOs active in Natal. In one publication, feminist activist Jacqueline de Souza Leite, the head of the Salvador-based NGO CHAME,[15] describes sex tourism in the following manner:

> By no means does sex tourism give value to women or transform their social situation. Rather, it contributes to the denigration of their image and the reproduction of sexist and chauvinistic relationships, in addition to racist ideologies … [It] has had a bad impact on the communities where tourist complexes are built, producing, among the young women, a desire for objects they receive as gifts. [This] feeds false dreams of changing their lives and getting material things easily. In a similar way, it feeds, in their circles of friends and relatives, patterns of behaviour and dreams of consumption inaccessible for their own class – a perverse way to be inserted into the consumer society. (Leite 2003: 68)

From this perspective,[16] sex tourism is necessarily harmful because it is premised on the (sexual, racial) objectification of women. Furthermore, it creates dependence on goods these women and their relatives should not wish for because these are 'inaccessible for their own class'. In other words, only those of the 'proper' class may fully participate in the consumer society. While Leite's critique of sex tourism is potentially cogent for its analysis of class inequality and commodity fetishism, it remains problematic for its essentialist assumption about sex tourism. It is indeed difficult to engage with questions of coercion and consent in sex tourism, as these are complex issues that are not easily resolved. Indeed, for Jacqueline Leite, exploitation occurs when women are not paid for their sexual (and other) services. As she told anthropologist Erica Williams, 'the sex industry is a legitimate industry' (2010: 129). The exploitation occurs when relationships are ambiguous, 'when he dates' (2010: 129) and expects to have sex, visit the city safely and have a girlfriend for his stay without paying. The assumption is that western tourists take advantage of women's vulnerable position – a valid concern, but one that raises several questions regarding what constitutes exploitation. Indeed, the issue is how to articulate a critique of sex tourism that does not reduce poor, racialized women to what Anne McClintock aptly describes as reductive images of 'sluts and slave dolls' or 'too poor, too victimized, and too prone to false consciousness to be able to represent themselves objectively' (1993: 7). According to Williams (2010: 130–131):

> How can researchers, or NGO activists for that matter, who are so far removed from the daily harsh realities that our informants must endure evaluate if it is 'less exploitative' to receive anywhere from R$30 to US$300 in cash payment for the sale of sexual services, or gifts such as new clothes, a month's rent, airfare, or dinner at a fancy restaurant to which they could never have access were it not for their intimate associations with seemingly moneyed foreigners? This is particularly challenging when faced [with] the prostitutes' articulations of the ways in which they are exploited that have nothing to do with the act of selling sex – to tourists or locals – but rather are ramifications of the criminalization of sex work (even though it is technically legal).

This conception of women as enslaved by consumer society prevents a critical analysis of the ways in which Brazilian women are playing necessary roles in foreign tourism and negotiating their quest for social mobility through one of the few means available to them. While concerns for the protection of women against potentially exploitative men are not completely ill-founded, the lack of a sustained critique of state economic policies results in targeting the women as individuals making naïve, wrong choices as they passively hope for a Prince Charming to save them. In this way, state economic policies favouring mass tourism development at the expense of other sectors remain unchallenged. In Natal, efforts are thus unquestionably made to preserve the reputation of Sun City as a city of pleasure for tourist consumption.

There are exceptions to this dominant narrative, but mostly in the margin. For instance, the feminist organization Coletivo Leila Diniz provides a sound critique of the ways in which sex tourism is often talked about in Natal. As Jolúzia Batista, a member of the collective, puts it: 'Feminism as an emancipatory movement advocates that all women have equal opportunities to be protagonists of their own lives. We do not pretend to "save" women as advocated by the institutional discourse' (2007: 2). Rather, the Coletivo Leila Diniz questions the role of social inequality in fostering sex tourism, including 'differentiated access and opportunities between men and women, concentration of wealth, [government] corruption and the racial question' (2007: 2). Ultimately, Batista asks: 'Where and what are the opportunities for these women?' While the collective does not specifically work on the question of sex tourism, it is often present and involved in public forums, academic conferences and municipal or regional meetings where sex tourism is discussed. What makes the viewpoint of Coletivo Leila Diniz distinctive is its understanding of sex tourism as a way for women to negotiate social inequality and achieve social mobility in a context of harsh economic policies favouring mass tourism. Thus the collective instead targets state policies and focuses on the development of social and economic rights for women, rather than seeking to 'save' or stop the women from taking part in sex tourism. Yet its voice is marginalized in Natal. Other groups rarely take seriously the collective's expressed concerns over state development policies and inequalities. Instead, they focus on protests against 'sex tourism'.

Thus, the vision of women as in need of saving from exploitative foreigners occupies the dominant public discourse in Natal. As Cole and Phillips discuss in chapter 1, feminisms – and their emerging publics – potentially re-inscribe inequalities, and not all voices are present/presented or heard equally. Thus, newly engendered democracies potentially produce awkward alliances and set in motion the deployment of troubled discourses and practices in the name of feminism, gender equality or women's interests. In Natal, claims of protecting women against exploitation (*exploração*) by foreigners were invoked by various actors – not exclusively feminist ones – and appropriated for all sorts of ends.[17] As we shall see, the rhetoric of saving women works to maintain the local social order against the disruptive presence of poor, mixed-race, black *garotas* in Ponta Negra. In other words, claims of fighting sex tourism and women's exploitation are used to protect spaces seen as belonging to the local middle class. The fight against sex tourism, then, represents an attempt both to get rid of the disreputable *garotas* and to reclaim a space seen as invaded by impoverished informal workers contributing to the 'deterioration' of Ponta Negra.

RACE, CLASS, CITIZENSHIP AND CIVILITY

During an interview in May 2008, Manolo,[18] the owner of one of the first pubs to open in the Alto de Ponta Negra explained that tourism significantly transformed the neighbourhood. Initially, only the (white) upper class, his targeted clientele, would frequent his bar. It was, as he said, those with money, 'who spend more and are well-behaved [*mais comportado*]' who represented his ideal clientele:

> It has changed a lot with time. When there was only [this] pub on this street, the public was more upper class [*classe A*]: the rich of the city frequented this place. After that then the middle class [*classe B*] came too and it remained like this for about six years I think, just this public. When foreign tourism began so too sex tourism began and people from Natal started to pull away and the public changed. From then on the upper class [*classe A*] left completely, with the middle and lower class [*classe B, C*] and tourists remaining.

For local business owners like Manolo and for members of the middle class, the presence of *gringos* and *garotas* was perceived as an invasion of *their* space. As discussed above, anthropologist James Holston (2008) provides an insightful interpretation of these senses of invasion. He also makes an important distinction between civility and incivility. Drawing on Balibar's notion of civility as the condition that makes civic participation possible, Holston employs incivility to allude 'to the entanglement of citizenships at the moment when equality is an actual threat, when those who demand it threaten existing inequalities and those who are privileged by them feel threatened' (2008: 354 n. 8). In many ways, the presence of *gringos* and *garotas* in space associated with the middle class represents an assault on the old entrenched differentiated citizenship characteristic of Brazilian society. For Holston, it is a form of incivility by insurgent citizens who, through spatial struggles, disrupt those with privilege.

The sense of threat, invasion and loss of privilege on the part of members of the middle class is well captured in the project of privatization of the beach by the association,[19] AR de Ponta Negra – an association dedicated to promoting the business interests on Ponta Negra's beach. This project was only in its initial design when I interviewed its creator, Nelson Melo, the president of AR de Ponta Negra. From the mid 1970s on, Nelson frequented Ponta

Negra, first with his parents, eventually building his own house there in 2001 – one of the few remaining. He saw the beach changing, for better and for worse. He welcomed the new city regulation of 2000, which resulted in the closure of the *barracas*, the improvised kiosks on the beach from which Vila fishermen served food and drinks to tourists. New kiosks, regulated by the city and meeting new sanitary regulations, replaced the fishermen's kiosks. Nelson approved of these changes as well as the new sidewalk built in 2000 to make the beach more accessible to the local middle class. Then things began to deteriorate as people from the Vila began again to set up informal vending operations along the sidewalk and on the beach. As Nelson sees it:

> this facilitates [sex tourism]. When the prostitutes came with their *namorados* [lovers] they mixed with what was already there, the environment was already conducive to this. If the beach had continued to be pretty, organized and safe, this would not have happened.

For him, the problems have a lot to do with the beach's informal economy, where vendors circulate offering all sorts of products, from food and drinks to sun creams, souvenirs or CDs:

> The environment has a lot to do with this. I mean sex tourism itself did not just develop on its own. It's because the ambience was already slightly deteriorated. And now we're working hard to try to reverse all this. We're working on a project to completely change the street [by the beach], to transform it into a wide promenade. Our idea is that it would become like a shopping mall, like a large public stroll. Beautiful, interesting, with nice shops … a cool thing! Safer, because it's going to be something private. The street will be public, of course, but the security, cleaning and organization will be private.

His project was thus intrinsically connected to his sense of spatial threat:

> My idea is not only [related to] the question of tourism, [it's also for] the people of Natal to have a good place to go, because today people in Natal don't have an area of good quality they can frequent. There's none. It was Ponta Negra, and it's no longer. So the idea is that it would return and be a definitive thing, you know,

of good quality, and that the people from Natal, the middle class, would come back to frequent it. Because there's no public space in Natal for the middle class. There are the shopping malls, but outside of them, there are no other places. There was, already, there was this tendency, and I want it to come back today.

In other words, it was a proposal for gentrification, allowing the return of the middle class to *their* space, not only invaded by *gringos* and *garotas* but also by the *ambulantes*, the itinerant sellers trying to make money from tourism using the informal economy. This project has yet to materialize, but it hints at the class tension and the incivility (Holston 2008) generated by the 'lower classes' and especially by the visible presence of *garotas*. In Ponta Negra, the *garotas* have indeed come to stand for the evil of tourism, as their racial and class background signal their differentiated citizenship. They have thus become an easy target of middle-class discontent.

The tensions over space were extremely palpable in 2007–2008 when I conducted fieldwork. In the Alto de Ponta Negra, it was possible to find, side by side, bars catering to very different clienteles. Indeed, whereas some business owners sought to benefit from, or even foster 'sex tourism' (by charging a cheap entry fee or offering free drinks to women), other commercial ventures claimed to repudiate it and posted signs opposing sex tourism. Others have adopted practices meant to reduce their undesired clientele and target their privileged one, as Manolo, owner of a pub, explains:

> We have a special client card for any resident of Natal affiliated with a business or going to university. If you don't have this card, the price to enter is very expensive ... The regular entry price without any discount is 40 *reais*. It's an expensive price to get in, so in this way we stop people we don't want to come in. It's not that we stop them from entering but we make it more difficult ... Some people, some of the girls who are involved in sex tourism pay 40 *reais* but it's rare, so we are able to maintain the level in this way.

Several other business owners catering to the elite and middle class echoed Manolo's vision. Some of them came together to form the association Ame Ponta Negra (Love Ponta Negra; see note 9), with the aim, as the president of the association, Eduardo Bagnolli, explained to me during an interview in May 2008, of fighting the 'problems of violence, sex tourism and pollution'. Originally from São Paulo, Eduardo opened a hotel with a restaurant in what remains a quiet area of Ponta Negra, where the most expensive hotels are situated. Much like Manolo, Eduardo found the change in Ponta Negra since the advent of mass tourism upsetting and drastic. While the campaign of Ame Ponta Negra is mostly against mass tourism and its environmental consequences, sex tourism is a significant matter of concern for the association – a problem seen as deriving from the overall degenerate state of Ponta Negra. Outside the door of this hotel and restaurant, a sign opposing sex tourism is visible. Eduardo explained his strategy to prevent the occurrence of sex tourism in his hotel and restaurant:

> E: If he [a tourist] stays in [this hotel], and goes on a dune buggy tour, there is no chance to see [prostitution]. But if he goes outside, he'll see it there. But in theory, you can't really promote this. Here it's a '*prostituta* free' zone[20] You can't do this.
>
> ME: What do you do then, to distinguish …
>
> E: On our website, we explicitly state … we have it written there as a rule that we repudiate any form of sex tourism. If you come here and go to the reception desk, or if you come to the restaurant, which is open to the public, it's written there: 'No Sex Tourism'.[21]
>
> ME: And meaning any form of sex tourism?
>
> E: Any form: adults, children. So much that here in [this hotel] you can come here at any time, you'll never see a prostitute inside here. Because they know we don't let them in. There is someone outside that will ask: 'Do you have a reservation? You don't, well it's all booked today' … If someone comes here with a prostitute, we don't let her in, in any way … We even had some fights, and had to call the police … given it's not a crime. Here [in this restaurant] it's forbidden to get in with a mini-skirt. In Fortaleza, owners and managers of hotels who refused to permit prostitutes were sued in court because there is always a lawyer bad enough to say 'You have rights, you are black … or you are Indian. They did not let you in due to racial discrimination. We have to file a suit against the hotel.'

Manolo also explains how he prevents some women from entering his pub when they are suspected of being *garotas*, identifying them by their race, clothes and body language:

> We cannot say 'you can't enter' to discriminate against prostitutes, Blacks. It's a serious infraction, and it could lead to an expensive

trial. I was on trial already as some people accused me [of discrimination] because I didn't let them in because they were wearing short skirts. I didn't want to say that they were *putas* [whores], but I said their skirts were too short, and they sued me. Several times it happened to me but each time I won. But we prevent them from entering with the price. If they look like a prostitute, or if they are foreigners we don't like, we charge the full price of 40 *reais*.

The use of 'sex tourism' – purposefully left undefined – gave legitimacy to the backlash against prostitution. It is here that we can see how awkward alliances, in Tsing's (2005) sense, also produce marginalization. Here, sex tourism allows owners such as Manolo to refuse the egalitarian terms upon which the *garotas* seek to establish their citizenship. Yet as Holston (2008) proposes, by engaging the law and claiming equality these women refused to abide by the unspoken rules of civility that govern differentiated citizenship, as we shall see. Their practices can be seen as a form of 'unorganized activism' (see Cole, chapter 2 this volume) as these women find their own responses to what they perceive as the failures of the state and the market. Unlike the older women discussed by Sally Cole in chapter 2, these women seek to make ends meet outside of their local networks, through transnational ties that dislocate the fields of power in Natal.

INSURGENT CITIZENS

When is it that a *negra*, a black person from the *favela*, from the periphery, will imagine herself living in the Zona Sul owning a car, helping her family? When is it that a rich Brazilian man will look at you? Never! This is one of the positive aspects, I think, the foreigner when he comes here he can give you a better life, one you've dreamed of but never imagined would come true. (Larissa, 7 December 2007)

Larissa's words capture in a nutshell what is at stake for many Brazilian women like her in Ponta Negra. Her words reveal her understanding of her limited access to upward mobility, her awareness of the hegemonic workings of race and class relations in Brazil, and her perception of foreign men as the path to escape her own biography, or, as many women would say, to '*sair dessa vida*' – that is, 'to get out of this life'. In these few words, she summarizes the significance for many Brazilian women like her of engaging in various forms of commercial sex with foreigners. In her comment, Larissa points to the restrictions in Brazil for 'a black person from the *favela*' to experience mobility through marriage. This is the reason she frequents the bars, beaches and nightclubs in Ponta Negra, hoping for this 'better life' she has 'dreamed of but never imagined would come true' in Brazil or with a Brazilian man. Yet there is more to Larissa's narrative: her search for mobility with foreigners is also closely tied to her sense of respectability. Because she has worked as a *garota*, Larissa thinks she has 'spoiled' her identity and, as a consequence, has no opportunities left in her hometown. As she explained to me during a conversation we had about her future:

> And so today I'm 28 years old, and I don't see myself with a future, working, like having a normal life. Not here in Natal. Because as I told you, because there is this thing. This thing is in my mind because I did *programa*. Like I said to you, a businessman, if he hires such a person, he'll be discriminated against too. And the atmosphere, the place will be badly seen, you understand? So it's a big chain. It's very easy to enter [the sex trade], very easy, but after … You need to have lots and lots of help [*ajuda*] from your family. In case you don't have that, I don't know what will become of that person. A marriage. In my case, I think the only thing that could happen to me is a marriage. And not with a *brasileiro*, with an *estrangeiro* [foreigner].

For Larissa, marriage to a foreign man means the possibility to escape her own life in order to begin anew, in a place where both being a 'black person from the *favela*' and doing '*programa*' with foreigners would not restrain her opportunities. Larissa, aware of the stigma attached to sex with foreign men in Ponta Negra, also sees in it, paradoxically, a way to achieve a respectable status and to access social mobility. The tensions between her sense of respectability, her sexual transgressions and her wish to marry a foreign man are not exclusive to her. Rather, her struggle echoes that of many other young, working-class, mixed-race or black Brazilian women in Ponta Negra. Indeed, many women emphasize that, unlike their fellow Brazilians, male foreigners like their skin colour and do not mind their social origin. Brazilian men, they say, judge them in terms of their racial and social backgrounds. They are also driven by the idea that their chances of experiencing upward mobility in Brazil are practically non-existent. Marriage to a foreigner is seen as allowing them to realize their dream of social mobility in a respectable fashion.

Given the racial and class barriers in Brazil (Goldstein 2003; Twine 1997), it is difficult for many Brazilian women to achieve social mobility within their own society, as Larissa's comments make clear. Moreover, doing *programa* with foreigners further stigmatizes these women. In their narratives, women made countless references to the shame they feel for doing something as dirty, vulgar or bad as having commercial sex with foreigners. If sex with foreigners brings with it the 'whore stigma' (Pheterson 1993), it also conjures newly imagined possibilities, including enhanced social status and cultural capital as well as respectability. In a transnational space like Ponta Negra, which presents new opportunities (both imagined and real), these women came to imagine, and sometimes even succeeded in, pushing past class and racial boundaries. Women thus capitalize on the ambiguities of sex tourism in order to achieve social mobility, a finding echoed by Piscitelli, in her research in Fortaleza, the capital city of the neighbouring state of Ceará. She proposes that, 'for lower-class women, ambiguous relationships with sex tourists open the ways to real social mobility' (2007: 498).

Yet in the public discourse on sex tourism in Natal, sex tourism as social mobility is too often reduced to warnings of danger, in which enchanting princes are transformed into lascivious wolves. If their dream often echoed the fairytale of Cinderella, as so brilliantly depicted by Joel Zito Araújo in his documentary on sex tourism in Northeast Brazil (2008),[22] women like Larissa are also complex social actors who grasp the structural inequalities they face and strategize to *mudar de vida*, or change their life, as they would say. The campaigns against sex tourism too often neglect the complexity of sex tourism and its imbrications in the political and economic contexts of Ponta Negra, Natal and Northeast Brazil. Furthermore, the campaigns and other spatial practices of bar, restaurant and hotel owners further stigmatize women for their engagement with foreigners, especially when they are black and poor.

Several of the women I interviewed who self-identified as *garotas* have experienced not being allowed inside a bar in Ponta Negra, usually under the pretext that what they were wearing was deemed inappropriate. Yet they were well aware of the underlying meaning of such practices and often expressed their critical view of them. As Perla explained to me, speaking about one of the bars that denied her entry because she was wearing a mini-skirt:

There, it's all *garotas de programa* disguised. Because there are a lot of university students, they come there to work [as *garotas*] but they are more discreet. They don't go directly to the Água de Coco they go to the Samba,[23] but I see them only with foreigners. Anyway so I talked with the owner of the Salsa. There was a foreign woman with a short skirt, when she was dancing, you could see her underwear. I told her 'We can't get in, but foreign women can come in, dance, show off and expose their underwear, and you say nothing!'

As Perla was aware, the reason for not letting her into the Samba had nothing to do with her skirt and everything to do with her race, class and sexuality. She also sarcastically referred to the Brazilian women frequenting this bar as '*filha de papai*',[24] who, according to her, pretend not to be prostitutes: 'Many of them say "Oh, I'm not a whore", but they go to the shopping mall [with a foreigner] and buy a pair of shoes for 150 *reais*.' Perla thus hints at one crucial stigma. In Natal, a woman who is identified as *morena*[25] (like Perla) or as black and found in the company of a tourist is almost automatically seen as a prostitute, whereas white, middle-class women are not.[26]

Like many other Brazilian women, Perla was hoping to find a foreign man she would eventually marry, but she was not a dupe. She was well aware of the potential disenchantments of a life abroad, especially given her own experience, having lived two years in Germany with her ex-boyfriend. She did not fit the widespread, stereotypical depiction of the victimized woman, as circulated by the state, local NGOs and the media. She was highly critical, indeed, of the state intervention to eradicate sex tourism and recounted being interviewed by a journalist during the massive operation of 2006:

I told her, 'The problem is not the foreigners. The problem is that the Brazilian population is very hypocritical.' I talked this way to her. Because it's not just the foreigners who come looking for sex. I told her: 'Go there in the Praia do Futuro [Future Beach] or go to the Avenue Roberto Freire by night. Who stops? Brazilians, with their cars, looking for *travestis* [transvestites].'

Indeed, Perla saw hypocrisy in the state and NGO campaigns against sex tourism, because both Brazilian men and women (including, she said, married women, lawyers, judges and deputies) also hire prostitutes. 'I think if this prejudice against foreigners would go, the Brazilian population would be much better', she told me, adding later that several of the cases of sexual abuse with minors also involved Brazilians. In her critique, Perla disrupts the dominant discourse that victimizes her and pathologizes foreigners, as she turns her gaze on the campaigns against sex tourism and the *gente de família*. Her narrative suggests that she was more affected by how local residents and business owners treated her than by engaging in commercial sex with foreigners.

The tensions surrounding race, class, civility and respectability were also manifested in the minutiae of everyday life. In the restaurants, bars, and at the beach, the fight against sex tourism translated into different practices of discrimination against black or mixed-race women dating and/or engaging in commercial sex with foreigners. During my fieldwork, I witnessed numerous instances of these exclusionary practices. In the bars that cater to university students and young professionals, waiters and customers stare disapprovingly when locally known *garotas* come in. Upon hearing about the topic of my research, my landlady, a Brazilian woman, whose (white) daughter I knew was dating an Italian, asked me never to bring 'one of these women here'. She then added – making an indiscriminate connection between criminality and women engaging in commercial sex with foreigners – that not long ago members of the Italian mafia had been arrested in Natal. Meanwhile, my roommate, a Swedish woman working for an NGO active in the struggle against the sexual exploitation of children and adolescents, requested that there be 'no prostitutes' at home. When I suggested that she come with me while I conducted fieldwork, in disgust, she refused to accompany me.

On my last night in Ponta Negra, I invited friends from different backgrounds (including women engaging in commercial sex) to a small bar catering to a mixed clientele. The night was particularly tense for my middle-class friends who are dating foreigners – Clara, a 25-year-old lawyer, dating an Italian who owned a hostel and my neighbour Lisa, a former hairdresser dating a French man working in real estate. I had previously noticed how both women sought to distinguish themselves from *garotas de programa*. I had heard several discriminatory comments such as '*puta um dia, puta pra sempre*' (whore one day, whore forever) from Clara, who explained that *putas* could not be honest, nor ever truly in love, and thus were always self-interested. On this night, things got particularly heated: disapproving looks were given, and both Clara and Lisa refused to speak to women they deemed *garotas*. Eventually, Lisa, whose French partner had recently cheated on her with a local sex worker, declared 'I hate this race', leaving me on my final night with a lasting taste of the tensions generated by the presence of black and mixed-race women in spaces previously frequented exclusively by the middle class.

CONCLUDING REMARKS

While the idea of 'fighting women's exploitation' is a powerful trope in the discourse on sex tourism in Natal, its alarmist tone does little to tackle the complex subject position of women involved in sex tourism or to engage with the plurality and potential ambiguities of their interests. The coalescence of the do-gooders has created yet another obstacle for women like Larissa and Perla, whose experiences of sex tourism are rendered invisible. Their narratives provide us with only a glimpse of the broad universe that sex tourism encompasses, and which cannot be fully exposed here. At times, sex tourism closely resembles a transnational marriage market; at other times, it departs from prostitution even when material benefits are present. Sex tourism is inevitably inscribed in the micro-politics of race and class that play out in a context of local and global inequalities. There is thus a fluidity of scale that is crucial to engage with analytically – between transnational marriage and local sex tourism – so what constitutes 'sex tourism' remains a fluid, contested terrain. Ethnography is well positioned to capture this fluidity of scale, and to engage empirically with this new public/political space.

I would like, finally, to turn to the concept of location, which – in chapter 6, 'A Pedagogical Conversation' – we allude to as sites of contestation where new notions of the public and feminism and other democratic practices may be in development. The 'public-in-formation' constituted by the new space created by sex tourism in Natal requires further critical feminist engagement. Tensions in feminisms are nothing new but assumptions of gender equality in newly engendered democratic spaces are often taken for granted. By exposing the contradictions of the fight against sex tourism in Natal, my hope is to begin unravelling the fault lines in these relations of domination, in order to expose the power of those invested in defining oppression and acting upon it. In this project, I am aware of my own limits, as I re-present the interests of these women. Indeed, the question of who can speak for whom is a highly contested and problematic one. As Laura Maria Agustín aptly suggests: 'A great deal has been written about the need to bring out voices that are silenced or marginalized, but there are dangers when, as Gayatri Spivak argues, it is assumed that everyone can "speak" in the same way' (2007: 175). And, in the context of sex tourism in Natal, everyone cannot 'speak' in the same way. For one thing, the Brazilian women involved in commercial sex with tourists in Natal are not invested in the production of knowledge about themselves, nor are they involved in the many public discussions and debates on sex tourism. Unlike sex workers in the rest of the city and country, they do not form part of any association,[27] nor do they seek to organize as 'workers' or defend their rights or refute the stigma attached to commercial sex with tourists. In short, they do not speak in the same way as the dominant social actors in Natal. By no means outside of the production of knowledge about sex tourism, I too wish to participate in this 'public-in-formation'. But my engagement is, after all, just one voice in this new sphere of debates, contestations and negotiations that sex tourism is slowly coming to be and thus it is also open to debate.

By considering sex tourism through the lens of '*public*', it has become possible to engage with the salient question of who is included/excluded, and why. It has also become possible to attend to the crucial question of what kind of cultural space this public is (see Cole and Phillips, chapter 1 this volume). In chapter 4 Phillips engages with the contradictory possibilities of a participatory public in Ecuador, and provides another ethnographic glimpse into the ways in which newly engendered democratic spaces are sites of political negotiation, and in which differential access to spaces of power mediates the possibility for social change.

Activist Testimonial: Susana and Luísa

'If you look at the feminist agenda today and you look at the decade of the 1990s, it's another world.'

Susana and Luísa work in a small NGO – the 'CF8', the Centro Feminista 8 de Março (8 March Feminist Centre) – in Mossoró, a town in the northeastern Brazilian state of Rio Grande do Norte. They describe the CF8 as a 'hybrid' NGO, one that has 'a foot in the local with an eye to the global'. That is, they say CF8 is both a women's organization that does the work of accompaniment to address the needs of local women and it is 'a movement' working for social transformation. Susana and Luísa describe the changes in CF8 from its founding in an era of 'institutionalized feminism' to the more 'critical' and 'holistic' approaches they say they now take as a result of their links to transnational feminism and to the 'mixed spaces' of activism on the solidarity economy, the environment and the anti-free trade campaign. They see these as intellectually stimulating and politically challenging spaces for both the possibilities of change they offer and the potential to entrench old class and gender inequalities. The following is from our conversation with them on 18 April 2008 in the office of the CF8 in Mossoró, Brazil.

Susana: We are a 'hybrid' NGO. We are both a movement *and* we accompany [*accompanhar*] women. We have to give support to women's small income-generating groups and make links to other movements. We keep a foot in the local with an eye to the global. We are always discussing, 'How can we work on local projects but keep an eye on broader transformation?' We work with rural women's needs but with a global vision and with the goal of transforming society. For us it is never only about poor women having a small source of income. It's not this. It's more than this. For us, it's *economia solidária*, an alternative view of the economy that is not a trickle down from above, not an economy where people work for profit, profit, profit. It's seeing the economy instead as about care and reproduction ...

We can't separate our alliance work from our work of accompaniment. This dual focus is the basis of who we are. We think they can't be separated. To reflect on the global you have to have a foot here in the local and you can't have a foot [i.e. work] in the local without having a more global vision. We are half-crazy! At the same time that we are participating in work with the other social movements, we also have to accompany women in the community. We have to keep this tie; it can't be separated.

Luísa: For example, the cistern project started with the self-organization [*auto-organização*] of rural women in Mossoró who wanted to develop economic opportunities for women. They were also concerned about problems of access to water and water quality in the recently established [MST/INCRA] settlement [*assentamento*] where they lived. They came to us for help preparing a proposal to the Million Cisterns Project.[1]

Susana: At that time, we were in dialogue with REF.[2] We had been looking for contacts with other organizations that were tackling the violence against women issue in terms of broader social transformation and we encountered the feminists of REF and the Marcha, the World March of Women (MMM). The Marcha conceptualizes the struggle against violence as related to the fight to end poverty. REF was working with themes that are very close to those we were already working with in Mossoró: agro-ecology, food sovereignty and the solidarity economy. Through its publications and through our participation in workshops, REF has helped us a lot. Working with REF helped us to conceptualize the work we were doing [*ajudámos a construir o nosso trabalho*] in broader terms. For example, the concept of the sexual division of labour gave us a new context within which to think about the 'capacitation' of the women we were working with locally. REF's feminist theory of the economy helps us in the work we do here, in the debates on the solidarity economy and agro-ecology. What we brought to REF was our knowledge of the everyday practice of the women we work with. For us, it's an exchange [*uma troca*] between people from here to there and from there to here. It's a *space* of exchange of knowledge, of experience.

Luísa: The contribution of REF is very significant for us. As a result of our dialogue with REF during the cistern project and of our experience with the women building infrastructure that meets local needs, we now view critically large-scale plans for development that will have no local benefits for the Northeast – for example, current national proposals to dam the São Francisco River to meet water and energy needs in the south. It is REF that has enabled us to link our work to broader contexts. In the cistern project, we combined all of our objectives as an organization: assisting women to develop organizational and leadership skills; meeting women's everyday needs [for water]; paid work for women; and, overturning the gendered division of labour by moving women out of domestic work into the typically male-dominated labour of construction work.

Susana: In the past we had a less critical approach than today because at that time it was violence we worked with – and health … Really, if we look at it, this has much to do with the tools – the repertoire – available in the feminist movement at the time. In that period, the feminist movement was institutionalized [*institucion-alizada*]. What was the feminist agenda? It was that of the UN conferences. And so was the government's agenda. Until we came to the March, we had a type of critique but it was more self-defence in the face of our relations with the UN and with the government that were very institutionalized, bureaucratized. What came with the World March of Women was the possibility for us to reinforce our objective to work with popular feminism and with popular women [*mulheres bem populares*] – women of the 'base'. And to elaborate a critique, not simply to maintain the organization but to initiate an alternative process to the logic of the UN – to this bureaucratized feminism that Brazil had at that time. The MMM came and shook things up [*mexou*]. If you look at the feminist agenda today and you look at the decade of the 1990s, it's another world [*é outro mundo*]. And more than this, this movement of the 1990s in Brazil has been dislocated by another agenda, the agenda of the campaign against free trade (ALCA),[3] for example. And agro-ecology. This is not solely a dislocation by another movement but a dislocation within feminism itself.

Luísa: Our holistic vision that links improving women's lives to broader social changes is, however, difficult to promote when we move into these mixed spaces. For example, we participate in the Brazilian Forum on the Solidarity Economy. Even at our pre-Forum preparation meetings here in Mossoró, there is machismo. The ambience is respectful but within the social movements there is still much machismo. Agro-ecology, especially, is a male-dominated space. Agricultural economists are very important within the agro-ecology movement and they are all men. There's a similar difficulty with *economia solidária*: the theorists are male economists. We try to introduce discussion of the particular difficulties that women's double day of work – in production and in the care economy – poses for women's groups, as solidarity economy movements seek to commercialize and distribute their products. Our proposals involve broader social transformations and especially changes in the sexual division of labour. The men think this is unnecessary.

4
Feminism and 'Post-Neoliberal' Publics: Working the Spaces of Ecuador's Constitutional Reform

Lynne Phillips

After several decades of repressive political regimes and economic austerity, a 'new' Latin America has emerged, one where national governments are declaring interest in economic alternatives and more participatory democracies. Ecuador is one of a number of Latin American countries where state–citizen relationships are being realigned. In 2007–2008, the country's president, Rafael Correa, invited all Ecuadorians to re-envision the country's future – to create 'another society' (*otra sociedad*) – by participating in the rewriting of the nation's Constitution. This invitation was framed as an opportunity for citizens – many of whom struggle with acute poverty and racism – to challenge the neoliberal framework of the existing Constitution last revised in 1998. Correa called it a 'citizen revolution'. In this chapter I explore the challenges to feminism of this state invitation and the new publics it produced.

My goal here is to understand the shifting relationship of feminism to the state and, specifically, to the complicated and contested terrain of a 'post-neoliberal' state. Feminist analyses of the participation of women's movements in conventional state projects in Latin America have shown how engagement can institutionalize, co-opt and de-politicize women's issues (Rakowski and Espina 2006; Schild 2002; cf. Franceschet 2003). These critiques have led to calls for greater analytical attention to how some publics are more 'inviting' than others for effecting change (Rodgers 2007; Cole and Phillips 2009). An underlying argument of this chapter is that we need to direct attention both to how spaces to which people are invited may be inhabited in innovative ways *and* to how the creation of new public spaces – what Miraftab (2004) calls 'invented' spaces of social mobilization – can shift the terms of state invitations. 'Invented' spaces are often marginalized, erased or criminalized –

associated with 'uncivil' behaviour – but they also often harbour ways of imagining and speaking 'otherwise' to social change. For this reason, I maintain a focus here on feminism's relationship to both inviting and invented spaces.

In Ecuador's last revision of the Constitution in 1998, women's organizations had fought hard and won important rights, and many were deeply suspicious of Rafael Correa's Constitutional project in 2008. Nation-wide support for the president was relatively strong, but Correa's 'socialism of the twenty-first century' – and his vision of '*otra sociedad*' – remained vague and at times derisive regarding women's issues. There were widespread concerns among activists that, with the 2008 Constitutional revision, rights would be lost. Would a focus on 'rights' – effective for challenging the 1998 Constitution – have the same efficacy in an era of building a 'post-neoliberal' Ecuador in 2008? Was it best to continue to fight for women's rights as defined by the international community through the Beijing 1995 UN World Conference on Women and CEDAW, the 1979 UN Agreement to Eliminate Discrimination against Women? Or should there be a challenge to the very ways in which liberal democratic publics have been constituted through such international organizations? Was this 'invited' space of the state really an opportunity to effect social change? Or was it only a new mode of 'governing' social movements (like feminism) in an era of promoting 'participatory' publics?

These were the dilemmas that activists faced in 2008. Throughout the five months I was in the country that year, debates about feminist engagement with the Constitution dominated my conversations; it was, in this sense, a topic that 'chose me'. I conducted interviews (see Appendix 1); analysed audio and visual media (radio, websites and television); read newspapers, reports and pamphlets; and participated in conferences, workshops and marches. During my research, I saw activists dealing with a multitude of issues – paid and unpaid work, health and maternity, sex education, women prisoners, territorial rights and election quotas, to name just a few. Most with whom I spoke agreed that it was essential to respond to the state's invitation to re-write the Constitution, but their objectives differed and their participation took different forms. Much depended on how they evaluated the Constitutional revision as a *public space*.

For some activists, the Constitution was a key site for advancing their projects, and it was important to work 'within' (*adentro*) the parameters of the Constitutional process. Other activists did not think that the Constitution was a significant site to support their projects; they thus gave priority to working on spaces 'outside' (*afuera*) the parameters of the formal Constitutional process. In addition, there were two distinct kinds of equality projects that crosscut the *adentro* (within) and *afuera* (outside) approaches to the Constitution, roughly following the fault-lines that Sally Cole and I (Phillips and Cole 2009) have identified. One project placed 'women's rights' at the centre of analysis, and highlighted the need for a coalition-based unity in the form of a 'politics of presence' to ensure that rights are maintained and expanded. The other feminist project linked to a vision of creating 'another world', one that challenges the economic, political and cultural underpinnings of the (neoliberal) 'model', as Cecilia calls it in the following activist testimony. That is to say, working alongside activists like Cecilia – who in 2008 challenged Ecuador's 'neoliberal' Constitution from *adentro* – we find activists who *defended* the rights of women enshrined in the 1998 Constitution.

THE LEGACY OF THE 1998 CONSTITUTION

In principle, the 1998 Constitution made Ecuadorian women equal citizens. To achieve this outcome, women's groups learned early on about the importance of engaging public spaces. In the 1990s, challenges to the oligarchic and exclusionary character of the Ecuadorian state had already been launched by strong indigenous movements and society-wide protests against government corruption. Drawing from the international discourse of women's rights as human rights in the 1990s, women's groups successfully mobilized around issues such as the violence against women law and the government's ratification of UN conventions (for example, CEDAW).[1] They also came together to address the government response to the Beijing Platform (1995–1996), at which time national organizations such as El Foro Nacional Permanente de la Mujer and the Coordinadora Politica de Mujeres Ecuatorianas came into being.[2] As issues were widely debated and distributed through the media, women's groups became a women's 'movement'. CONAMU, the government's advisory council on women's issues, was created in 1997 with strong support from the women's movement. CONAMU encouraged women from all over the country, rural and urban, to participate in the development of a national equal opportunity plan (1996–2000); it worked hard to develop a 'base' in rural areas.

The women's movement during this period changed the public discourse on gender; many important issues, including violence against women, were debated and taken seriously. As one activist I interviewed summarizes: 'Today if a man is discovered to be an abuser of women, he's dead politically; before it didn't matter' (I-B45). Many feminists noted that such efforts were all the more remarkable as they were accomplished during a highly unstable political period which had greatly weakened most of the country's institutional structures.

The existence of a robust women's movement in 1998 did not, however, mean that making changes to the 1998 Constitution came easily. On the contrary, one activist recalled:

> When we arrived with our proposals, we had to fight for our voice to be heard. The men didn't want to hear anything about it. So our strategy was to have a woman sit behind each [Constitutional] Assembly member to give him information on how an issue affected women. They would ask 'why?' and we would say 'because of this or that'. (I-B3)

The 'unceasing presence of women' at the Constitutional Assembly (Ruiz 2000: 56) and the development of innovative strategies led the women's movement to declare the Constitutional reforms of 1998 a success.[3] A key achievement was the incorporation of sexual and reproductive rights – particularly freedom of sexual orientation and 'free maternity', that is, broad state support for maternal health care. Achieving 'success' also meant avoiding certain issues. As Cecilia notes in the testimony following this chapter: 'When we introduced sexual and reproductive rights into the Constitution we worked miracles to avoid the subject of abortion so that it wouldn't impede its passing' (I-A4).[4]

The 1998 'neoliberal' Constitution was also significant for its promotion of political decentralization. But devolving power to municipalities has had mixed results. In a recent study of six municipalities in Andean Ecuador, Peru and Bolivia, John Cameron found that municipal democratization has opened new publics in the Andes:

> Indigenous and peasant struggles to control and democratize municipal power have had important positive impacts on the sense of dignity and respect perceived by formerly excluded rural populations, and which are most notable in the reduction of racist exclusion by municipal employees and politicians. (2010: 308)

A positive influence on gender relations, however, cannot be assumed. Indeed, Cameron argues that:

> The *de facto* exclusion of women from municipal governance was most pronounced in the municipalities with the largest indigenous populations, where gendered inequalities in literacy were also greatest ... Viewed through lenses focused exclusively on gender power relations, there was little evidence of municipal democratization in any of the six municipalities despite profound transformations of class and ethnic power. (2010: 316)

Cameron's observations on highland regions contrast with my own in the coastal region of Ecuador, where the decentralization process, combined with gender quotas, brought in relatively large numbers of women who took formal positions in their municipal councils (*juntas parroquiales*) and who led projects for their communities (I-B9, I-B11, I-B12).[5] Women's political participation at local levels was also an impetus for the formation of a national organization, AJUMPRE (Associación de Mujeres de la Juntas Parroquiales Rurales del Ecuador), comprised of rural women who are associated with the *juntas parroquiales* throughout the country. Members I spoke with emphasized the goal of AJUMPRE to garner greater dignity and respect for rural women at the national level. Thus, although the 1998 Constitution is considered 'neoliberal', the process leading to its adoption supported a wide range of human rights and enabled democratic changes at the municipal and national levels.[6]

At the same time, political instabilities (or 'presidencies interrupted', as Valenzuela [2004] has put it), combined with continued neoliberal policies, generated hardship for increasingly large sectors of the Ecuadorian population. 'NGO-ization' (Alvarez 1998) took hold and 'movements' became 'organizations' dependent on external sources of funding. This trend challenged the vitality and strength of political movements in the country, and perhaps especially of the women's movement. In 2008, activists told me that the women's movement in Ecuador had become 'almost invisible'.

During fieldwork in 2008, however, I observed many women's organizations acting a lot like social movements as they engaged with President Correa's invitation for Constitutional revision. By this time, the significant political changes in the Latin American region and around the globe had reshaped where feminists undertook their activism. Transnational social movements, such as the World Social

Forum (WSF), the World March of Women (La Marcha Mundial de las Mujeres), and La Vía Campesina – pushing especially for alternatives to free trade (that is, alternatives to ALCA, the Free Trade Area of the Americas) – had begun to propose the possibility of rejecting neoliberal policies and creating 'another world'.[7] These movements – at once local, regional and transnational – are today seen by many Ecuadorian feminists as important sites for activism precisely because they are perceived to be 'beyond' the (often recalcitrant) nation-state. Perhaps not surprisingly, aspects of that alternative vision – comprising new publics with compelling ideas that appear to include feminism – found their way back to the nation-state in the context of the Constitutional revision process I am considering here.

CORREA AND THE 2008 CONSTITUTION

This mix of political, economic and cultural changes in Ecuador supported Rafael Correa's call to 'break from the past' – the neoliberal past – in his run for presidency in 2006. Although a president who claims to challenge oligarchic rule and appeals to the masses is certainly not a new phenomenon in Ecuador, Correa's invitation to all Ecuadorian citizens to participate in creating a 'post-neoliberal' model for the nation held wide appeal. He called for a new era of sovereignty (alluding to less dependence economically and politically on the US) and for a new society not rooted in the accumulation of wealth but in the 'well being of everyone' (*El Comercio* 12 February 2008: 3) – *una convivencia social*. The election of his Alianza País 'movement' (as he called it) was to mark the beginning of a 'citizen revolution' (*revolución ciudadana*) to bring about this post-neoliberal society.[8]

Once the Alianza País was voted into power, Correa disbanded the Congress in 2007 (viewed by most as corrupt and representative of oligarchic interests) and opened elections for a new Constitutional Assembly. Because this broad and democratic election process sidelined the traditional political parties, Constitutional Assembly membership was unusually diverse and included representatives from rural, indigenous, Afro-descendant and women's organizations. Although, in elite circles, many of these representatives were considered 'ignorant' or to be 'people who do not matter' (*gente que no pesa*), many activists commented to me that the young age of the *asambleístas*, signalled an Assembly that was more open to new ideas and a willingness to learn. In contrast to the 1998

Constitutional process, women activists could also clearly identify allies working inside the Assembly. As one activist put it: 'Thank God our proposals were received by the women *asambleístas*, who themselves were working with some interesting themes' (I-B10).

Rafael Correa's effective communication with the public distinguished both his presidential and Constitutional campaigns. He was the first president to be fluent in Quechua (though he is not indigenous) in addition to Spanish, and could address Ecuador's largest indigenous population in their language. He also engaged with the internet community, designing an up-to-date and detailed website that permitted viewers from all over the world to track and comment on the progress of the Constitution. Even *asambleístas* blogged on the website, clarifying their positions on a wide range of issues. As a space in which daily events were logged and debate was encouraged, the website stood as a relatively successful cyber-public.

Correa's extensive use of the radio to reach 'the people' was also strategic. Although previous politicians had used the radio, Correa's radio broadcasts and Q&A each Saturday cannot be characterized simply as 'rhetoric' or 'populist'. Taking place in a different part of the country every weekend and often addressing local issues, his radio programme included day-by-day reports on what the government was doing, how these activities related to the country's movement forward and lessons learned when they didn't. This strategy was significant, not only because the traditional print media was often hostile to the government's efforts, but also because it engaged the many Ecuadorian publics-in-formation that – not dependent on the reading of newspapers – did not correspond well to the classic (Habermasian) 'public sphere' (see chapter 1, this volume).[9]

The historical political and economic fissures in Ecuador between the highland, coastal and *oriente* (Amazonian) regions, combined with powerful indigenous demands for sovereignty, and a relatively autonomous southern identity (in the provinces of Azuay, El Oro, Loja), have always presented problems for national governance (Blanksten 1951; Clark 1998; Prieto 2004; Radcliffe and Westwood 1996). For the 2008 Constitutional process, the potential for national unity was symbolically represented by the image of Eloy Alfaro, the Ecuadorian revolutionary who took action to free the country from its oligarchic past during the Liberal Revolution in the late nineteenth century. Eloy Alfaro achieved an almost deity-like status during the Constitutional process, his image perched high above the deliberations of the Constitutional Assembly. In Correa's speeches, Alfaro stood for 'freedom' and 'independence' – values that, in decidedly different ways, appealed to different sectors of the population. At the same time, Alfaro stood for revolutionary change, signalling the break from the country's neoliberal past that Correa was proposing. (During telecasts of the Constitutional proceedings, it was not unusual to hear '*Viva Eloy Alfaro, corajo!*')

The geographical site of the 2008 Assembly – named Ciudad Alfaro – also challenged the usual (competing) centres of power (Quito and Guayaquil) as a *new* venue for constructing a building specifically for the Constitutional process. Located on a hill in the town of Monticristi, Manabi, it evoked Alfaro's birthplace. Inside this hilltop building, people from across the country presented their proposals for Constitutional change to ten special Constitutional Panels or *Mesas*. The Panels addressed the topics of: Fundamental Rights and Constitutional Guarantees (*Mesa* 1); Citizen Organization and Participation, and Systems of Representation (*Mesa* 2); Structure and Institutions of the State (*Mesa* 3); Territorial Regulation (*Mesa* 4); Natural Resources and Biodiversity (*Mesa* 5); Work, Production and Social Inclusion (*Mesa* 6); Development Regime (*Mesa* 7); Justice and the Struggle against Corruption (*Mesa* 8); Sovereignty, International Relations and Latin American Integration (*Mesa* 9); Legislation and Fiscal Issues (*Mesa* 10).

That the Constitutional revision was meant to be a nation-building process was undeniable. At the Constitutional closing ceremonies in July 2008, referring to Ecuadorian citizens' wide and inclusive participation in the process, President Correa proclaimed: 'Finally, we have a truly national project' (2008: 1).

WOMEN'S CONSTITUTIONAL ACTIVISM

The activists I spoke with knew too well that being present in public, being heard and being able to circulate one's own texts was an unspoken but crucial strategy to make their issues public. For those who chose to speak to the Assembly, their 'public' was not anonymous – everyone had some familiar contact inside the Assembly – but neither was their public necessarily 'like-minded' (Wells 2010). Persuasion was therefore not straightforward, and what was considered a 'legitimate' public issue remained tricky.

To prepare for the Constitutional process, most women's groups met in Riobamba in advance to develop an agenda, *Agenda de las Mujeres* (Women's Agenda), to present to the Constitutional Assembly. The point was to educate one another about the process and come to a consensus about what kinds of proposals to develop. By all accounts, consensus did not come easily. In part this was because some felt that they could rely on past strategies, while others felt that Correa's invitation required new strategic and thematic approaches. Others complained that UNIFEM (the United Nations Development Fund for Women) was directing the process. Its logo was everywhere on government texts and banners. Divisions between young and old, liberal and left, and multicultural and pluri-national perspectives also created difficulties in finding shared ground. The women's movement had changed since 1998. As one young activist put it: 'after years of NGO-ization, everyone was most interested in protecting their own spaces'.

Workshop preparations in different parts of the country did not always go according to plan. In one workshop I attended in the northern coastal province of Esmeraldas – organized to discuss the Constitutional process with CONAMUNECE (Coodinadora Nacional de Mujeres Negras del Ecuador [Esmeraldas], the Black Women's Organization of the province of Esmeraldas) – issues took on a dynamic of their own. Women simply talked about what they wanted to talk about instead of their assigned topics. For example, one group, charged with the question of how to maintain free maternity health care in the new Constitution, discussed instead 'the right to our sexuality without discrimination'. A woman in the group, Marta, questioned this discussion, saying that she disagreed with changing the marriage law. Another woman responded: 'it's not about changing the marriage law. It's about not having *homofobia*.' Marta clarified: 'Okay, that I respect.' Then another woman, continuing the theme of rights to sexuality, said: 'What I want is to be well satisfied [*Quiero ser bien satisfecho*].' This produced snickers, and another woman shouted out: 'Now *that* should be in the Constitution: men should satisfy their women!'

The 'refunctioning' of the workshop by CONAMUNECE women – who inhabited its public space in an unintended way – hints at a 'public-in-formation'. Discussion at the beginning of the workshop centred on how CONAMUNECE members felt that they had been ignored since the last Constitution. Similar to the concerns of Brazilian rural women that activist Mariza discussed in her testimony, the main priority of CONAMUNECE had been to obtain citizenship documents for marginalized rural women in the region, a concern not registered in the women's movement's Riobamba Agenda. The concerns of CONAMUNECE women about being 'used as sexual instruments' seemed to parallel their expressed concerns about being used as Constitutional fodder.

Clearly, not all women found Correa's Constitutional invitation an 'inviting' one. But the dynamics of this workshop also speak to how feminist publics may reproduce notions of people who do not 'matter' – or who matter only when it is politically expedient.

Adentro (Inside) the Constitutional Assembly

Most of the women's organizations involved in the Riobamba pre-Constitution workshops chose to work 'within' the framework of the Constitutional Assembly. It seemed like familiar territory, but there was a significant difference: the 2008 Assembly members did not represent oligarchic power. The 2008 Constitutional Assembly was viewed by many activists as a liberated space where the old, clientelist ways of relating to government authority had been swept away to permit new modes of social interaction. One activist contrasted the difference culturally by mimicking the required subservience of activists in 1998 with a high voice and liberal sprinkling of the diminutive ('*Por favorcito* ...'). This deferential comportment was no longer necessary in 2008. On the other hand, few *asambleístas* had experience in legislative issues or knew anything about women's issues. More than one activist spoke of their frustration:

> Unfortunately, the patriarchal ideology of *asambleístas* was impressive. Presidents of *Mesas* didn't know anything. When I went to [the Assembly], one asked me: what is parity? Could you explain to me in one page what that is? I said: We voted for you, and you are asking me what parity is? You think it takes only one page to explain what it is? It is hard to have a strategy when people don't know anything. (I-B14)

Yet most agreed that *asambleístas* were willing to learn. Even those who were critical of the process spoke of the 'will' (*voluntad*) of the *asambleístas*:

> At least the *asambleístas* are accepting our proposals; I think that is good. Everyone has gone there, with all their political proposals. And the *Mesas* that have received us appear to be listening. I think this is good. The media criticize the Assembly a lot because of how much time it is taking, but I think that it is fine that they are taking time – it takes time to hear everyone. Some of them began without knowing anything. So I think this process has been very good for them too. (I-B5)

> The *asambleístas* are good people. And they are *young*! (I-C5)

Groups wishing to address the Constitutional Assembly followed a standard procedure. They occupied the plaza outside the main building of Ciudad Alfaro (held back by a fence and security) and then made a lot of noise (*bulla*) in order to be seen and heard inside. The women's groups I observed waved banners, chanted and called out to the particular *Mesa* that they wanted to address. And, they constantly 'texted' – cell phones being essential for communication with allies inside the building as well as in other parts of the country. Once a group had made plenty of noise, and allies within had convinced members of a *Mesa* to hear them out, a message would be sent out to the 'plaza' and two or three representatives of the groups would be permitted to pass security and enter the building. They went inside with their pamphlets, photos and/or written proposals to 'educate' the *Mesa* members.

The distinction between the plaza and the Assembly building – between the inside and the outside of the Constitutional Assembly – was permeable. Not only did some of the *Mesas* travel to different parts of the country to hear proposals, but the *asambleístas* inside the Assembly sometimes voluntarily came out to the plaza area to greet or question those waiting. One gathering I witnessed involved a group of about 100 women (from different organizations throughout the country connected through CEPAM, Centro Ecuatoriano para la Promoción y Acción de la Mujer). Dressed in black with T-shirts that read 'Women don't deserve to die for giving life' (*Las mujeres no merecen morir por dar la vida*), the women had used the platform of the International Day of Women's Health to raise the issue of reproductive rights. Over a black casket, they held banners listing statistics about teen pregnancies and poor sex education. One spokeswoman took the opportunity of being interviewed by the press to speak indirectly to the *asambleístas* of *Mesa* 1, the panel on rights:

> Don't have a double morality! Listen to our demand to have women's health rights. It sometimes means abortion. It sometimes means doing something about domestic violence. It sometimes means HIV/AIDS treatment. And it sometimes means making sure our children are educated about sexuality. That's why we have a coffin here, to say *we don't want any more women to die*!

Everyone in the group chanted these last words. A male Assembly member suddenly came out from the building to talk to them. Addressing the group, he said he had two teenage daughters who had never been offered sex education in school – and then added, 'they should be!' Then, much to the delight of everyone, he lay in the casket for a photo-op. In the meantime, another man who had come out from the building entered into a heated debate about abortion with two of the women from the group. This ethnographic moment disturbed my initial assessment that activities in this public space were highly ritualized: there appeared to be fluid engagement – a genuine sharing of ideas through dialogue and debate – between some *asambleístas* and protagonists to create alternative publics that were indeed 'inviting' and 'participative'.

In what follows, I outline three ways in which feminist activists worked within the space of the Constitutional Assembly. Activists who were convinced of the value of the 1998 Constitution proposed that they would not 'take one step back' (*ni un paso atrás*) from it. Their strategy was to 'stretch' the concepts of the Assembly in order to protect women's rights. Other activists were insiders who worked closely with the *asambleístas* to bring a feminist perspective to the 'post-neoliberal' framework of the Assembly. A third group of activists contested the space of the Constitution itself, directly challenging its assumptions about what constituted a legitimate Constitutional issue.

'Ni un Paso Atrás': Standing Ground by Stretching Concepts

The dominant perspective expressed among women's organizations I consulted was that the main purpose of working within the parameters of the Assembly was to ensure that the rights of women won in 1998 were not taken away. This was the case for most of the women who had engaged in the 1998 Constitutional process (sometimes referred to as the 'old' feminists, *las viejas*), including CONAMU and UNIFEM, as well as for women's organizations that focused on issues of visibility and respect (for example, AMJUPRE and OEML, the Organización Ecuatoriana de Mujeres Lesbianas).

The fear of loss of rights was apparent in many of my interviews with these groups, as well as in more public discussions such as conferences on Constitutional issues. For example, ads for one conference spoke of 'the danger of trampling [*conculquen*] our rights'. In another workshop I attended, some speakers claimed that the *asambleístas* 'want to erase the word "woman" entirely from the 2008 Constitution' (*quieren borrar todo la palabra mujer*). Echoing many women's sentiments, a woman elected to one of the coastal *juntas parroquiales* argued that if any of the rights won in the 1998 Constitution should be lost, it would be 'fatal' (*fatal*): 'We can't have advanced so much only to retreat'.

So, in 2008 activists again drew on international conventions such as CEDAW, the UN Convention to Eliminate Discrimination against Women, and practised an intense 'politics of presence' (A. Phillips 1996) to maintain their rights in the Constitution. A politics of presence required women's organizations from across the country to become familiar with the Women's Agenda of the pre-Constitutional meeting in Riobamba, and to coordinate times and individual representatives to travel to the Assembly to do the work of educating (and lobbying) the members of appropriate *Mesas*.

> We went [to the Assembly] with CONAMU ... We were there for two hard days of work, visiting any of the *Mesas* that involved women's issues, gender equity, all of that. We had eight themes, for the different *Mesas*, with discussion about budgets, about the law, etc. (I-B11)

> In the Block [Correa's party, Acuerdo País] there are many people who don't know anything about the theme of gender [*género*]. They don't have any idea, and so they are against it. So we go visit them. We show them documents, and talk to them so that they come to understand. But it is difficult. (I-B5)

> We went practically every week [to the Assembly]. Initially we went to all the *Mesas*. We presented the Women's Agenda of rights. I was the spokeswoman [*vocera*], which helped to make the word 'lesbian' visible in the spaces of the Assembly. (I-B29)

A politics of presence – seeking to be 'heard' within the space of the Constitutional process – also required 'stretching' (*estirando*) the meanings of concepts the Assembly was working with – concepts such as diversity, sovereignty and the economy. Women spoke of working the particular interests of their organization into these concepts in order to give them 'content'. The Ecuadorian Lesbian Organization, the OEML, took up the idea of diversity (*diversidad*) to speak to diversities other than the established ethnic ones, such as diverse families and diverse sexual identities. Others understood the importance of the concept of *sovereignty* to the Assembly and 'stretched' it by introducing the concept of 'sovereignty of the body' (*la soberanía del cuerpo*). A coastal women's organization framed its activism with sex workers in terms of discussions on 'sovereignty of the body'. Similarly, the idea of 'economy of care' (*economía de cuidado*) was introduced to those *Mesas* that were discussing economic issues. An organization from the highlands interposed the issue of the precarious work of domestics (*empleadas*) into the concept of the care economy. In this sense, activists managed their input into the Constitutional process by inserting women's issues into the narrative framework of the Assembly in novel ways.

For most activists taking this strategy, it was not just a matter of maintaining rights but of 'deepening' rights (*profundizar derechos*). This was the main focus of Mujeres por La Vida, for example, a popular sector movement of indigenous and *mestiza* women:

> So, this year, in 2008, one of our goals was precisely active participation in the Constitutional process. [This decision] was very much marked by the political moment [*el momento politico*] in which we are living in the country. We have participated since the Riobamba pre-Constitutional process. And we have participated in all the processes of the women's movements in general – the various meetings, workshops – for the construction of a common agenda of the women's movement.
>
> When we went to the pre-Constitution we had to develop the concepts that we wanted to bring to the Assembly. The fundamental concept, for us, is 'rights' – the theme of sexual rights, reproductive rights, etc., and we are framing [*planteando*] them as 'sovereignty of the body' – the right for women to decide about their bodies ... We organize ourselves to be close to certain *Mesas*, to deepen rights, to deepen rights at the national level. We have other issues like 'a life of dignity' [*la vida digna*] which weren't well understood, so we 'deepened' them [too] at the *Mesas*. We go to the *Mesa* of rights [*Mesa* 1], to the *Mesa* of political participation [*Mesa* 2], the development model [*Mesa* 7], and also to Work and Production [*Mesa* 6]). So, for four months we have been there, but not every day ... We go on the march [up the hill to the plaza], and ask to go inside. (I-B5)

The women's groups taking the position that losing rights would be *fatal* worked tirelessly to have their voices heard. They did not just focus on the 'rights' *Mesa* (*Mesa* 1); they wove women's rights in a transversal way across most of the *Mesas*. And they employed innovative concepts such as 'sovereignty of the body' to push at the defined borders of the *Mesas*. Although this concept met considerable resistance, it forced debate and opened a new space for the public to think about who has the right to control the 'territory' of women's bodies.

Still, always haunting the rights-based strategy of the *ni un paso atrás* position was the question of whether a different focus for the 2008 Constitution – the vision for 'another world' (or *otra sociedad*) – trumped women's rights.

Working as an Insider: Post-liberal Feminism or Cooptation?

I was not a participant observer of the *Mesa* proceedings inside the Assembly, but I did follow the televised proceedings and I was an observer-participant at two conferences on the theme of women and the Constitution attended by some of the women *asambleístas*. I also spoke with two women who worked as liaisons inside the Assembly.

Cecilia, whom we meet in the activist testimony following this chapter, has been organizing against ALCA and creating feminist spaces within the WSF for the past decade – since the last Constitutional revision. For her, the state's invitation for proposals for the 2008 Constitution revision offered a unique opportunity to introduce a feminist post-neoliberal orientation. Working from the 'another world' perspective, Cecilia sees the rights approach as problematic. The rights won in the 1998 Constitution, she says, are steeped in a neoliberal vision of society based on a capitalist market economy. For example, her view is that the 'free maternity' clause in the 1998 Constitution was put forward precisely because neoliberalism had eaten away at the public health system ('it was a defence strategy'). In contrast to most feminists I spoke with, she did not see it as a sacred cow. The question for her is not what rights need to be held on to but *what kind of state* is necessary to enact a new way of living. For her, linking the economy of care with the concept of solidarity economy (*economía solidaria*), provides the base for re-thinking society from a feminist perspective.[10] She considered it essential to work the spaces of the Constitution from the inside in order to successfully move a broad concept such as the economy of care into the legal framework.

Tied to analyses of 'another world', the concept of the care economy becomes more than just taking domestic labour into account. For example, a liberal approach to the care economy often documents, through time-use studies, the time women spend working without getting paid (see CONAMU, INEC, UNIFEM 2006). For Cecilia, the care economy:

is more broadly about how we mobilize resources to maintain life ... In the Assembly [*Mesa* 6] there is a very narrow notion of work. It is primarily from the perspective of employee and employer, as in the Labour Code. We are getting them to think of work more broadly as about how resources are distributed.

Fighting for an economy where redistribution is based on the recognition of inequality provides 'a much broader space for fighting for women's issues'.

It was not unusual for activists to say to me: 'Perhaps the Constitution will be fine on economic change and on political change, but on the theme of gender, I doubt it' (I-A5). But, in Cecilia's view, the themes of the economy and gender cannot be separated. This is a message she shared generously with the public. She participated in the pre-Constitutional meetings and workshops and, throughout the Constitutional process, wrote public statements to explain her position that working for gender equality cannot be extricated from re-thinking the economy. However, many of the women's organizations did not respond positively to Cecilia's position. To them, the interests of women were becoming lost in the discourse about 'revolutionary citizens'.

Activists working inside the government considered these concerns of the women's movement to be misplaced, arguing that women's rights were much more threatened by the interventions of the conservative sectors of Ecuadorian society than by the government or the Assembly. As another 'insider' told me:

If you are talking about the progression of rights, not all rights are going to progress. There *is* a risk of losing some. We are right now in that moment of political tension. Because some sectors say that nothing should be lost [from the 1998 Constitution], and, yes, that would be progressive, but other sectors are arguing for losing certain rights. Right now, for example, there was a demonstration by the Catholic schools, and I think Evangelist schools, demanding to take the theme of sexual liberation out of the Constitution, because they think this is something horrible to have in the Constitution. So with some themes we are in tension, and the focus or lens *has* changed [since 1998].

But it is understandable. Why? Because in the 1998 Constitution the conservative sector, the Right [*la Derecha*], didn't worry about [the presence of] these rights, because they knew that the [neoliberal] model was untouchable. But today all the attention is on this theme precisely because the government is intervening in the hegemonic, exclusionary model ... [and] the Right is advancing on all sides. The political tension is huge. (I-B20)

Not surprisingly, those not working inside the Constitutional Assembly provide a different view. As an activist from the south related:

There are many women from the movement today working as part of the political power. They are working within the government on the issues, but not militantly. That has hurt the potential of the women's movement in terms of its strategic orientation and as a political movement. I see a lot of weakness compared to the 1998 Constitution [because of that]. (I-B14)

This statement implies that the women's movement in Ecuador has lost its autonomy and is being 'governed' by the invitational spaces of the 2008 Constitutional revision. There is, however, no consensus on this issue.

Levantar Espacio: Clearing the Public Space

A third strategy of activists working the spaces of the Assembly was undertaken by urban collectives critical of the way in which the Constitutional process was controlled by the government. These activists viewed themselves as part of the women's movement, but remained autonomous from UNIFEM and CONAMU. As one said to me: 'The UNIFEM orientation robs the autonomy of women's movements and weakens them. They talk of 'gender', not feminism. They tell us to conform. But we should have the freedom not to conform' (I-C4). Identifying themselves as 'left, not liberals', this activist was tired of having LGBT (lesbian, gay, bisexual and transgender) concerns and abortion put on hold in the name of the 'more important' projects of governments. 'They tell us "It isn't the right time"[No es el momento]. We say: "Si es el momento" [Yes it is].' These activists sought out other publics (independent media [indimedia], such as alternative small radio stations) to talk from their perspective about 'taboo' subjects – subjects otherwise bracketed from public debate.

Another activist whose collective took this autonomous position argued that CONAMU and its affiliated women's groups: 'are there to negotiate [negociar], but we are there to position [posicionar]. That differentiates us. We are more critical. We assume we are going to enter discussions about abortion. They go saying they represent the base. But they don't' (I-B38). As a member of a feminist group working with women prisoners from the perspective of the criminalization of poverty, this activist had originally supported the government. As a close observer of the Constitutional process, however, her view was that:

> Little by little the Assembly has become a space of concentrated power – a concentration of political power. When we went [to the Assembly], others with whom we spoke were there with their proposals. By then, civil society organizations were asking when they could enter *their* own spaces of dialogue, *their* thematic issues, *their* proposals. Everyone was developing a critical perspective in distinct contrast to [Correa's] 'citizen revolution'. This government claims that it is progressive in economic terms. But it is profoundly reactionary and conservative in cultural terms, and fundamentally in terms of women's control over their bodies.
>
> We know that our themes, as militant feminists, are not part of the government's idea of solving the problems of poverty. We don't conform well to this space of concentrated power. The Assembly is a hostile space to these kinds of feminist perspectives. So, we decided to make an alliance [*alianza*]. We decided to make a strategic alliance with two other groups for this [Assembly] action – a collective that works on abortion and a transgendered collective, from the Les-Trans movement. As a group formed specifically for the Constitutional process, we became the Collective for De-criminalizing Abortion, Poverty, and Alternative Families. (I-B38)

All three of the collectives mentioned here saw themselves as working toward '*otra sociedad*', another society:

> We decided on the [larger] collective because there was no citizenship space for learning about other ways of being social [*otras socialidades*], those of LGBT, for example. We are expected to enter the canons of civilization. We made the alliance because the government in its present configuration is fundamentally hostile to discussions about our lives. We went to the Assembly to clear [*levantar*] spaces for our themes. Our collective thought it was necessary to put it to the *Mesas*: you can't have a citizen revolution without us ... Take us into account or don't pretend you are transforming the country. (I-B38)

The collective focused on *Mesa* 8 (Justice) and *Mesa* 10 (Legislation). They brought testimonies of women prisoners, photos of the inside of the women's jail and they brought family members of imprisoned women. They strategically invented new 'Constitutional space' by creating a political presence in the Assembly lunch (*almuerzo*) room where they interrupted *asambleístas* as they were eating saying 'Excuse us, we have something important to talk to you about, because women are, at this moment, dying from abortion, forgotten in prison, and criminalized because of who they love …' They distributed pamphlets that, for example, asked readers, 'How do you think women should be punished for having an abortion?' And, they filmed the whole event. 'We drew attention to ourselves. You need to know that the Right are always on top of the *asambleístas*. You need to get [the *asambleístas*'] attention.'

The President of the Assembly reprimanded the collective, told them to turn off their cameras and to cease their demonstration. He said that the Assembly couldn't permit themes that destabilized 'the delicate equilibrium' of the Assembly. 'We were furious, of course, from a feminist perspective. The Assembly wasn't just receiving proposals but it was interpolating [*interpolando*] them.'

So, while the collective saw the Constitutional process as 'progressive' it also saw it as tied to a particular kind of civilizing process that 'razes' (*arraca*) certain people. It thus became important to produce new publics – new public spaces (outside of CONAMU, UNIFEM as well as the Assembly) to truly revolutionize society, to effect a 'cultural revolution in who gets to be considered part of civilization'. It is not surprising that those who undertook this strategy tended to work both inside and outside the Assembly.

Afuera (Outside) the Constitutional Assembly

Activists strategically working in spaces outside the Assembly – the official public space of Constitutional revision – can generally be divided into two groups. One comprised those who understood that, if issues were to be accepted within the Assembly, the public and the government (especially the president) needed to be on side. The other group viewed the Constitution as a limited way to effect social change and thus declined or minimized their participation. In what follows, I briefly discuss how some women's organizations engaged audiences through public engagement. I then describe the situation of two women who distanced themselves from the Constitutional invitation. Finally I consider a third case – the collective that works with imprisoned women – for its unique strategy of creating its *own* invited spaces.

Working the Plaza Grande as Public Space

'We need to work a lot more at the level of society ...'

One morning in late March I received word that there was going to be a large women's demonstration in Quito's Plaza Grande, a traditional space for protest as it faces the Palacio de Carondelet, the place of government. I arrived to find the plaza half full of school children waving anti-abortion signs and shouting 'No to abortion; yes to life!' (*No al aborto; sí a la vida*). I asked one of their teachers what was going on and he said: 'They are trying to put free abortion into the Constitution, so all the public schools and colleges are here to protest.' I stayed to watch but, disheartened, soon made my way to leave. Suddenly, a huge 10 foot long banner made a dramatic entrance on to the plaza, hundreds of women following behind. The women bore placards stating their Constitutional demands. The school buses quickly left, and women – *indígenas*, *costeñas*, young, and old – from three different popular movements (Mujeres por la Vida, Luna Creciente and CONFEBEC) passed out pamphlets and spoke passionately to an attentive audience. It was a very impressive use of public space.

Later, when I was interviewing the leader of one of the movements, it became clear that the plaza demonstration was part of their critical analysis that saw the Assembly as only partially reflecting the locus of decision-making power; the small circle of the executive government also needed to hear their demands. The Plaza Grande served a dual purpose:

We always go to the plaza on Sunday, because there are lots of people who can see us. We have *cartas*, our proposals, and the Acts of the Assembly. We make sure we bring this [information] in front of society and also in front of the government. For the society, we want people to identify with our issues, the women from the barrios, and we also want to inform people. We need to work a lot more at the level of society ... There is this problem of misrepresenting us at the level of the society, and at the government level. The president is very conservative about these themes. He says, for example, 'What is this sovereignty of the body? How can you have decisions of a body?' We think it is very important to be able to decide over our 'territory'. We went to visit the president twice. He said that he knew that the women's organizations are proposing social security and sovereignty of the body. He thinks all these things are for more developed countries. *Punto*. That's it.

This activist argues that it takes 'very strong action for them to hear us'. For example, they went to the Ministry of Housing with their proposals for months.

It is very frustrating. Those people are supposed to be in power for us but they are extremely closed ... Only when there are actions of force do they decide to listen to you. You have to pressure; if you don't, nothing happens. (I-B5)

Working the Spaces of Everyday Life

'We need an economy that is of life.'

Many activists have been working for years without government support to improve the conditions of daily life in their communities. For example, Clara, an indigenous woman, has been working in her community in the Amazonian *oriente* to raise awareness about women's legal right to contest their husband's decision to rent their land to petroleum or forestry companies. Like Cecilia, Clara worked as a liaison within the Assembly, but she was much less optimistic about the potential of the Constitution to support her community. As an indigenous person, she experienced the Assembly as decidedly racist, and she came to see its subtle culture of exclusion as a reason to reject it:

For us, there isn't anything there ... And so the indigenous problem stays behind because the indigenous person isn't really there. That's precisely why we are defending pluri-nationalism, because it speaks of *interculturalidad*. That is different from multiculturalism, in that it involves respect for our rights and for who we are. (I-B31)

For Clara, the indigenous person 'isn't really' in the Assembly because, though physically present, she or he is not 'heard' as an equal. So, instead of pinning hopes on the Constitution, Clara views the future in terms of the work she has been doing with women in her community. Her goal in participating in the Constitutional process had been to garner public support to create a reserve to protect the lands of her community from oil and forestry development, but her experience in the Assembly encouraged her to place her political energies elsewhere.

In the southern region of Ecuador, other activists have for some time been working with *campesino* and women's groups to put into practice a concept of solidarity economy rooted in principles of environmental sustainability. One project that has been in operation for over eight years links highland *campesino* families and their organic produce with women consumers in the lowlands (I-B14; I-B 35). Elizabeth, who is part of the solidarity economy movement, has long been involved in fair trade and agro-ecology initiatives. Although, unlike Cecilia, she has not participated in transnational 'another world' movements, Elizabeth's idea of a solidarity economy is very similar to Cecilia's. Elizabeth, who is based in southern Ecuador, strongly disagrees with efforts like Cecilia's to incorporate the notion of the solidarity economy into the Constitution. In her view, the Constitution is 'just in the sphere of laws and people don't change through laws'. Elizabeth views solidarity economy as a broad movement toward a way of life, where people change 'through conscientization, through action'.

She disagrees with the proposal that some of her male *compañeros* from the solidarity economy movement have submitted to the Assembly:

The document says that a solidarity economy needs to be recognized and paid attention to like the other [capitalist] economy. But it isn't like that. If you know anything about the concept of solidarity economy, you know that these economies can't be together. It is impossible – because we are speaking of solidarity economy as another way of life. For this reason, I think that here [in Ecuador] there is still a need for further analysis, because the concept could be badly translated. Because we don't think it is a matter of getting finances, or an office, or having processes for small producers. That is totally absurd. It isn't that at all.

We need an economy that is of *life*, not just of people, but also of the land, and of the animals. Plastic products [from China] don't live, [or at least] they have a short life. That's why we say that a solidarity economy isn't only related to producing and selling, because that is a very limited [*muy reducido*] idea. That's why we say it is part of an economy of care. To have an economy of care, it is necessary to change our way of thinking. (I-B16)

Alluding to the ways in which capitalist economies can absorb alternative ideas about how to live, Elizabeth sees the space of the Constitution as somewhat dangerous because the ideas of the movement may become distorted. Like Cecilia, Elizabeth links solidarity economy with the concept of an economy of care, but she does so in a way that forces a consideration of *everyday life* as the site for gender change. For Elizabeth '*machismo* is contrary to the values of *economía solidaria*'. For her that means bringing feminism into the places where people work, buy, socialize, cook and consume – be they farms, markets or communities. She struggles with what she identifies as *machismo* within the 'mixed space' of the solidarity economy movement.

Clara and Elizabeth appear to be working with a very different sense of 'public' than the activists working within the spaces of the national Constitutional revision. For these two women, participating in the Constitution takes precious time away from producing 'another' way of living/thinking in their own communities. Elizabeth also hints that such participation potentially makes the work of developing an alternative economy – an economy of *life* – more vulnerable to national governance. Though speaking from very different positions, their similar response to the official space of the Constitutional revision process – disassociation – indicates again that the invitation to participate is not experienced as 'inviting' by everyone.

The Prison as an Invited Space

'We are all negotiating our own liberty.'

After the episode in the Assembly lunch room, the collective working with imprisoned women decided to invite the *asambleístas* – many of whom had never set foot in a prison – to visit the women's jail in Quito. They made this invitation based on work the collective had already done with imprisoned women (some of whom are themselves members of the collective) to break down the barriers between 'inside' and 'outside'. They knew that 'you had to have a "heart of stone" [*un corazon de piedra*] not to be moved by this forgotten space'. Their approach was not one of 'social assistance'. On the contrary, they argued that imprisoned women are criminalized for being poor and have become expendable 'others' – disposable citizens.

> If you are outside the productive sphere, you are not just excluded, you are superfluous. It is a way of 'governing' poverty, in the Foucauldian sense; criminalizing poor women is part of the discourse of governing poverty. Security, as it is defined within neoliberalism, plays on collective paranoia and emphasizes the need for self-security. (I-B38)

The collective worked to break down the walls of a security-based society by exchanging life experiences and challenging accepted divisions of included and excluded. In the jail, they 'learned to listen' and held twice weekly meetings to discover that 'we are all negotiating our own liberty'. They explored the prison as an invented space – one that needed to be abolished. In a collectively written publication, they depicted the lives of violence imprisoned women lead, 'not in the sense of torture, but in the sense that there is an everyday, daily punishment [*castigo*]'.

In a wonderful reversal, the collective assumed the privilege of extending invitations and defining invited spaces. They convinced the president of *Mesa* 10, the Legislation panel, to visit their own 'space of mobilization', the women's prison. This strategy was a success in that, after the visit, an agreement was secured that excessive prison sentences would be reviewed and pardons would be considered for some of the imprisoned women. Mainstream media reported on the event. The news coverage gave legitimacy to the work of the collective and, while not an indication of structural transformation (was it just a symbolic act? the collective wonders), they consider this one step toward opening public debate on who is included in Ecuador's 'citizen revolution'.

CONCLUDING REMARKS

In January 2008, when I arrived in Ecuador for field research, a male academic, on hearing that I planned research on regional efforts to 'mobilize' gender equality, told me that women's movements in the country had 'gone out of style'. The ethnographic research presented here suggests otherwise. After years of neoliberal rule and NGO-ization, the state's invitation to re-write the Constitution may have been viewed with suspicion by many, but it also moved women's organizations to action. Responding to the invitation, women's organizations acted again like movements – that is, with flexibility, imagination and strategic alliance-building. Some designed innovative ways to argue that women's rights still need to be attended to in a new economic regime. Others integrated new ideas about gender and the economy into the Constitution. Still others invented novel spaces to illustrate the cultural limits of the new regime – or consigned the Constitution to a peripheral status in alternative visions of social transformation. All these orientations helped to shape the multiple and contesting publics that the Constitutional revision process produced.[11]

Ecuador's experiment with 'post-neoliberalism' indicates that feminism does not disappear: it moves – and it changes as it moves – into the many dimensions of inviting *and* invented spaces. Rather than fragmented, invisible or anachronistic, Ecuador's women's movement is better understood as diverse. Its diversity reflects the country itself. If the country's public spaces – its publics – are to be truly inclusive, it is a diversity that should be embraced.

We have seen that some stories remain at the margins of projects to build 'participatory' publics. Attention needs to be paid to unheard voices – as Clara, Elizabeth and the women in Esmeraldas remind us – as well as to assumptions about what are 'good' spaces for women. Elizabeth's encounter with *machismo* in the assumed good space of the solidarity economy movement gives pause for thought. We have heard echoes of her view in the activist testimonies of Mariza, Susana and Luísa. In the following testimony, Cecilia describes how her work to advance gender equality at multiple scales requires working in 'mixed spaces' – a novel experience for her. And, in chapter 5, activist-researcher Erica Lagalisse experiences similar challenges working in a 'mixed' activist network dedicated to developing solidarity with the Zapatista movement.

APPENDIX 1: ORGANIZATIONS AND MOVEMENTS CONSULTED

AMJUPRE: Associación de Mujeres de la Juntas Parroquiales Rurales del Ecuador (Association of Women from Rural Municipal Councils of Ecuador)

CEDIME: Research Centre on Social Movements of Ecuador

CEPAM: Centro Ecuatoriano para la Promoción y Acción de la Mujer (Ecuadorian Centre for the Promotion and Action of Women)

CONAMU: Consejo Nacional de las Mujeres (National Council for Women)

CONAMUNECE: Coordinadora Nacional de Mujeres Negras de Ecuador, Esmeraldas): (National Coordinator of Black Women of Ecuador, Esmeraldas)

CONFEMC: Confederación Ecuatoriana de Mujeres por el Cambio (Ecuadorian Confederation of Women for Change)

Coordinadora Juvenil: Youth Coordinator for Gender Equity

CPME: Coordinadora Politica de Mujeres Ecuatoriana (Political Coordinator of Ecuadorian Women)

Foro de la Mujer: Foro Nacional Permanente de la Mujer Ecuatoriana (Permanent National Forum of Ecuadorian Women)

Junta Parroquiales: Municipal Councils in provinces of Guayas, Santa Elena, Esmeraldas

Luna Creciente: Crescent Moon movement

Movimiento Nacional de Economía Solidaria: Solidarity Economy National Movement

Movimiento de Mujeres de El Oro: Women's Movement of El Oro province

Mujeres por La Vida: Women for Life movement

Mujeres de Frente: Women's Front

OEML: Organización Ecuatoriana de Mujeres Lesbianas (Ecuadorian Organization of Lesbian Women)

Organización Runashito: indigenous community organization in Napo province

REMTE: Red Latinoamericana Mujeres Transformando la Economía (Latin American Network of Women Transforming the Economy)

Secretaria de Pueblos y Movimientos Sociales: Government Secretariat of Communities and Social Movements

SENDAS: Service for an Alternative Development for the South

UNIFEM: United Nations Development Fund for Women (now named UN Women)

Activist Testimonial: Cecilia

'Gender inequality is a problem, and it has to change.'

Based in Quito, Ecuador, Cecilia is a member of the continent-wide feminist network, REMTE, Red Latinoamericana Mujeres Transformando la Economía, the Latin American Network of Women Transforming the Economy. Cecilia describes her activism as a feminist and public intellectual in national and international contexts: the anti-free-trade campaign in Latin America, the World Social Forum and the Constitutional reforms in Ecuador – all 'mixed spaces'. She critiques the neoliberal framing of women's issues as 'social issues' on public policy agendas. Cecilia sees women's organizations as partly complicit in this and she strongly argues that the organizations themselves need to make an economic analysis of gender inequality central to their programmes. The following is from our conversation with her in Quito, Ecuador on 27 February 2007.

REMTE (the Latin American Network of Women Transforming the Economy) is almost 10 years old. In Ecuador, we have been participating in it since 2000. REMTE began in the context of [the UN conference in] Beijing, because the idea emerged there, but later it came to be [developed] through groups in Brazil, Peru, Mexico and Bolivia. [That work] confirmed that [the discussion of] economic matters was very weak in the Beijing debates and in the existing networks. For 20 years in Latin America we have had networks related to health and education that had influence and permanency but there was a feeling that there was a gap in terms of economics. We've been able to critically analyse that gap as part of the [neoliberal] model, where issues of women and poverty are converted into *social* issues and economics is defined in terms of business and markets, removing issues like work. This is not just in the public, state and political structures but even in the language of the press. In the press the economy sections are called 'Money' or 'Business'. Topics such as poverty, work, women become 'social' topics. In a way, organizations have been co-opted by this vision because economics has lost its place on the agenda of women's groups and in their vision and perspective. This [neoliberal] economic model is the context in which women are arguing for their social rights. Partially this is due to institutional management and also in part it is a trap into which the organizations have fallen.

In this process, for us what has been very important is the resistance to free-trade agreements (ALCA) and then developing an alternative proposal to integration. At first, women's organizations set out to intervene in the negotiations in order to obtain women's rights. Later we would see that they were incompatible, because you can't have women's rights within free-trade agreements, because in the heart of those agreements is gender inequality, the sexual division of labour and the exploitation of women. This has permitted an evolution from the initial stance of saying, 'We are intervening to negotiate our rights from inside', to a stance of saying, 'No, we are against the agreements.'

REMTE does not have projects. We have activities and initiatives that deal with debate, diffusion and influence. To a certain extent, we don't believe much in campaigns. Since we began, the main activity has had to do with resistance to free-trade agreements. On the one hand, this entails questions of analysis, the production of materials and the carrying out of workshops. The workshops are almost always organized with other women's organizations, especially with indigenous and rural women, because our basic alliance has been with women who have economics on their agenda. Economics has always been on the agendas of peasant unions – it has never ceased to be on the agenda – unlike other women's groups in which the topics of violence, policy and participation have been priorities. Although we do have proximity and an affinity with other women's organizations, our basic rapprochement has been with union women of the indigenous-rural sector because we have a common agenda around the theme of economics.

What do we do in the workshops? Above all, we share knowledge of the economic model, how it functions, what are the free-trade agreements, and how they are going to affect women. The majority of us are economists or professionals, and feminists.

The economy has become something that is more and more specialized, sophisticated. And, furthermore, with neoliberal language, it is something that has distanced itself from people. The women with whom we interact have a different type of experience and knowledge [of the economy] that perhaps is not in the same language. The idea is to find a meeting point and to construct a shared discourse. That is the perspective. Different from other workshops. It is to advance the understanding of the themes, in the sharing of information and also to build an agenda of action. At the end of the workshops we ask how we can adjust our activities, actions and interventions.

Do we work with the idea of creating gender equality? Yes. Our focus is on the economy, but, of course, we do see the intersection of issues. For example, we have organized workshops on questions on violence from an economic perspective in order to see the economic uses of gender violence: how the economy produces violence against women; the commodification of the body. We see how issues or fields come together. One of the biggest changes that we've seen is the recognition that there are gender inequalities, that society and public policy have accepted that there is inequality. They recognize that there is a problem that involves society and the political economy. That has been a result of the struggle and the organization of the women's movement in general. Gender inequality is a problem, and it has to change; no one can deny that it is a problem now. It's on the public agenda. The issue of gender inequality is the biggest step that's been made.

More specifically, there has been progress dealing with the political participation of women. That is an issue in itself: recognizing the equality of political participation. Women have seen this as being connected to accomplishing the rest of the agenda. If we don't have political participation we are not going to achieve other changes. It's a requirement for other changes. If women are not present at the moment of decision, those moments are not going to take on our agenda. The coordination of national women's organizations has occurred around political participation, around the demand for equality of participation. From there, in Ecuador, an elections quota law took off involving various coordinating initiatives, for example, of the women in local government, of the Association of Municipal Women [AMUME, Asociación de Mujeres Muncipalistas del Ecuador]. This association attempts to strengthen the presence of women [in local government], still a minority. It tries to have a shared agenda, to offer training, mutual support that sustains itself with time. To have collective spaces helps women empower themselves. Many say that it's not enough to be a woman who is elected; it has to be a woman who is also committed to the women's agenda.

Of course, changing gender inequality involves changes that take more time in practice. The first step is to recognize it as a public issue. In all countries, there is resistance. People say gender violence is a private matter that every family knows about and each couple manages. Recognizing it as a public matter, of public interest, a subject of legislation and policy is already a step. This allows for linking violence with other issues and for it to be recognized on the agenda of certain organizations. There have been women's organizations and mixed organizations. Poor women are more often in mixed organizations, of women and men. Indigenous women, for example, have had a long journey to building organizations of women – to detach themselves. And, their organizations are related and often dependent on mixed organizations. It's a complex process but it's very interesting – challenging – because it requires different approaches to 'read' gender in a different cultural context. It's very different in indigenous communities due to the community logic, the cosmology, a series of elements. Anyway, the fact that the issue of violence is on those agendas is a step, because it's normal that it is on the women's agenda, but not necessarily normal that it is on the agenda of mixed organizations. That's been an important step forward.

More recently, in Ecuador, in the Constituent Assembly of 1998 in which the Constitution was passed, one of the most significant accomplishments was including reproductive and sexual rights, which before were not recognized in the Constitution. I participated directly in this. We succeeded in putting this notion of self-determination, of freedom of sexual orientation, even in the Constitution. Ecuador's was the second Constitution in the world to include freedom of sexual orientation – after South Africa.

Not abortion. We didn't get that. [But] doors were opened. We put reproductive and sexual rights in relation to different topics, not just the right to everything dealing with maternity, paternity – except abortion – but with [bodily] integrity, non-violence. This framework has allowed for legal advances. For example, one of the current debates has been the morning-after-pill – to have legal access to this pill and for it to be available in the public services – and converting the whole notion of maternal health care into a broader conception of sexual and reproductive care.

One of the social projects that we have is free maternity, meaning to have free access to public health services for maternity and childbirth. Initially, poor women had free delivery in the hospitals. But with the neoliberal model, public health began to have costs. For this reason, free maternity was invented. Before, there was free care for all; now the focus is on maternity only. [But] the panorama of what one understands to be maternity has widened. This has permitted the problematization of the subject of abortion because before, for cultural reasons, it wasn't on the women's movement agenda. It was impossible to discuss this subject or to even put it on the table. When we introduced sexual and reproductive rights into the [1998] Constitution we worked miracles to avoid the subject of abortion so that it wouldn't impede its passing. People who were in the Assembly, and had the possibility of passing the law, associated sexual and reproductive rights with abortion. How could we disassociate the two? How could we stop the church from intervening? We achieved that. Now abortion can be on the agenda of women's groups, particularly young women. There have been demonstrations for that. However, at the same time, the pro-life movement has grown, which is a movement of anti-abortion rights which wasn't seen here before. Last year, in debates around the Health Law, we saw a structured pro-life movement which was strong, that had resources, with activists, with very young women.

Another important [political] space, like the World March of Women, which is also global, is the World Social Forum. We have participated since the beginning in the Forum. It has been a very important international space for REMTE. We have had activities in all of the Forums. REMTE is a member of the International Council of the Forum. It's like another stage from which to look at women's issues, gender and feminism. We have been one of the drivers of women's, gender and feminism issues and of a policy on gender equality that we invented for the World Social Forum.

There are two feminist currents within the Forum. One is more institutionally influenced, by UNIFEM. It's a current that says: 'The Forum is a new space for argument for us. We come to argue for our rights.' But, we say: 'No, the Forum is a space of collective building and our vision is that feminism becomes a shared vision of the Forum.' We don't come to argue, we come to build with a new feminist vision, and our view is that another world is possible. That is the slogan of the Forum: 'Another world is possible.' Our proposal for another world also has to be feminist.

The Forum is a huge space. The most structured aspect of the Forum is the International Council, because by its own design it is a meeting point, a space. As a space, everyone fits who identifies with the general proposal. A level of organization is inevitable; if not, we wouldn't have been able to organize the Forums that we have, one per year, in addition to the continental Forums as well. For example, in 2004 there was the first Social Forum of the Americas in Quito that we organized, we coordinated. That was our space. It is a space of resistance to the [neoliberal] model, of struggle against free trade. The World Social Forum based its forces, in good part, on that mobilization. The 'alternatives' camp has been a space in which we, as REMTE, and the MMM, have been questioning the model. Working with the Forum has been an experience which reconnected us with a much wider agenda and with the mixed movement. Personally, until the Forum, I had only moved in women's circles. Now I'm in mixed environments but with a feminist agenda. The experience is different.

5
Gossip as Direct Action

Erica Lagalisse

> *Ring the bells that still can ring,*
> *Forget your perfect offering,*
> *There is a crack in everything,*
> *That's how the light gets in.*
> (Leonard Cohen)

My generation of anti-capitalist activists insists that revolution must grow out of the concrete realities of people's day-to-day lives, speak to the particularities of their situations and decentralize governing power. We feel that political activities must provide ways for people to get in touch with their own powers and capacities, to name themselves and their experiences instead of forming lobby groups or arranging spectacles to gain the favour of powerful agencies – what we call 'direct action'. These activities, in and of themselves, are meant to create and constitute an alternative set of social relations that prefigure a new social order on a larger scale, aligning means and ends – prefigurative politics. Anarchist social movements seek to effect social change through developing alternative ethics, affects and forms of 'counterpower' (Graeber 2004) within collective relationships which will spread rhizomatically and virally – 'seeds' of a new social order within the shell of the old (see Graeber 2009; Juris 2008; Maeckelbergh 2009).

The following ethnography of a Zapatista solidarity collective based in Montreal, of which I was a member, proceeds by considering our activity on these terms, that is, precisely with an eye for decentralized direct action, prefigurative politics and 'seeds' of a new social order within existing formations. I 'speak nearby' (Chen 1992; Trinh 1992) the activists in question for multiple reasons. I use a conceptual framework that is familiar to them and that they respect; it helps them to hear me. Speaking nearby also helps all of us 'find the movement' differently (see Enke 2007), to 'decentre the movement', perceive its 'ripple effects' beyond where we would otherwise delimit it in social space (Nelson 2003). By doing so, perhaps we may productively decentre common understandings of 'social movements'.

Although social movements have often been ontologized as 'civil society' and seen through the lens of particular 'organizations', they involve various scales of social activity, rely on 'backstage' interaction and confound boundaries of 'public' and 'private'. As ethnographic research necessarily concerns itself with everyday life, I investigated the Zapatista solidarity collective beyond its formal meetings and specifically considered the 'backstage' – the private – activity that defined the collective's work and trajectory. This methodology is well-suited to observing and documenting women's activities, including the ways women in our collective agitated to advance our specific concerns as women and feminists. We faced many challenges and did not have much room to manoeuvre, but we found a crack or two.

By 'speaking nearby' we may also achieve a certain understanding and intervention foreclosed by merely 'speaking about' in a foreign vocabulary. Activist and non-activist readers alike will appreciate the irony of anarchist men criticizing women's action to subvert their power on the basis that it is decentralized and autonomous. In this chapter, I invite us to look at a 'backstage activity' that anarchist men pejoratively dismiss as 'gossip' and to analyse it not only as a form of everyday resistance by women but as direct action. Considering the movement – a political space that Cole and Phillips might consider an emerging public (see chapter 1) – on its own terms, then, does not mean foregoing criticism. In this essay I illustrate disjunctures between ideals and practice within the movement, particularly male activists' aversion to challenging gendered power. This is where women's direct action comes in. Women's conversations in 'private' homes about 'personal' relationships embodied attempts to steer the movement in a feminist direction and to call male power into question. While this activity was maligned by many male comrades as 'gossip' and 'conspiracy', anarchist women were doing no more and no less than practising the direct-action political philosophy as expounded by anarchist men themselves. They took back the power to name their experiences, and cooperated autonomously outside of the hierarchical institutions biased against them – in this case the anarchist collective, as well as the state – and they planted 'seeds' of a new social order within the shell of the old.

HISTORICAL AND ETHNOGRAPHIC CONTEXT

The Zapatista movement in Chiapas, Mexico, which began in 1994, might arguably mark the inception of the 'alter-globalization' movement. The Zapatistas' use of internet media to make their struggle known and call for a global mobilization against neoliberalism resonated strongly among diverse activist groups all over the world (Khasnabish 2008). The Zapatistas' engagement with the racialized, gendered and capitalist logic of neoliberal globalization resonated with many anti-capitalists who had become disillusioned with 'old' class-based politics yet who saw the limits of 'new' rights-based identity movements (Day 2005; Graeber 2009). The Zapatistas' particular autonomist approach also signalled a new anti-capitalist relationship to the (Mexican) state: As opposed to the 'old' anti-capitalists who sought a dictatorship of the proletariat, the Zapatistas sought to 'change the world without taking power' (Holloway 2005).

All of these aspects particularly appealed to autonomist, anarchist and anti-authoritarian movements all over the world that, by nominal definition, are against all forms of domination. These movements critique the state form as oppressive, unnecessary and part of the world capitalist system. For this reason, when the Zapatistas organized the Second International *Encuentro* (Gathering) for Humanity and against Neoliberalism in Barcelona in 1998, more than 3,000 activists from 50 countries arrived, a significant portion of whom identified as autonomist or anarchist (Juris 2008). Many of these people were North American and European activists whose movements combined the ideals and rhetoric of the western anarchist traditions of the nineteenth and early twentieth centuries with the organizational forms of feminist movements responding to the authoritarian New Left. Their ideals included prefigurative politics (means matching ends), consensus decision-making and participatory rather than representative democracy (Katsiaficas 2001; Lamoureux 2004). At this Zapatista *encuentro* the activists syncretised these ideals with those of the Zapatista movement when they organized the People's Global Action (PGA) network.

The PGA network, born at this meeting, proliferated into many regional direct action networks that in turn coordinated the series of large-scale mobilizations against the World Trade Organization, the International Monetary Fund and other neoliberal initiatives, the first of which took place in Seattle in 1999. It was the regional PGA network in Montreal that organized the demonstration against the Free Trade Area of the Americas in Quebec City in 2001 (see Graeber 2009). Approximately half of the activists in our Zapatista solidarity collective were politicized in this context or shortly after. The others had arrived in Montreal more recently from Mexico, bringing with them experience in anarchist collectives, Zapatista solidarity campaigns and student movements in Mexico (for example, the student strike at UNAM in 1998–1999). All identified as 'anarchist' or 'autonomist' anti-capitalists, and shared the ideals of means matching ends, consensus decision-making, and autonomous direct action.

Our collective had a shifting core of a dozen people, with another few dozen rotating in and out of meetings and events. We formed in 2005 in Montreal, concurrent to *La Otra Campaña* (the Other Campaign) in Mexico. *La Otra Campaña* was the Zapatistas' campaign organized parallel to the Mexican federal election campaign of 2006 to build a broad national movement against neoliberalism 'from below and to the Left' (*desde abajo y a la izquierda*). Following the EZLN's (Zapatista Army of National Liberation) call in their Sixth Declaration from the Lacondon Jungle, transnational activists organized collectives and adapted this programme to a variety of contexts.[1] In Montreal, our collective organized demonstrations to raise awareness of social movements and their repression in Mexico, held film screenings and speaking events on related topics and organized benefits to support political prisoners in Chiapas and Oaxaca.

METHODOLOGY

My decision to research my peers' and my own activism was inspired by my familiarity with both the compelling and problematic aspects of our praxis, and my desire to articulate constructive critique in this regard. I knew that turning my 'home' into the 'field' would involve both psychological and ethical challenges (Dyck 2000), but I also knew that my insider/outsider positionality as both activist and researcher would allow a unique opportunity to critically reflect on this activism. I proceeded according to the tenets of feminist participatory research methodology put forth by Maguire: 'development of critical consciousness of both researcher and participants; improvement of the lives of those involved in the research process; and transformation of fundamental societal structures and relationships' (2008: 418). During the research process I worked to identify participants' own perceptions of significant problems in our activist practice (2008: 422), and ultimately I concentrated on the themes that I did based on the fact that many of my peers – granted, mostly women – felt it was important to do so.

Beyond one year's participant-observation (2006–2007) within meetings, public events and informal gatherings, I conducted informal interviews with activists in our collective, activists who attended the larger events and activists in collectives with whom we often collaborated. I mention the broader scope of my research here because, although this ethnography focuses specifically on gender dynamics within the Zapatista solidarity collective, the reader may keep in mind that the patterns I present here are not idiosyncratic (Lagalisse 2010).

The quotations I offer in this discussion all come from my field notes rather than recordings. They were either collected during the course of my participant-observation and written down the same day, or scribbled down during conversations and interviews. One of the challenges in researching anarchist, anti-capitalist movements is activists' wariness that recordings and photographs proving their participation may be used against them if they were to fall into the wrong hands. Thus, although audio recordings, videos and photographs can bestow certain legitimacy to research, the fact that they do constitute indisputable 'evidence' is the reason I could not and would not pressure activists to offer them. For the same reasons, pseudonyms are used for the names of individual activists and collectives that appear here. In any case, names are irrelevant as the purpose of my research is not to critique any particular person or collective's practice, but to speak to certain discourses, logics and practices common among them. I call our collective *La Otra Campaña* (The Other Campaign), or simply *La Otra*, as it was inspired by the Zapatista initiative that went by this name, and note for my readers that this collective no longer exists at the time of writing.

As a final point regarding my method, I would like to mention a way in which I 'write and speak nearby' my ethnographic subject and feminism at once: the reader will find that throughout this chapter I am transparent within the ethnography as a participant. After all, I came to do this research through my previous and ongoing participation as an activist. In the same gesture, I also respond to the feminist challenge to ethnography – often neutered as 'the reflexive turn' – to be transparent as a researcher as well as a participant.[2] I bring the reader into the story of my fieldwork, explaining how my research focus developed, the dilemmas I experienced due to my dual roles and why I decided to spread the gossip I do.

THE HONEYMOON: SUMMER 2006

I joined *La Otra* collective in 2006 shortly after the brutal repression of activists, including a *La Otra Campaña* delegation, in Atenco, Mexico. They had been occupying the flower market in solidarity with the vendors who did not want to see it destroyed by the building of a shopping mall. The police attacked the camp (*plantón*), and widespread reports of rape and other prisoner abuse among the arrestees proliferated. *La Otra* collective in Montreal organized in response to the violence in Mexico. The actions were creative – artistic and colourful, involving flowers, music and puppets; the preparatory art sessions were as much fun as the actions themselves. I was happy to be part of this group of a dozen activists who were all friendly with each other and carried out their collective work seriously but with a good dose of humour. Indeed the informality and convivial nature of our collective work was more like the activist culture in Mexico than in Montreal, and it was refreshing.

Over the course of the summer, we organized parties to fundraise for political prisoners, arranged political art installations all over town, participated in 'No One Is Illegal' demonstrations and planned a speaking tour of two activists from Oaxaca for fall 2006. Meanwhile, I became better friends with the collective members and even found myself a lover in the group.[3] My fieldwork came to focus more specifically on *La Otra* collective as opposed to other initial leads simply because I liked them so much and ended up spending the most time with them. I also found the collective especially interesting because it embodied such a diversity of encounters: it involved men and women, Francophones and Anglophones, bilingual and monolingual Spanish speakers from Mexico, some with legal immigration papers and some without, straight and queer members.[4] It was an ideal site to witness the coalition politics that were the professed foundation of our activism. And as the months wore on, I was feeling more and more satisfied that I would be able to report that, notwithstanding minor conflicts, these coalition politics were realized in practice.

In fact what was happening was that I was so eager to render this activist space in a good light that I kept discounting an emergent pattern of problems as 'exceptions'. One strength of ethnographic fieldwork is that one can read one's notes later in order to cross-check oneself to preclude this sort of filtering. A series of events during a speaking tour in the fall of 2006 forced me to re-orient myself in precisely this way.

I was forced to concede to myself that there was a gendered division of labour in our collective whereby women performed the operational tasks without equal power in decision-making. These tasks included taking the minutes of meetings, email communication, translation, layout of flyers and posters and the social labour of facilitating meetings, mediating conflict and welcoming new members. Women were more likely to volunteer for such tasks. New female members were particularly keen to take on such responsibilities in order to gain the respect of the group.

During the summer a few women collective members stopped coming around. At the time I attributed this to reasons extraneous to the collective itself. One woman, Elizabeth, confronted Carlo about patronizing women in the collective and treating them like sex objects, and Carlo accused her of being 'a white feminist and imperialist'. Elizabeth left the collective in tears. Other collective members, both men and women, attributed the dispute to a 'crush' Elizabeth had on Carlo. This encounter I had also stubbornly marked up as an exception. In retrospect there was a clear pattern. Young women between the ages of 20 and 25 consistently joined and participated only to burn out a few months later and be replaced by new enthusiastic peers. Meanwhile, the same group of men would remain in the collective, adding to their gender privilege the prerogative of seniority. Many of the women who left did so due to a variety of gender-related problems within the collective. These were rendered 'private' issues (such as Elizabeth's 'crush') to be dealt with on an individual rather than collective basis. These gendered patterns of recruitment and seniority curiously resemble those that second-wave feminists – *las viejas* – report as prevailing in leftist movements in the 1960s and 1970s.

As I said, I did not begin to put this together until the fall of 2006. A series of overtly sexist comments and acts, and some crucially important 'gossip' afterwards, brought me to consciousness as to what had been going on.

THE SPEAKING TOUR: FALL 2006

In October 2006 several anarchist collectives in Montreal, including our *La Otra Campaña* collective, collaborated in organizing a speaking tour of two indigenous activists, Juan and Magdalena, from Oaxaca who had been involved in the Popular Assembly of the Peoples of Oaxaca (*Asamblea Popular de los Pueblos de Oaxaca* – APPO).[5]

The month-long tour involved events at universities, community centres, union offices and the indigenous communities of Kahnawake, Six Nations and Kanehsatake. Juan spoke of union movements, the formation of the APPO, and the state repression of his people. He spoke in the third-person, assuming the objective voice of a generalized 'other'. Magdalena spoke in the first-person, and about specific people who were tortured and why, and what they told her afterwards. She recounted stories from her experience as a community health worker (*promotora*), and described how government representatives attempted to persuade her to promote sterilization among indigenous women.

The audiences as well as the organizers responded much more enthusiastically to Juan: 'Remember when that guy asked why the APPO is against political parties and Juan answered 'Because we are *indigenous*'? Wasn't that *awesome?*' Magdalena, however, inspired much less discussion. In the second week of the tour, a shift was perceptible: whereas at the beginning of the month Juan and Magdalena shared the speaking time at public events, gradually Juan was occupying the microphone for longer periods of time. He would pass the microphone to Magdalena to introduce herself in Zapotec (an indigenous language in Oaxaca, her first language) and then take it back, speak for an hour, and pass it back to her to thank the crowd and say good night. While one could partially attribute this to disrespect on the part of Juan, the situation was clearly more complicated; a dialectic between Juan, the audience and the organizers was encouraging his speech at the expense of Magdalena's. Some women activists noticed this and were troubled.

We approached the collective members who were to form the next relay of accompaniment during the tour and suggested we discuss the situation. One of the men replied, 'Magdalena doesn't want to talk, she's very shy, and we have to respect cultural differences. We shouldn't force her to do something she does not want to do.' Other men echoed the need to respect 'cultural norms', citing anti-racism as an important collective value. Yet another said it was important to keep our 'white feminism' to ourselves, as it was not appropriate to 'impose our personal politics'. One of the women responded by asking if any of them had actually asked Magdalena how *she* feels, including whether she would like to be speaking more. The first man shrugged while another replied, 'Let's face it, Juan has more of an analysis, he is more articulate, educated, and he's had more experience in politics and the union movements.'

During the same week another incident occurred which riled some of the women in the collective. While I and the three main male members of the collective were at Six Nations, Ontario, accompanying Juan and Magdalena on the speaking tour, three people involved in the APPO, including an American journalist, were killed by paramilitaries in Oaxaca. It was 27 October, a few days before the Day of the Dead in Mexico. We decided it would be powerful to organize a demonstration to coincide with the holiday. But that did not leave us much time. We would have to start working that very night. As I had done all of the driving that day (about 12 hours) I went to sleep, while the three men stayed up to mobilize the event over email and cellphones. Instead of getting in touch with the women collective members back in Montreal according to the 'telephone tree' we had previously established, the men called other activist men, a *Chavista* group (supporters of Hugo Chávez, the socialist president of Venezuela). The next morning I asked them why they had not contacted the rest of the collective, and one of the men responded 'Because we are all here!'

Meanwhile the women collective members back in Montreal had also heard the news from Oaxaca. When they could not get in touch with us, they began on their own to organize a demonstration on the Day of the Dead, having had the very same idea. It didn't take them long to hear that the *Chavistas* had announced an Oaxaca solidarity demonstration they were organizing 'in cooperation with *La Otra* collective'. The women confronted the *Chavistas* about adding *La Otra* to their flyers without the collective's permission, at which point they realized that Carlo, Ricardo and Stephane had contacted the Chavistas and not them.

MID-FIELDWORK (RE)ASSESSMENT: NOVEMBER 2006

All of this got me thinking. I mulled over the conversation about Magdalena during the speaking tour, and remembered the dispute between Carlo and Elizabeth. I thought back to times during the summer when I suggested we collaborate with some other collectives on various projects but men in the collective said that some women in these groups were *hembristas* (an inverse of *machista*, whose operative meaning was something in the vein of 'man-hating separatist feminists'). Carlo in particular was concerned about women ex-members who had 'personal' grievances against him and had maliciously spread 'gossip' (*chismes*) about him in the past. At one point he called one of these women a *manzana de discordia*; literally, 'apple of discord', an (ironic) derogatory reference to Eve (eating the Fruit of Knowledge!). At other times, men in the group referred to local feminist activists as 'racists that hate Mexicans' or 'lesbians that hate men' or some combination of the two. Racist man-hating lesbians were so ubiquitous that our group had to eschew contact with almost every other activist collective in the city. I had somehow managed to bracket all of this.

I considered how some women in our group had participated in insulting these women, and wondered if they actually knew them or if they were taking the men at their word. I made inquiries. Some women in the group had indeed had negative experiences interacting with local anarchists; anarchist men and anarcha-feminist women had alienated at least one Mexican woman in our collective by patronizing her, apparently because of her feminine gender presentation – many women in the anarchist scene adopt an androgynous 'punkesque' style. Most collective members didn't know any of these women, however, and didn't know what had transpired between them and the men in our collective. Neither did I, but I began to think that there may be something to all this 'gossip', given our own recent, frustrating experiences.

I also wondered whether the men were purposely pre-empting contact between current and past collective members by casting them in a negative light, an activity facilitated by language barriers: at least half the collective were monolingual Spanish speakers, most others were Mexicans who spoke Spanish and French, and most of the rejected women – ex-members or otherwise – were bilingual Anglophones. Perhaps this dividing line indicated a series of schisms defined by racism or cultural differences, perhaps not. Either way, language divides almost exactly overlapped racial divides and made characterizing past conflicts as due to race, separatist lesbianism or personal hatred very easy indeed, as it was unlikely that new collective members would hear any other version.

I was one of the few trilingual speakers in the collective, the only Anglophone at the time, and I knew many of the rejected women personally from past experience in the activist scene. I realized I was in a unique position to investigate this situation, but was conflicted in my dual roles as participant and researcher: as an activist I felt a responsibility to my collective to find out what had been going on, but was troubled by the fact that it was only due to my writing field notes that I had come to consider all of this. I decided to wait and see if other women in the collective themselves felt that there was a problem with the gender dynamics within the collective. I didn't have to wait long.

NEGOTIATING THE *AGENDA DE RESISTENCIA*: DECEMBER 2006

In early December 2006 we met to discuss amendments to the Zapatista *agenda de resistencia*, including the proposition to add 'patriarchy' to the *agenda*. Adherents of Zapatista collectives both in Mexico and beyond had suggested that patriarchy should be on the agenda. So all Zapatista collectives in Mexico and elsewhere in the world were to discuss this proposal and weigh in, either in person or by email, during the upcoming Zapatista *encuentro* in Chiapas that winter.

We discussed all the other pre-*encuentro* questions for discussion first. Where should the 2010 *Intergalactico* be held? How can we learn from the successes and failures of the Peoples Global Action network? Can one be a pothead and a Zapatista at the same time? What does it mean to be a leftist? I don't think the word 'procrastination' would be an exaggeration here. Valeria, one of the few self-identified feminists in the collective (and the only one who was Mexican, and therefore partially shielded from attacks of 'white feminism') finally said:

> The other thing put forth is that patriarchy be included as an axis of struggle. We are explicitly anti-capitalist, but we have to clarify that you can be anti-capitalist without being anti-patriarchal and this has been a fault in the movement.

And so it began.

Some women in our collective insisted a critique of patriarchy should definitely be integrated. The men generally disagreed. One man called it 'a first world issue', the concern of 'imperialist *hembristas*', and referenced the egalitarian nature of indigenous communities. Some women in the collective took issue with this argument and countered that indigenous women also experience male domination and critique gender relations in their communities, albeit not always using the word 'patriarchy'.

At this point a different man countered that 'patriarchy existed before capitalism so it's a separate issue', seeming to contradict the first man, but nonetheless putting the women back on the defensive. Some women, including myself, then attempted to explain how the dispossession of women figures in 'primitive accumulation', how neoliberalism relies on racialized women's underpaid labour and how profit is created in the domestic sphere. This political economic analysis is well-substantiated and appeared a useful rhetorical response. But then we were back at square one: 'You see? The problem is capitalism not patriarchy.'

Valeria and I then took turns trying to explain that 'neither capitalism nor patriarchy can be seen as first cause'; that 'male domination often emerges in non-capitalist societies, although not necessarily'; that 'regardless of the initial gender system, capitalist colonialism has most often resulted in increasing male dominance due to the gendered organization of capitalist economies'. But a man interrupted us and summarily redirected the conversation to concentrate on feminism as imperialist. He said he just did not want to be 'part of a social movement [that is, feminism] that supported rich white women just so they could have poor indigenous women working for them'.

To dispel the rising tension, some men and women suggested settling on a phrasing whereby capitalism 'preys on the marginalized' (who was marginalized in the first place, and why, would be left unspoken). Some women, however, continued to argue that women are oppressed 'in a particular way', this time making specific reference to the triple burdens of poor indigenous women. 'Yes, but that's because they are *indigenous*' was the response. At this point we were all quite exhausted. No one seemed to remember the earlier argument that indigenous communities are egalitarian and harmonious, or, if they did, they weren't prepared to argue about it any more.

We went back and forth a while longer, and managed to settle on the phrase 'patriarchy is a form of exploitation within capitalism and it is urgent that we recognize it' – not bad. I read off our response to this and other questions at the *encuentro* in Chiapas later that month, and we never broached the subject again.

BACKSTAGE 'GOSSIP': THE SAME NIGHT

Despite the tense evening, or perhaps because of it, we decided to go to a restaurant afterwards to relax and hang out. The conversation was dominated by the women discussing a collective member's abusive ex-boyfriend. Rather than sit silently and listen to our conversation (which is what we women usually did when the men spoke of something that did not interest us enormously), the four men began to have their own conversation and then declared they were bored and were going to leave. This stirred us all to get up – we had finished our food after all. Three women including myself went back to Valeria's house and continued our discussion. The conversation expanded to each of us sharing similar stories, which ultimately led into us debriefing our earlier collective meeting. I paraphrase our conversation, originally in Spanish and much, much longer:

'It's so delicate, I mean you never want to fight with your collective, or with your partner for that matter, not with anyone you are close to...So you end up not saying anything! And, then what? I mean if it takes a two-hour meeting just to establish that patriarchy is a problem then we obviously have a lot of work to do!'

'Yeah, to think that it's that hard just to mention the fucking problem, imagine trying to actually *organize* around it?'

'Yeah, every time I mention gender they start complaining about the *hembristas* in D.F. [*Distrito Federal*, that is, Mexico City].'

'What really enraged me [*me dió corage*] was when I had to justify that the oppression of women exists by using the example of indigenous women.'

'No shit! That was really horrific!'

'Yeah. Then they just say "yeah, but it's because they're *indigenous*" after all.'

'Yeah and it makes it hard, y'know, if within your own group you can't even talk about the things that are so real in your life. If it's not even accepted by the group, what are you supposed to do? Have a separate group where you have to deal with women's stuff? And have twice the work?!'

'If *La Otra* is about solidarity and being "from below and to the Left" ... there's no fucking way that we should have to organize around patriarchy *outside* of *La Otra*. The whole point is that it's supposed to be inclusive of everyone and about a convergence of struggles. We even said that earlier, we defined the Left as *convergencias* and *pluralidad*.'

'Yes we say we want to have our politics and our daily lives match up, meanwhile in our relationships there's all this abuse and men are continually taking up more space and never admitting that ...'

'I mean things in this group have been a *little* better recently but, I dunno, Stephane calling the *Chavistas* instead of you, Valeria ... that was *bad*. You were there Erica, how did *that* happen?'

'I was sleeping at the time, and when I found out the next day I was really not impressed and I told Carlo and Ricardo so. They said it was all Stephane, that it was he who made the call, and said "Oh man *las viejas* [roughly, 'the old ladies', in the sense of 'the ol' ball and chain'] are going to kill us, they gotta know it wasn't our fault!"'

'*Las viejas?!*'

'Yeah I know, but at least they seemed to notice it was wrong that he didn't call you ... which is better than usual. But then I suggested that we talk to Stephane about it and they started finding all sorts of reasons not to!'

'Sometimes they say stuff, like how it should be one guy and one girl to do some task, and I mean that's something but it's not enough. Just because there is a woman there, doesn't mean there is no power imbalance at play.'

'It's a representation game!'

'Like how they recruited us to their soccer team for the anarchist soccer tournament 'cause the team had to be gender equal, but then wouldn't let us on the field!'

'Remember how proud they were of themselves that they invited a *compañero* and a *compañera* from Oaxaca – 'cause at first it was just *dos compañeros* ...'

'And then they think that they have done their good deed or whatever and pay no attention to what actually unfolds during the tour!'

'Y'know once we were leaving an event, and I was talking about where to park the car, and Juan proceeded to repeat everything for Magdalena as if she hadn't understood! And she was obviously getting fed up with him at times. She even asked to stay in a different house from him at one point, remember?'

'Yeah, and yet when we try to talk to the guys about it, they say ...'

'Yeah they don't give a shit [*les vale madre*].'

'And they think they treat her with such respect ...'

'But the kind you give a fragile little flower. They all fuss over her and get delighted when she laughs and plays in the snow ...'

'Totally infantilizing her! When in reality she's ...'

'... tougher than all of us put together!'

Towards the end of the conversation, I mentioned that I suspected many of the women activists whom the guys complain about had had similar frustrations. Perhaps what the men called their 'malicious gossip' was no more than complaining like we are now?

And maybe the women had had reason to? Perhaps, Valeria and the others agreed. In any case, this evening of 'gossip' marked a turning point of sorts. Up until that point, the men had always been the core group of friends and we women had connected mostly through our mutual friendships with the men.

ENCUENTROS AND ENCOUNTERS IN MEXICO: WINTER 2006–2007

Valeria, Carlo and I went to Mexico that winter. Carlo and Valeria went to visit their friends and families; I went to visit friends and do fieldwork. Part of my original research idea was to investigate both sides of transnational anarchist/indigenous movements' collaborations. In doing so, I ended up discovering that some of our collaborators' agendas and our own were possibly operating at cross-purposes. This was interesting in terms of my research. But, as a member of our collective, it was my responsibility to 'report back' to my group. So I emailed my collective with the information for them to discuss and come to a decision by consensus as to what to do, if anything. At this point, before meeting with the collective, Stephane (who was the one who had originally forged links with the group in question) forwarded my email to some of the implicated people. I can only imagine that he felt threatened, worried that this development would reflect negatively on his own integrity (although there was no way he could have known the information beforehand). In any case, the battle-lines had been drawn: a polemical Internet War ensued from London to Argentina. The stakes were so high (at some point I was accused of being a spy for the Mexican government) and the intrigue so impenetrable, that I abandoned the possibility of incorporating any substantive account into my ethnography. And I only recount as much as I do now because this conflict had the effect of throwing into relief the gendered divides in our collective.

The women and one man (my boyfriend – coincidence?) pointed out that if it had been one of the men who sent back such information, he would have been seen as fulfilling his responsibility as a member of the collective, rather than being charged with spreading 'calumnious gossip', of which various men had accused me. Also, it was oft-repeated that a reference to 'domestic abuse' in my email was what made it gossip. That this interpretation of my email constituted major ammunition in the Internet War was 'sexist', said some in my defence. I tried to stay focused on my projects in Mexico as my inbox filled up with escalating arguments.

Both Carlo and I were in Mexico City at Christmas time. We got along well those weeks in D.F. and I even spent Christmas with his family. Soon afterwards Valeria, Carlo and I all went to the Zapatista *encuentro* together. Valeria and I chatted constantly in between the plenaries and many, many dances. We discussed our collective, how our dissertations were shaping up and shared many personal stories. Our friendship was further strengthened when we got into a bus accident on the way home that almost sent us over a cliff and stranded us on the highway, building bonfires as flares all night long – a perilous experience we still joke about today.

Valeria and I were particularly inspired by the women's plenary session (*Mesa de Mujeres*) – the first of its kind. A dozen Zapatista women emphasized that there is much work that remains to be done, but that the organization of women within the EZLN, thanks to a few original women militants, has inspired unprecedented advances. During the question-and-answer period, one question in particular caused Valeria and I to look at each other and smile:

Do you think it would be good to have a meeting with all the Zapatista women with other women of the world, without men? Or do you not think it necessary?

Two Zapatista women answered in turn:

I think it's necessary to have a meeting with all the women to raise ideas and strategies of resistance, to go forth organizing all together. That's all. *Gracias compañeras.*

The second woman said:

I think it's very important, women *compañeras*, to make a meeting among all the women because there are women *compañeras* who don't speak up, who don't get up and participate [*que no se animen*] in the presence of the men *compañeros*. Among women, more ideas would come forth about how to strengthen and widen the struggle.

'LA OTRA OTRA': SPRING 2007

When the collective reconvened in Montreal in February, the group was different. Whether due to conflicts the previous autumn, the polarizing effect of the Internet War, my reflections and Valeria's on the Zapatista *encuentro*, new friendships among women in the collective, or some constellation of all the above, certain things began to change. Women members began to meet separately in order to plan events about Zapatista and APPO activist women while also continuing to meet as *La Otra* (we never adopted a name; *La Otra Otra* is my twist on the pseudonym).

The first time this happened was leading up to 8 March, International Women's Day. Valeria had been invited to participate at an event organized by the Chavistas, and in turn invited the collective to present something together. Most members were non-committal. Some men said no because Women's Day was not 'for them'. Valeria and I decided to do the presentation together; she would take care of an introduction and I would follow by reading the Zapatista women's speeches from the *encuentro* I had just finished transcribing. After our presentation, some women came up to us and asked if we would host a workshop at the *Centre de Femmes d'Ici et d'Ailleurs* (a community centre in Montreal for women 'from here and abroad') in a month's time. Perhaps we could discuss women's role in the APPO? Organize some participatory activity? Valeria and I said yes. We invited the collective to participate, at which point two other women joined, making us a group of four.

We met three times leading up to the event, during which time we divided the presentation into four parts, 15 minutes for each of us. We chose some YouTube videos to show about the APPO women who occupied the national television network Canal 9, managing to hold it and broadcast themselves for three weeks (see Stephen 2007). We remarked how each of us completed the tasks we took on in between each meeting, and how smooth our meetings were. We self-facilitated, took minutes and integrated our ideas such that the workshop was truly a collective product. We noted how different this experience was from our experience in *La Otra*.

The workshop itself was also a success, and the women who attended were so inspired by the women of Oaxaca that they asked us to come back in April and help them put together a radio clip of their own to honour the Oaxacan women for CKUT, a Montreal community radio station.

THE BEGINNING OF THE END: SPRING 2007

All was not well in *La Otra*. There was an increasing polarization and animosity among certain collective members, largely but not exclusively along lines of gender.

Upon my return from Mexico in February 2007, I decided to speak to various women ex-participants about their experiences in our collective, as well as women activists in the other collectives who had participated in organizing the speaking tour. I took advantage of many parties and social events to strike up such conversations. One woman explained to me that she and Carlo had been good friends but a rupture occurred when she confronted him about manipulating young women to do all the leg-work in the collective while he acted as ideas-man. He responded by accusing her of being a 'white feminist', which especially provoked her, she said, because she is not white! She said he proceeded to 'trash' her to activists in both Montreal and Mexico, effectively cutting her off from many projects. While this was all in the past, as she told the story it was clear this experience still hurt and frustrated her.

Someone apparently told Carlo I had been talking to these women, because within a week Carlo had told some collective members that I was 'conspiring' against him. The week following, my boyfriend accused me of having another lover in Mexico and not telling him. Carlo had told him, he said. My soon-to-be-ex also said that my new activist women friends in other collectives were 'racist *hembristas*' and 'lesbians' who only want to hang out with me 'in order to seduce me'. This information also apparently came from Carlo.

It occurred to me that I was in danger of becoming the next pariah. While I had some good friendships with some women in the collective, most men and women respected the men to such a degree that their analysis would prevail – if Carlo had it in for me, I was probably doomed, especially if my ex 'switched sides'. The collective members would not side with me or give me the benefit of the doubt, just as I had not supported Elizabeth ten months before.

Meanwhile, *La Otra* continued to meet. Our main project now was to forge ties with native youth at the Montreal Native Friendship Centre and to fundraise to help send those interested to the *Encuentro de Pueblos Indigenas de America* the next year. At the Zapatista *encuentro*, activists had problematized the fact that the Montreal participants were largely privileged middle-class students rather than people from indigenous communities that had most in common with the Zapatistas themselves. This *Encuentro Indigena* was then convened and we decided to mobilize resources to facilitate others' travel instead of our own.

After shooting pool at the Native Friendship Centre for a few weeks, we were invited to bring a movie about the Zapatistas and do an informal workshop about the struggle of indigenous peoples in Mexico. When the day arrived, Carlo, who had taken on the task of bringing the video, was nowhere to be found. A phone call to Carlo yielded the information that he did not recall that this had been his responsibility. We thus had no movie on hand and our collective looked incompetent as a consequence.

This 'misunderstanding' appeared disingenuous to me. Carlo liked to be the nexus of our contact with other groups. Most of the links suggested by other members were rejected. If these initiatives ever did come to fruition (helping out with the drive to unionize Mexican migrant workers or giving a presentation on International Women's Day), it was because the people who had suggested the idea in the first place ended up doing it by themselves. The only projects we would take on as a 'collective' were projects that Carlo suggested or strongly supported. Attempts to point this out earlier were dismissed not only by Carlo but by other male members of the collective.

The phenomenon was subtle. Each time a project was not followed through, another explanation was easily found. A look at the big picture clearly evinced a pattern, but very few members at any given time had the big picture at their disposal. The women members who had tried to point out the problem a few months before had since left the collective and new members had joined. Only a few of us retained an 'institutional memory' of the collective during the past year. And I had not wanted to challenge the collective on this point because, as I've mentioned, I was on thin ice. I did not want a campaign against me to escalate, forcing me to break ties with the group. At the time they were my closest group of friends.

But this act of 'forgetting' the movie for the Native Friendship Centre was, for me, the last straw. At the next collective meeting I challenged Carlo about his selective memory. I suggested that perhaps he was not interested in following through with our project with the Native Friendship Centre because, unlike most other social milieus we operated in, the centre was an Anglophone environment. This meant that the three English speakers of the collective – *all of whom were women* – would be privileged nodes in the project network. We would have unmediated contact with our collaborators, whereas his contact would be mediated by us. In other words, he would not be able to control the project. Carlo said that this was not so. In his defence he offered an alternate explanation: he had trouble socializing with indigenous people, he said, as he can't help but see them as 'backward'. He admitted this was a problematic prejudice, but could not seem to work through it, and so thought it best to remove himself from the situation. This comment was followed by an awkward silence, and a few, rather measured, sympathetic responses – at least he was honest, being reflective, it was said. I did not particularly believe Carlo (at first he said he 'forgot', and now this?). And even if it were true, I thought it an unacceptable excuse. I ventured the observation that if any of the white women of the collective had said something in such a vein, he and others would spare no time in denouncing their unacceptable racism.

'Are you not conscious of this double-standard?' I asked. A messy, heated discussion ensued which I cannot render exactly here. Basically, the remaining women in the collective piped up about all the women who had left, and conjectured the reasons why, directing their criticism to all the men in the collective. This line of questioning was then overshadowed by a diatribe by my ex-boyfriend, who began to lay into Carlo viciously and relentlessly, blaming him for a litany of our collective's problems.

Carlo, rather uncharacteristically, began to cry. Also uncharacteristically, he suggested he leave the collective as a solution. Was he showing remorse? Was he having a revelation? Or was this a devious manoeuvre? After all, perhaps it was easier to drop out than to assume responsibility. And he was smart enough to know that, faced with the choice to either continue the collective without him or disband the collective, we would feel compelled, by either guilt or integrity (depending on how you look at it), to choose the latter. (This is, indeed, what happened.) Furthermore, Carlo was one of the few collective members with enough social and symbolic capital in the activist scene to be able to create a new collective later, with new members, so this could be simply a way of getting rid of us. But maybe he was being sincere. It was impossible to tell, and I don't think I will ever know for sure.

The collective never met again. *La Otra Otra* continued to organize the events at the women's centre, but once we no longer had this immediate purpose, we too stopped meeting. During the summer of 2007, some former collective members left the country for Mexico or elsewhere. Some didn't, and I heard through mutual friends that some considered me a divisive white feminist who also had some sort of grudge against Carlo and that I, single-handedly, broke up the collective to 'get at him'. The people saying these things were mostly women. These outcomes depressed me, but I tried to put it out of my mind and turn my attention to writing my thesis.

There continue to be friendships among many of the ex-members, but also fault-lines that have prevented us from getting together as a group. Those of us from *La Otra Otra* have stayed in touch, on and off, although we all live in different countries now. We have each moved on to new anarchist collectives, jobs in NGOs and further academic degrees. While the dramatic end of our collective saddened us, those I have spoken to have said in retrospect that we learned from and value our experience – both the fun and difficult parts. Most agree that ending the collective was the best thing we could have done – besides, no one 'collective' is 'the movement', *we* are. The movement has moved on. We bring our experience to bear on the next project. I'm sure that we learned a thing or two about the need to talk to one another, the value of working together as women, and the importance of backing each other up. At least I certainly did.

There are many lessons to be drawn from this story. We may observe, for example, how contemporary anarchists continue to characterize feminism as 'single-issue', reflecting the classic argument between Marxist and anarchist women and their male comrades since the turn of the twentieth century (Chinchilla 1992; Moya 2002). On the other hand, we may note a change on the Left whereby the economic reductionism that romanticized the working class is in some ways replaced by an ethnic reductionism that romanticizes the indigenous as the new revolutionary subject (and yet, notably, still marginalizes gender). I have explored these questions elsewhere (Lagalisse 2010, 2011). What I want to focus on in the following section is the question of gendered communication dynamics and their intersections with the 'micro-political and quotidian elements' (Osterweil 2004: 185) of oppositional publics through a persistent conceptual public:private divide in activists' 'revolution of everyday life'.

GENDER, COMMUNICATION AND THE PUBLIC:PRIVATE DIVIDE

Despite our collective's espousal of prefigurative politics and a 'revolution of everyday life', an insidious public:private dynamic informed what the collective considered 'political'. 'Consensus' governed (public) meetings of the collective, but outside of meetings ('in private') informal hierarchies – including relations of power based on gender – governed social relations. Activists' comments suggesting that communication on the internal dynamics of the collective should only take place within official collective meetings reflects their construction of the meeting as *the* public space, that is, the (only) legitimate sphere of political dissent. When men complained of 'gossip', their strategy of criticism centred on its *form*: 'conspiring' (in private) – rather than on its content. Given that collective meetings were often hostile to gender concerns, and given that this appears to be why women members aired their thoughts and feelings in women-only spaces, such a citation of the 'public' must be seen as serving specifically to de-legitimate discussion of gender politics within the collective – thus creating a situation that called for direct action.

One challenge to solidarity among women in our collective was our own relatively uncritical acceptance of the discourses of public and private. Women too participated in the criticism of 'gossip'. As noted above, 'gossip' was criticized in terms of its form (communication 'behind someone's back'), rather than its content, notwithstanding the fact that if the content had been anything but gendered grievances, it would not have been marked as 'gossip' – but simply as 'conversation' – in the first place. In fact, what marked the communication as gossip was not only its gendered content but the simple fact that women were the ones communicating it: when men discussed my supposed sexual adventures in Mexico or maligned my electronic report back from Mexico behind my back, no one ventured to call *their* speech gossip. Women in our collective largely failed to notice this.

Indeed the word 'gossip' has a gendered valence broadly speaking. In English it is rarely used to refer to talk among men, which is usually rendered instead as 'shop talk', 'shooting the breeze', etc., and if they are said to be gossiping, it carries the connotation – a derogatory one at that – that they were acting like women (Rysman 1977). The adjective we used in Spanish may be rendered masculine as well as feminine (*chismoso/a*) and can be used in reference to men, but this usage was a rare occurrence in our collective (and continued to be rare during my subsequent fieldwork in Mexico City). Based on its use in context it is clear that *chisme* carries some of the same gendered baggage of 'gossip' in English. But why should women's talk be maligned as 'gossip', whether in the collective or the world at large? In English the etymology of the word and the history of its changing meaning suggest an increasing sanction against communication and friendship among women related to the consolidation of collective male power (Federici 2004; Rysman 1977). Indeed the story of our collective, like other ethnographic work on narratives (for example, Cole, this volume; Fonseca 2003), shows precisely how talking among women can challenge and mediate male power.

The critique of gossip as a form of communication was effective in part because women collective members, myself included, agreed with the principle that criticism should be 'to one's face' versus 'behind one's back'. Of course, if the activist praxis of our collective matched our ideals, then there would be no problem with upholding this virtuous principle. However, given that our meetings did not, in fact, exemplify a democratic, anti-authoritarian space, autonomous direct action – gossip – became necessary. When we did not act autonomously we merely buttressed the existing gendered power hierarchy within the collective. The failure of the women, myself included, to effectively analyse this pattern, and to reconcile our need to communicate 'privately' with our political values, worked to divide us.

Besides not 'talking behind people's backs', the other shared collective value that appeared to define 'gossip' was the principle that one not repeat second-hand information. This principle serves a righteous end in most cases. However, consider its implications in terms of how the negotiation of the relationship between 'public' and 'private' collides with the logistical realities of public and private space: when information concerns comportment in intimate relationships, especially regarding sexual activity, it is often the case that there simply are no 'witnesses'; the comportment is 'private' practically speaking. Any rule against hearsay thus becomes a rule against discussing a large swath of women's experience and problems. And, any call to refrain from hearsay lines up (rather perfectly) with the imperative to 'protect' the private sphere as an unpoliticized space. In other words, when anyone discusses the private sphere (outside the private sphere), subversion is seen to reside in both the form and content of the discussion.

Communication must be seen, then, as crucial to the constitution, creation or consolidation of the power of publics. Consider how this was the case in both the node (the collective) and the network (of collectives). The men who dismissed our concerns about Magdalena during the speaking tour were the two 'contact persons' of the collectives most involved, which made it difficult to cross them. When Stephane called the *Chavistas* instead of Valeria to organize the demonstration, there wasn't much we could do about it once it was done. The fact that the men in each collective were in closer contact with each other (either as 'contact persons' or due to informal – 'private' – ties among them) than they were with the women meant that women's attempts at intervention were less successful than they might have been.

A particularity of our situation was the fact that the communicative power of men in our collective was partially contingent on their transnational contacts. The longest-standing members in the collective were those (men) with contacts with social movement organizations and activists in Mexico, which made others disinclined to cross them. Carlo's high standing on this basis was a factor that made me hesitate to side with Elizabeth early on, and this same phenomenon appeared to be at work when I found myself in Elizabeth's position later that year.

Why male activists enjoy the privileged position of formal or informal 'contact person' in the first place requires further ethnographic research. Initial observations suggest that men enjoy these positions due to a higher level of confidence in public-speaking (both 'live' and on the internet); a greater inclination towards self-promotion and 'representing' others (in Mexico one would say *protagonismo*); and having more free time and energy because they are relieved (by women) from doing much social, emotional and imaginative labour in a variety of social fields. Once in the position of 'contact person', men attempt to retain such power in various ways. I am still quite certain that Carlo's sabotage of the Native Friendship Centre event falls into this category. Also consider, for example, what transpired – the Internet War – when I reported back to my collective from Mexico. The man who was the original link between the two groups became agitated and – ego and/or control thus compromised – he retaliated by gossiping about how I was a gossip. The extent to which this initiative was successful – despite its inherent irony – was due to male members of various collectives recognizing each other as authorities and treating each other as such, thus manifesting that very authority.

AGITATING THE NODE, THE NETWORK

Anarchists do not respect borders in practice or in theory. Thinking nearby those involved in *La Otra*, it is clear that the collective's identification as a 'Canadian', 'Quebecois', 'Latin American' or 'transnational' movement is immaterial to them. If there is an anarchist 'public', it is certainly not a nation-based 'sphere' or an 'audience' – national or otherwise. Rather it is a transnational network that publicizes certain issues, organizes certain public events and honours certain space as 'public' (for example meetings, *encuentros*) – versus (the bracketed) 'private' that serves to constitute the public.

Considering *La Otra* as a window into a rhizomatic 'movement public', one that spans the Americas, raises a variety of theoretical, methodological and political challenges. How may we discern one collective's relationship to – and influence on – a larger, unbounded network, and vice versa? And, for the purposes of this chapter, how can gender change occur, given a collective's embedded relationships with other nodes and networks?

Scholars of contemporary anarchism (Juris 2008) and historians of classical anarchist movements (Turcato 2007) have found the node/network framework most appropriate for understanding anarchism. Turcato notes that, since anarchism does not propagate itself through formal institutions in which 'an impersonal structure exists, with roles in which actors are mutually substitutable' (2007: 411), we must consider anarchism in terms of a 'network', that is, 'a set of nodes (i.e. its militants or groups), and links between such nodes (i.e. contacts, correspondence, resource exchanges, etc.)' (2007: 414). While we can expect patterns at one scale to be partially replicated at another in perpetual feedback loops (so that the interaction of individuals will affect interaction between activist collectives, which will affect regional networks, transnational networks, and vice versa), it would be a mistake to render the relationship of the 'macro' (network) to the 'micro' (node) as linear. Their relationship is not linear or binary (local/global) but rather contingent on many messy pathways. Within non-linear systems, small disturbances may have large effects, and vice versa. Relations of *scale* in such a network are constituted of 'partial' repetitions and connections (Strathern 2004).

So many drops in the sea make up an ocean, and in a non-linear system, one drop may create an ocean. As a transnational solidarity collective, we fundraised thousands of dollars and sent the money to various organizations in Mexico –and not others; we sent money to some political prisoners – and not others; we politicized certain assassinations of political activists – and not others; we organized demonstrations in response to some events – and not others. In all of our work, we privileged solidarity with activists and organizations that did not engage seriously with gender as a system of domination. And we systematically sidelined gender as an axis of struggle – we did not integrate solidarity with women's movements in Latin America into our transnational solidarity work and women who attempted to do otherwise were largely eliminated from the collective. If a fraction of the collectives in this transnational movement network failed to engage with gender dynamics in local and global contexts, from the smallest to the largest scale, this no doubt affected the network itself.

In 2011, I attended an anarchist *encuentro* in Mexico City – after the first draft of this chapter had been written – and participated in its anarcha-feminist caucus. While Mexico City and Montreal are different contexts in important ways, the women activists present voiced many of the same problems discussed here (and more). They were also worried that when we presented our summary (*relatoria*) in the plenary session, we would be accused of 'divisive gossip', and indeed some men later ventured to use these words. I think it highly likely that there are anarchist women all over facing similar challenges, and yet we do not necessarily realize it because this is not the kind of information that tends to 'flow' through the network; rather it gets locked 'in place' at the level of the collective. After all, there are all sorts of links between the anarchist movements in Mexico City and Montreal (and elsewhere), but the books, zines and information that circulate along the chain are largely written and circulated by male anarchists, who themselves appear to travel and circulate more often than the women. Some gossip on a continental scale is in order here. It now occurs to me that I could compile a veritable *anthology* of gossip to circulate to anarchists elsewhere and to which they could contribute their stories.

One could argue that, in forcing the private into the cracks of the public of one collective, the women of the *La Otra* had a small impact. But, while our women's meetings and workshops – as well as what we learned about feminist solidarity through all that transpired – were just drops in an ocean, they caused some big waves that continue to ripple. May the gossip spread like 'seeds' that germinate and grow where one most or least expects. May the weeds force open more cracks.

6
A Pedagogical Conversation: Public Scholars and Public Scholarship

Sally Cole, Marie-Eve Carrier-Moisan, Erica Lagalisse and Lynne Phillips

Are we doing an 'anthropology of publics' or 'public anthropology'? We began this project interested in an anthropology of publics. We were concerned to theorize the emergence of new political spaces, new publics. We wanted to explore how the meanings of the public can change. Yet, as feminist ethnographers who envision ethnography as social action (Gordon 1993) and as anthropologists who take activism as a research subject, we also envision public audiences for our research beyond the academy. And we undertake research for social transformation. We want our research to make a difference (Phillips 1995). So, perhaps, in that regard, we are also doing a form of public anthropology. But, if this is the case, then our understanding of publics as contested political spaces of tension and contradiction that produce 'awkward alliances' is itself in tension with the public in mainstream public anthropology. There we find the idea of the public has not been theorized but is assumed as a known and unified space. Thus, we conclude this volume with some thoughts on how we might practise a public anthropology for contested publics.

Although Louise Lamphere (2004) describes the call for public anthropology in the twenty-first century as a 'convergence' of anthropologies of different stripes – applied anthropology, public interest anthropology, advocacy, engaged and activist anthropology – the call for a public anthropology has not been *met* in a uniform way. Some – like ourselves – view it with suspicion (in whose interest is this project?), others with denial (have we ever *not* done public or engaged anthropology?), and others – ourselves as well – in agreement that writing *for publics* should figure more prominently in the future work of the discipline.

Public anthropology, simply put, refers to the view that practitioners of anthropology should undertake research not simply for readers in the discipline, but for publics. That is, knowledge should be produced explicitly for social change, moving ethnographic situations (including publics) to effect (positive) change. But this simple definition erases the many ways in which anthropologists are practicing public anthropology today, a diversity that is also blurred when described as 'convergence', or through the use of the term 'engaged' (are there any anthropologists who view themselves as 'unengaged'?).[1] Public anthropology reflects a wide range of different epistemological and ethical positions, different political orientations and different kinds of 'field' locations in which anthropologists work, both as employees and as researchers. Obvious examples of such locations are the employment of anthropologists outside academia (working in NGOs, international organizations, government – including the military – and the corporate world); the increasingly precarious and unequal conditions of employment within universities; and the location of the academy itself in the world (Field and Fox 2007; Lins Ribeiro and Escobar 2006; Sundar 2007). Not only do these locations complicate arguments regarding research 'at home' versus 'elsewhere', they indicate that what is called public anthropology is a product of quite different relationships to economic resources, political power, ethical obligations and political responsibilities and allegiances. What Rabinow et al. (2008) call the 'ethos' of anthropology can be hard to locate across such diverse contexts.

Practitioners undertake a range of different activities and define terms in quite different ways, all in the name of 'public anthropology'. If public anthropology is to have a transformative edge, it will be important to delineate those features which buoy it as such. As feminist anthropologists, we have experienced how more radical and critical elements of alternative visions can be 'tamed' by the academy, quietly sidelined as inappropriate for the profession (Cole 1995, 2003).

In chapter 1 we reviewed the theoretical literature on publics illustrated by ethnographic examples that reveal how investigating publics necessarily requires investigating 'privates'. A key conclusion we reach is that the different methodological and theoretical orientations of public anthropology demand an alternative pedagogical orientation – toward a position of learning *with* others, rather than an imperial 'doing good'. This is a point made clearly in the narratives of the Latin American activists in *Contesting Publics*.

In this book we have taken a learning-with 'standpoint' (Harding 1986) that recognizes that all social worlds produce knowledge; knowledge production is not the exclusive prerogative of the academy. We have engaged dialogue across generations and within a diversity of activist settings, and we have conducted ethnographic analysis across multiple scales – from the household to the city to the nation-state to the transnational. We have tried to reflect this in the structure of the book by interweaving activist voices and different styles and tones of ethnographic writing.

To conclude *Contesting Publics*, we address three pedagogical questions that we consider to be central if we are to fulfil the possibilities of the transformative public anthropology we envision: What are the *sites* for change and with whom – and how? What are the roles and forms of *collaboration* in public anthropology? What are the epistemological implications, responsibilities and possibilities that are raised by, and in, public anthropology research?

SITES

Although there has been consistent attention in anthropology to the 'communities' or 'people' with whom we undertake research, the sites of public anthropology are not selected to 'answer' a pre-designed theoretical question – as is typically the case in academic research. Rather, sites are places that demand social change and ethical co-engagement. This may mean research is 'multi-sited' (Marcus 1998), but not necessarily. In *Engaged Observer: Anthropology, Advocacy, and Activism* Victoria Sanford and Asale Angel-Ajani (2008) offer illustrative examples of the kinds of sites in which self-defined advocacy and activist anthropologists conduct research. Angel-Ajani (2008) undertakes research with women in an Italian prison. She defines working ethically as refusing to present the women's lives as 'facts' so that the discipline of anthropology – in its own juridical way – can judge them (do these women 'deserve' to be in jail or do they need to be saved?). Similarly, Marie-Eve Carrier-Moisan in chapter 3 (this volume) writes to challenge the representational practices at play in the campaigns against sex tourism, which tend to reduce Brazilian *garotas de programa* to sexually victimized women in need of rescue. She seeks to destabilize common assumptions about these women, and acknowledges the limits to accessing the standpoint of the women, given their own restricted access to public knowledge production and their lack of an articulated space for activism (see also Robertson and Culhane 2005).

Increasingly the internet and social media are recognized as significant public sites for diasporic communities and human rights research (Bernal 2006; Lozada 2003; MacClancy 2002). But sites for public anthropology can also include: the past, recovering stories from the archives and oral histories that challenge the public historical record (Cole 2003, 2009; M'Closkey 2002; Silva 2004); the classroom (Gordon 1993; Low 2011), the university (Barlett 2011), the communities in which we teach (Phillips 2011); and, the discipline of anthropology itself. For the latter, we have in mind efforts to 'decolonize' anthropology by activists like Faye Harrison (1991; see also Hymes 1972).[2]

Finally, we note the intriguing efforts by some anthropologists to *invent* publics in research sites, enabling new knowledge for critique or change (Satterfield 2009; Smith-Nonini 2009). Erica Lagalisse, for example, in chapter 5 of this volume, uses her position as an activist-ethnographer to create a space to re-frame 'gossip'. She initiates the compilation of what she calls an 'anthology' of gossip with which others can engage. Other examples of innovating publics include Jennifer Schirmer's (2009) work that brings together long-time enemies in Colombia – the military and ex-armed guerrillas – through a process she calls *conversatorios*. Schirmer finds that creating an alternative space where disparate parties must listen respectfully to very different points of view challenges their entrenched 'habits of mind' and offers an alternative 'model for deliberation' (2009: 229).

These are sites in which anthropological knowledge can come into play to make the 'private' public and to effect social change. At the same time we must also be aware that some publics may take up private matters in repressive ways (public debates about the veil or abortion are a case in point). These are all sites of contestation where new notions of the public and feminism and other democratic practices may be in development – 'emergent' in Rabinow's terms. If we heed the point that publics are in formation all around us, the research sites we could consider are endless.

COLLABORATION

Collaboration refers to *how* anthropologists engage with sites. Typically, in conventional anthropology, this involves techniques such as participant-observation, interviews and life histories. The distinction of public anthropology is that research is undertaken not 'on' but in alliance with research participants, or 'consultants' or 'co-intellectuals' (Lassiter 2005: 23–24). That is, fieldwork involves the development of relationships as part of the co-investigation of research questions of mutual concern; collaboration is a consideration for all stages of research. Here public anthropology can draw from feminist methods which have long eschewed both the objectification of research participants as a 'source' of data and the promotion of knowledge production as a matter of technique (Abu-Lughod 1993; Haraway 1988; Jaggar 2007; Naples 2003; Oakley 1981). In chapter 2, Sally Cole collaborates with migrant women workers to record their narratives of *liberdade* in order to document their experiences navigating Brazil's new political spaces and their creation of new public discourses on gender relations in their own neighbourhoods. When Lynne Phillips (chapter 4) arrived in Ecuador she did not expect to be focusing on the country's constitutional changes; she accompanied feminist activists not because they provided her with 'data' on this theme but to learn 'alongside' them as they engaged with a feminist concern that matters to them.

Luke Lassiter has done much to generate debate and interest in collaboration, through *The Chicago Guide to Collaborative Ethnography* (2005) and creating the journal *Collaborative Anthropologies* as a way to 'engage the growing and ever-widening discussion of collaborative research and practice in anthropology'.[3] Lassiter highlights the important contributions of feminist anthropology to public anthropology (2005; see also Gutmann 2007). Collaborative research seeks to develop less hierarchical, more reflexive ways of working with others in research, developing concepts such as speaking nearby, co-narration, reflexive ethics and accompaniment (Bridgman et al. 1999; Chen 1992; Cole and Phillips 1995; Howard 2011; L. Phillips 1996, 2004; Robertson and Culhane 2005; Trinh 1992). Indigenous scholars are developing research methods that highlight the social relations of research (Smith 1999); some have described research as 'ceremony' (Wilson 2008). Collaborative research, from this perspective, points to the need for reflexive *observation* of one's participation when undertaking 'public ethnography' (Tedlock 2007).

Ethical issues are central to public anthropology, not least because of the close temporal link between 'public' orientations and the question 'For whom is knowledge being produced?' Collaboration necessarily involves attending to this question. When Erica Lagalisse chooses to speak nearby her activist peers in the language of 'direct action', she does so in an effort to make her research constructive for and responsible to the anarchist movement itself, as opposed to academic voyeurism. Engaging a lay readership – or public – in this case a transnational anarchist one, implies more than writing 'accessibly' and translating drafts. It implies meeting collaborators on their own terms, including speaking a common language. One of the biggest challenges Erica faced in working with *Contesting Publics* was the fact that the language of publics is not only unused by her activist peers, but is also always suspect for its connotation of 'civil society' as well as of a passive 'audience', with which anarchists (including herself) emphatically do not identify. On the other hand, a gendered public:private analytical framework applied all too well (unfortunately) to her ethnographic situation. And so Erica decided that even if anarchists are not familiar with this feminist mode of analysis, they should be. She therefore sought a balance and synthesis of terms, a language at times familiar to feminists and theorists of publics (but not necessarily anarchists), and at times familiar to anarchists (but not necessarily feminists). She had two implicit goals: on the one hand, to suggest to feminists, and to others who theorize publics, ways in which 'the political' and 'the public' need to be reconceived to respond to a large terrain of contemporary social activism – the direct action of anarchists; and, on the other hand, to emphasize to anarchists the continued relevance of feminist analysis to the movement and in the world.

Indeed, it is interesting that collaborative public anthropology is emerging today precisely when two processes within universities – corporate control of knowledge production and medically based ethics procedures – dominate and monitor the research landscape. The former may welcome research teams, but seldom with the sense of collaboration assumed in a public anthropology, while the latter appear to manage the research process with legal complications (to the university) uppermost in mind. But ethics for public anthropologists can seldom be articulated before the research process begins – embedded as they are in the 'particular' (Abu-Lughod 1991) – and they can often emerge in ways that challenge research ethics councils. For example, following the rules of ethics in Canadian universities, the 'subjects' in Sally and Lynne's research project on Latin American feminist activism signed consent forms ensuring them anonymity and thus we could not use the activists' real names in this volume. In retrospect, we wonder if this process only reproduces a north/south dynamic where women activists remain unrecognized as the public intellectuals that they are. Moreover, one finds that the ethics of caring and generosity – that Sally and Lynne certainly experienced in working with feminist activists – are erased from view altogether (see Tornquist and Resende Flescher 2012). Yet it is precisely the practice of these kinds of values (rather than, for example, hubris) that are central to collaborative research, to healthy publics and to the transformative possibilities of the public anthropology we envision.

Marie-Eve questions the ethics of collaborative research itself, in light of her first-hand encounter with the complex political interests that traversed her field site. Witnessing awkward alliances between feminist activists, business owners and state agents that led to further entrenching the stigmatization of and discrimination against poor Brazilian women, it became more important to shed light on the tensions, contradictions and implications of these alliances, rather than to seek collaboration. In other words, Marie-Eve thought that, in order to reveal the working of power in the campaigns against sex tourism, it was necessary to 'speak against' rather than 'nearby'. For, as she underscored in a conversation the four of us had about our experience working together on this book:

> It is difficult to 'speak nearby' when one seeks to point to relations of power between different groups of people, or to recognize the many ways in which, within a group, different interests may be expressed. The Brazilian women I interviewed share multiple social locations and did not speak in a unified voice, but spoke in multiple voices. Yet, at the same time, I also see the value of challenging processes of knowledge production and I want to see the women, the *garotas* I am writing about as public intellectuals, creating meanings and critique alongside and with me.

The point here is that, while fieldwork is always a collaborative interaction, a public orientation requires a much more self-conscious examination of collaboration as a process. It requires vigilance about how more radical forms of collaboration – those which break down the divisions based on expertise and training – will be more difficult to do and more likely to be disciplined.

CO-THEORIZING AND EPISTEMOLOGY

Perhaps the most challenging dimension for public anthropology has been that of *co-theorizing*. If we accept that public anthropology demands collaborative research in alliance with others, this implies that collaboration also informs the knowledge production process, including its epistemological assumptions. Given the many years of training in individualist, competitive university environments, practitioners are seldom able to relinquish such control easily.

Joanne Rappaport (2005, 2007), based on her long-term research with indigenous activists and intellectuals in Colombia, argues for a collaborative anthropology that co-constructs research agendas driven by political, not theoretical, concerns. She recounts how her work involved engaging with alternative notions of time, space, knowledge and action – an alternative epistemological universe that challenged Rappaport's ideas of culture, collaboration and the construction of indigenous identity. She concludes that collaboration is less about the paternalist gesture of giving up the power to calculate than about subordinating oneself to a very different sense of the political – of not just 'knowing otherwise' (Berglund 2006: 198) but of acting otherwise. We see this levelling of the epistemological terrain as fundamental to co-theorizing.

The decision to make *Contesting Publics* an inter-generational dialogue, for example, helped Sally and Lynne, as '*viejas*', to think differently about emergent epistemological possibilities – for example, alternative publics-in-formation – as well as about the book's potential audience(s). We had assumed a 'like-minded' audience, but it became clear that many new scholars saw public anthropology as a benchmark, a 'best practice', rather than a radical orientation to change.

Marie-Eve engaged the idea of publics at first reluctantly, as it did not resonate with the language used by the many participants in her research. Yet, as the inter-generational thought-process in the *Contesting Publics* project evolved, she came to see publics as an analytical concept that allowed her to engage the various political interests that were expressed in the context of sex tourism. Indeed, the notion, while seemingly detached from the local reality of the Brazilian women, made it possible to recognize the women as protagonists in the new political space that sex tourism has become. Thus, through the concept of publics, Marie-Eve is able to engage co-theoretically with Brazilian *garotas de programa* who elaborate a cogent critique of their social locations and of the campaigns that stigmatize them.

Charles Hale (2007, 2008) has launched an ambitious project to build an 'activist anthropology' that is in solidarity with his research participants in Central America and that, at the same time, will be recognized and supported as academic 'knowledge' within university settings. The key to Hale's argument is that activist knowledge is a distinct kind of knowledge – as we invite readers to discover in the activist testimonies presented in this volume – one that often brings to light contradictions in our understanding of the world. Hale decries the tendency of activist anthropologists to hide the contradictions that inevitably arise due to the action orientation of their research. He argues that these contradictions are pedagogical moments – it is precisely there that knowledge 'bridging' is possible (see also Edelman 2009; Speed 2006). For Hale, activist anthropology can, in this sense, meet the new demand for educational institutions to teach knowing 'how', not just knowing 'what' (see Greenwood and Levin 2001). However, neither private nor public academic institutions are well known for supporting action leading to radical change. Whether the institutionalization of activist knowledge, as Hale envisions it, will simply lead to it being defused remains to be seen. On this point, perhaps lessons can be learned from the institutionalization of feminism – the assimilation of its 'respectable version' – in the university curricula of Women Studies programmes (Brown 2005; McRobbie 2008).

While there are hints of engagement with different types of publics in the above examples (the community and the university), it is rare for public anthropologists to position their collaborative research explicitly in relation to *changing* publics as *Contesting Publics* seeks to do. Aimee Cox (2009) is a feminist public anthropologist whose research is driven by this goal. Working with and drawing from the experiences of young black women and the performance collective BlackLight in Detroit, Michigan, Cox and her research participants identify the public sphere as racialized, sexualized and age-ist (black youth being viewed as a threat in Detroit). Cox specifically asks whether it can be part of public anthropology to negotiate the public in ways that support both the personal and collective transformation projects of young black women. Because the public is always subject to political manipulation, caution must be exercised in *how* engagement takes place. Thus, while the 'public:private women' of the Mujeres de Negro activists in Mexico (see discussion of Wright 2010 in the Preface to this volume), provide a rationale for 'private' women to participate in public, their activism paradoxically re-inscribes dominant gender norms and ideas of public:private relations. For the Detroit activists, Cox says, the goal is directly to challenge the meaning of the hypervisibilty of young African American women in public. A major issue then becomes: how can intervention in the public take place without becoming a product to be consumed by 'the public' in mainstream ways? The young women of BlackLight do this by combining text and performance to communicate and exchange in public spaces their experiences and the 'emotional impact of living in under-resourced communities'. Cox argues that BlackLight performances are 'forums for deliberation, where community members begin to consciously represent themselves and contradict the identities constructed for them through the systems of the state' (2002: 59). Strategic public performance, then, is another way to challenge the 'hierarchies of knowledge production' (2002: 53), at the same time as it begins to shift the ways in which the public imagines young African American women.

QUESTIONS FOR FURTHER DISCUSSION

To initiate discussion toward a critical pedagogy of public anthropology, we conclude *Contesting Publics* by offering to our readers – students, activists and citizen-scholars alike – the following questions. In concluding with these questions, our purpose is, first, to aid in problematizing the idea of the 'public' in public anthropology; second, to indicate some of the tensions, inequalities and contradictions involved in claiming public anthropology as a distinct way of doing anthropology; and, finally, to support the hope and potential of a critical, reflexive public anthropology to offer an alternative pedagogical and theory-driven practice for understanding – and transforming – worlds.

- *Situating publics*: Is there a discernible dominant public? Are there counterpublics? Parallel publics? Popular publics? What are their relationships to one another? How are the boundaries drawn, and what is the dynamic interplay among them?
- *Inclusion/exclusion*: Who is included in publics and how do they participate? Do some people dominate publics and with what consequences? Are there people in public spaces who remain invisible? Are they seen but not heard? By what criteria (civility? 'habits and culture'?) are their modes of communication and argumentation judged, and by whom? Who is absent, and through what rationale? Is it a matter of cultural exclusion ('matter out of place')? Or is it a matter of economic 'privatization'? Or is it self-imposed absence? What voices are lost?

- *Women/gender*: How are norms of 'proper' behaviour and communication in the public sphere gendered? How are masculinities/femininities/transgenders formed and performed in publics? What are the consequences for behaving otherwise? To what extent are the issues that are bracketed as 'private' gendered? How does this bracketing reproduce inequalities (class, race, sexual orientation, age, ability)? How does this bracketing shape agenda setting?
- *State and market*: How are the state and the market situated? What are the modes of governance? How are publics – and the media that aim to represent them – commodified? Are there invitations to become involved – to 'participate'? If so, from whom? And, for what purposes? What are the risks/gains of participating?
- *Space*: How are publics spatialized? Across what kinds of borders? How does spatialization limit or expand participation? What potential scales can be identified? What implications does scale have for circulating knowledge? How does scale affect debate and decision-making? What are the dynamics of 'mixed spaces'? What are the dynamics of women-only spaces? What are the dynamics of bureaucratic spaces?
- *Time*: Are there emergent publics? Are there publics (or privates) being invented or 'in-formation'? Are there generational disparities and possibilities – legacies? Convergences? Tensions? Why, and what discursive form do they take? 'Old fashioned'? 'Avant-garde'?
- *Setting agendas for change*: What issues are discussed in publics? How diverse or exclusionary are publics? What role do the media play in circulating or erasing diverse perspectives? How is decision-making achieved on 'matters of concern'? What contradictions or ambiguities can be identified? How should emergent publics be represented – e.g. kinship diagrams, photographs? Which matters are not accepted for – and are therefore 'bracketed' from – public discussion and decision-making and why? How can we identify publics that are working for gender equality? What would a public that offers alternative feminist futures look like?

Notes

PREFACE: CONTESTING PUBLICS

1. See: www.youtube.com/watch?v=3vOCnZOcr8w;17/05/11; see also Kapur (2012). Writing recently on SlutWalk and the Pink Chaddi (panty) campaign in India, Ratna Kapur argues that statements such as the police officer's that focus on women's dress 'reflect anxieties around women occupying public zones as citizens, professionals and consumers' (2012: np). She argues these anxieties – not women's dress – are what we need to analyse. And this is what our theorizing of publics seeks to contribute to.

1 TOWARDS AN ETHNOGRAPHY OF PUBLICS

1. We recognize, however, that our project does have roots in some of the early work of feminist historians such as Landes (1988) and Ryan (1998).

2 AUTO-CONSTRUCTED FEMINIST PUBLICS

1. The research was conducted as a project of the Team for Advanced Research on Globalization, Education and Technology funded by the SSHRC-INE programme. I would like to thank the many women in Cascavel who so generously shared their lives and knowledge, and Marie-Eve Carrier-Moisan for her research assistance. We interviewed 95 women (numbered I-1 to I-95 in the text). Translations from Portuguese are ours. Names in text are pseudonyms.

2. The Bolsa Família (family support) programme was introduced in 2003 as part of then-President Lula's Fome Zero (Zero Hunger) initiative. It builds on former president Fernando Henrique Cardoso's Bolsa Escola (education grant) programme and replaces other smaller food and gas subsidy programmes. Households must apply to be categorized as *baixa renda* (low income). In 2005, the base amount was R$50.00 per month with a possible additional R$15.00 per month per child for up to three children for a maximum of R$95.00 per month.

3. Of the women interviewed, 26 per cent were aged 18–29 years; 19 per cent were aged 30–39 years; 54 per cent were over the age of 40. Twenty-six per cent were formally employed at the cashew factory (almost all were over 30 years of age); 49 per cent worked in garment factories (32 per cent formally employed; the rest informally); 18 per cent worked in other informal activities; 4 per cent worked in government or social services; and 3 per cent were unemployed. Of the women interviewed, 39 per cent of those under 40 years of age and 35 per cent of women over 40 were working without benefits or security (Cole and Carrier-Moisan 2005).

4. Our interview questions addressed: parents' employment, interviewee's employment, migration history, education, marriage and children, household membership, income, resources and expenses. Conjugal violence was not a

149

topic we had anticipated discussing. Yet almost half (49 per cent) of the women introduced the subject during interviews and explained that it was one of their reasons for migrating, for seeking factory employment, for leaving a marriage or for not re-marrying.

5. Forty-six per cent of first marriages had terminated; only 7 per cent of these women had remarried. Less than half (44 per cent) of the women were in their first marriage; 9 per cent were in a subsequent union; 22 per cent were divorced or separated; 6 per cent were widowed. 18 per cent of the women had never married.

6. Following the 1988 Constitutional reform, retired agricultural workers became eligible for rural pensions. These pensions effectively are a form of social security because they are not based on contribution payments but rather are dispersed to rural workers (with *documentos*) who can document a minimum of ten years' work in rural activities. Although the rural sector has received expanded benefits since 1988, social insurance remains predominantly contribution-financed and thus reserved for formal sector workers. The increasing proportion of (urban) workers working in the informal sector (more than 50 per cent) means that labour market protections (minimum monthly wage, hours of work and pensions) provided for in the Constitution, apply to an increasingly smaller percentage of workers (Rudra 2008).

7. Abundant research documents that when women are the primary decision-makers in a household, a greater share of the budget is allocated to the needs of children and to the collective well-being of the household, and a smaller proportion of the budget is spent on individual consumption, especially of tobacco and alcohol (Benería and Roldán 1987; Grasmuck and Espinal 2000; Hoodfar 1996; Pfeiffer et al. 2001).

8. Margarida's ability to ensure that her daughters graduated from high school is a remarkable achievement. The highest educational levels of the women we interviewed were in the age 30–39 cohort, 39 per cent of whom had graduated from high school. Only 17 per cent of women over 40 had more than a few years of elementary schooling. Women in the 18–29 age cohort had more variable levels of education: 36 per cent had graduated from high school but 40 per cent had less than five years of schooling. This may indicate that the first generation of migrants was able to keep their children in school longer (one of the expressed goals of migration) and that the next generation is experiencing more economic insecurity, requiring children to go to work at an early age. It may also indicate rising consumer needs of younger women and a lessened desire to defer income earning to remain in school.

9. The average number of births per woman was 2.7; 17 per cent of the women interviewed had no children.

10. On women's 'sexual tactics' in a shantytown in Recife, Northeast Brazil, see Gregg (2003). See also Rebhun (1999) on love, romance and 'new economic gender deals' in Brazil and Kandiyoti's classic article 'Bargaining with Patriarchy' (1988).

ACTIVIST TESTIMONY: MARIZA

1. Historically, the main programme of MMTR-NE was to help rural women workers obtain papers (*documentos*) that document the years they have worked as agricultural workers in order to be eligible to receive retirement pensions.

2. Sempreviva Organização Feminista, SOF, is a feminist NGO founded in São Paulo in 1963. According to Faria and Nobre (2003), its objectives in that era were 'to articulate a feminist politics within the popular democracy project in order to transform gender relations and build women's self-determination'. Its principal themes were women's health and reproductive rights. These themes have since expanded to include: feminist workshops; lobbying and monitoring public policy; feminist analysis and publications; and articulation of women's movements with other social movements.

3. The first Marcha das Margaridas was coordinated in 2000 by CONTAG – the women's commission of the rural workers union – in partnership with MMTR-NE, MMM and REDLAC (the Network of Rural Women of Latin America and the Caribbean).

4. The MST (Movimento dos Trabalhadores Rurais Sem Terra), the landless rural workers' movement in Brazil, has fought for land access and entitlement since the 1970s (Ondetti 2006; Wolford 2010). INCRA, the National Institute for Colonization and Reform in Brazil, is responsible for resolving land claims and awarding legal land settlements.

3 SAVING WOMEN?

1. I would like to acknowledge funding from the Social Sciences and Humanities Research Council of Canada and the University of British Columbia Faculty of Arts and Liu Institute for Global Issues. In Natal, I would like to thank the Coletivo Leila Diniz – Ações de Cidadania e Estudos Feministas for institutional support provided during field research and Joluzia Batista and Analba Brazão Teixeira for their kindness, hospitality, friendship and generous assistance. Their feminist work linking theory to praxis is a constant source of inspiration. Faculty and students at the University of British Columbia provided critical insights on earlier versions of this chapter: thanks to Bill French, Juanita Sundberg, Gastón Gordillo, Becki Ross, Alexia Bloch, Rachel Donkersloot, Robin O'Day, Susan Hicks, Manuela Valle and Oralia Gómez-Ramirez. I would like to express my warmest thanks to Sally Cole, Lynne Phillips and Erica Lagalisse for an invaluable experience in collaborative writing. And I thank William Flynn for his constant intellectual and emotional support.

2. The protest was co-organized by SOS Ponta Negra, a collective of different actors dedicated to combating the problems resulting from urbanization and mass tourism and the NGO Pau e Lata (Wood and Tin Cans), which uses music and arts to engage the public on different issues.

3. Flights come from Portugal, Spain, Italy, the Netherlands, Germany, England, Sweden, Finland, Denmark, Norway and Argentina (Governo do Estado do Rio Grande do Norte 2010).

4. As of 2010, the state of Rio Grande do Norte ranked first in Brazil in terms of foreign investment, with US$24 million, in contrast to US$17 million for the state of Rio de Janeiro (Governo do Estado do Rio Grande do Norte 2010).

5. The city of Natal is divided into the Zona Norte (North side) and Zona Sul (South side), a division that marks a contrast between the more privileged city centre of the Zona Sul (where the university, NGOs, government offices, shopping malls and Ponta Negra are located) and the outskirts of the city in the Zona Norte (the periphery with poor infrastructure, services, roads, houses and sanitation).

6. As I explore elsewhere (Carrier-Moisan 2012), in Ponta Negra the relationships between male foreigners and Brazilian women operate along a continuum of commercial relationships, from strictly contractual commercial exchanges, to more romantic engagements.

7. *Gente de família* does not have a direct English translation but it has a class connotation and alludes to people from well-off families.

8. The term *garota* is from *garota(s) de programa*, which literally translates as 'programme girl(s)' but means prostitute. It is sometimes translated as 'escort' or 'high class prostitute' (Rohter 2006). I prefer to use the term *garota(s) de programa* and its colloquial diminutive, *garota(s)*, in its original language, given it bears a slightly different meaning than *prostituta* (prostitute) or *professional do sexo* (sex worker). It does not have an equivalent in English and was the most common term used by Natal women.

9. *Ame*, which means love in the imperative tense, also stands as the abbreviation for the association of the residents, businessman and friends of Ponta Negra – in Portuguese, Associação dos Moradores, Empresarios e Amigos de Ponta Negra.

10. In 2001, more than 160 representatives from the governmental sector, civil society and various NGOs came together to craft the code and logo, inspired by its international equivalent, as developed by ECPAT (Bonorandi 2006; Resposta 2010a, 2010b).

11. The media reports covered both Natal and Fortaleza, the capital city in the neighbouring state of Ceará, also known as a sex tourism destination.

12. It is illegal in Brazil not to carry an official identity card; foreigners have to carry their passport.

13. The Forum Social Nordestino is a mini-version of the World Social Forum; it brings together different organizations involved in all sorts of social movements in Northeast Brazil.

14. This is also the title of one of their publications; see Coletivo Mulher Vida (2003).

15. CHAME stands for Centro de Apoio Humanitário à Mulher, or the Humanitarian Centre for the Support of Women.

16. It should be noted that the feminist perspectives that prevailed in these various meetings and were promoted by NGOs are not the only feminist positions that exist on sex tourism in Brazil. There are many 'feminisms' indeed, and a wide range of perspectives on sex tourism in both feminist scholarship and activism in Brazil; see Piscitelli (1996, 2004a, 2004b, 2007) for her rich exploration of this complex universe and insights beyond the victimisation/liberation debate.

17. For instance, following one of the raids during Operation Free Ponta Negra, Luís Fernando Ayres, regional chief executive of the federal police, declared in one of the local newspapers, that:

> sex tourism is malevolent because there are people who earn money by exploiting women, by exploiting the human needs of these women. These women didn't find a job, they didn't find anything in the social area, the only thing they envision is being a *garota de programa*. (*Tribuna do Norte* 2006b)

According to his logic, it was thus the police's responsibility to raid Ponta Negra's beach, in order to protect women from 'exploitation'.

18. I have changed the names of all informants, with the exception of those who spoke to me in their professional capacities, as head of an NGO or association for example.

19. AR stands for Associação Representativa de Ponta Negra (Representative Association of Ponta Negra), but its founder explained it was an association representing the interests of business owners.
20. Original expression, in both Portuguese and English.
21. He used the expression 'No Sex Tourism' in English.
22. I borrow from Joel Zito Araújo's film title the metaphor of the fairytale and the image of the enchanted prince, wolf, and Cinderella.
23. The Água de Coco (pseudonym) is a bar associated almost exclusively with *garotas* and *gringos* whereas the Samba (pseudonym) has a more varied clientele.
24. Literally, 'daddy's daughter', meaning a woman from the middle or upper class.
25. *Morena* literally translates as 'brown woman' and is used in Brazil as a racial descriptive term in reference to women of mixed racial origin.
26. It should be noted that race is context-dependent in Brazil. While it is polarized with black and white at two poles, it also operates along a continuum and creates a sense that 'class mitigates color' (Degler 1971: 106). Yet, 'colour' is also highly suggestive of class and, as several scholars have shown, in spite of fluidity, racism prevails (Goldstein 2003; Twine 1997).
27. According to Maria de Andrade, the head of the local association of sex workers ASPRO-RN, women in Ponta Negra are not interested in joining the association as they make a distinction between servicing local men (which they often times despised) and servicing foreigners. None of the women I interviewed identified with the association.

ACTIVIST TESTIMONY: SUSANA AND LUÍSA

1. The Million Cisterns project is a multi-partner development project involving international, national and regional organizations to ensure year-round access to water in the arid Northeast region of Brazil. For Oxfam International's role, see: http://www.oxfam.org/en/grow/development/brazil-bringing-life-desert.
2. REF (Rede Economia e Feminismo) is the feminist group that helped to found REMTE (the Latin American Network of Women Transforming the Economy) in Brazil.
3. ALCA (Acuerdo de Libre Comercio de las Américas) is the Free Trade Area of the Americas (FTAA) to which there has been widespread opposition in much of Latin America. For feminist critique of ALCA, see León and León (2002).

4   FEMINISM AND POST-NEOLIBERAL PUBLICS

1. I want to thank everyone in Ecuador who contributed to this study by generously making the time to talk to me about the issues discussed here. I begin the study in the 1990s because, as one activist put it: 'much of the momentum for the women's movement [in Ecuador] came from the Beijing process, and the fact that the government had signed on to it. The government couldn't feign ignorance of the issues' (I-A3). However, clearly there is a much longer history of Ecuadorian women and their publics. For an engaging assessment of this history, see Goetschel et al. (2007).
2. Acronyms of women's organizations I consulted for this study are explained in Appendix 1, at the end of the chapter.

3. For excellent analyses of feminist work on the 1998 Constitutional reform, see Rosero et al. (2000) and León (2000).
4. The Catholic Church has a long and important history in Ecuador and its influence (along with the Right to Life movement in 2008) ensured that the topic of abortion would present problems for the women's movement. President Correa apparently stated that if the 2008 Assembly proposed abortion, he would be the first to vote against it. While it could be said that, at the women's pre-conference in 2008, there was also agreement to avoid the subject of abortion, this chapter makes clear that not everyone agreed that it should be left off the table.
5. Rosa Lopez (2004) notes that, thanks to the Ley de Cuotas (Quota Law), participation of women in local government in the southern coastal province of El Oro rose from 19 per cent in 2000 to 33 per cent in 2004. For more on the impact of the Ley de Cuotas on women's political participation in Ecuador, see Cañete (2006).
6. Deere and León's impressive cross-country study (2001) supports the argument that neoliberal governments, with pressure from women's movements, have had a positive impact on formal (legal) gender equality in Latin America, but that this equality has not translated into equality of property ownership (land, housing). Thus a seemingly contradictory situation has arisen where, as activist Mariza says for the case of Brazil: 'Women are empowered in their knowledge and awareness but economically they are poorer every day.'
7. See Desmarais (2007); Dufour et al. (2010); Faria (2003); León & León (nd); Gibson-Graham (2006); Sousa Santos (2006). Boaventura de Sousa Santos was invited to speak to the Constitutional Assembly as an expert on new economies.
8. For more on Correa's citizen revolution, see Aguilar and Haro (2008).
9. Some women's groups sought mainstream media coverage but others tried to avoid it because of its tendency to manipulate issues. National newspapers, and particularly *El Comercio*, showed little interest in the Constitutional activities of the activists I interviewed. Outside the issue of abortion, my review of *El Comercio* between February and June 2008, for example, reveals minimal coverage of women's issues. This is in contrast to the coverage of indigenous issues (see, for example, *El Comercio* 26 May 2008: 7; *La Hora* 14 May 2008: B3). The mainstream press often caricatured feminist issues as silly and a waste of the nation's time.
10. Both of these concepts were eventually incorporated into the Constitution as part of a 'regime of good living' (*regimen de buen vivir*). The concept of 'good living' – in Quechua, *sumac kawsay* – is attributed to an indigenous epistemology that values life, human and non-human. The 2008 Constitution is credited for being the first in the world to grant rights to nature.
11. Almost two-thirds of Ecuadorians (64 per cent) voted to support the Constitution in 2008, and Correa handily won re-election as President in April 2009. However, activists continue to be concerned, especially within the indigenous movement, that they are being 'managed' by the government (CONAIE 2010).

5 GOSSIP AS DIRECT ACTION

1. A full English version of the Sixth Declaration of the Lacondon Jungle (*La Sexta Declaración de la Selva Lacondona*) is available at: http://enlacezapatista.ezln.org.mx/especiales/2 (accessed 26 February 2009).

2. See Behar and Gordon (1995) on the relationship of feminism to anthropology's 'reflexive turn'.
3. For discussion surrounding the ethics of romantic and/or sexual involvement 'in the field' see Kulick and Wilson (1995).
4. Montreal is a bilingual city; however, the Francophone and Anglophone activist scenes are somewhat segregated.
5. For description of the APPO movement, see Sánchez (2008) and Vásquez (2007).

6 A PEDAGOGICAL CONVERSATION: PUBLIC SCHOLARS AND PUBLIC SCHOLARSHIP

1. This is not to discount the many important contributions that have been made in the name of engaged anthropology. See Culhane (2011), Farmer (2003), Fortun (2001), Gill (2005), Goodale (2009), Scheper-Hughes and Bourgois (2004), Speed (2006) and Warren (2007).
2. Other examples of early contributions to politically engaged anthropology were the special issue on anthropology and imperialism in *Current Anthropology* in 1968 and Stanley Diamond's launching of the journal *Dialectical Anthropology* in 1975. In Canada applied anthropology has a long tradition, as seen in the pioneering work of Harry Hawthorn, Marc-Adelard Tremblay and Sally Weaver; see also the contributions of Jim Freedman (1977), Robert Paine (1985) and Penny Van Esterik (1989). Jim Waldram (2010) and Marie-France Labrecque (2000) offer useful reviews of this 'tradition' in Canadian and Quebec contexts.
3. For more on the journal *Collaborative Anthropologies*, see: www.marshall. edu/coll-anth/

References

Abers, R.N. 2000. *Inventing Local Democracy: Grassroots Politics in Brazil*. Boulder, CO: Lynne Rienner.

Abu-Lughod, L. 1991. *Writing Against Culture*. In R. Fox (ed.) *Recapturing Anthropology*. Santa Fe: School of American Research Press, pp. 137–162.

Abu-Lughod, L. 1993. *Writing Women's Worlds: Bedouin Stories*. Berkeley: University of California Press.

Ackerman, J. 2003. Co-governance for Accountability: Beyond 'Exit' and 'Voice'. *World Development* 32(3): 447–463.

Agarwal, B. 1997. Bargaining and Gender Relations Within and Beyond the Household. FCND Discussion Paper No. 27. Washington, DC: International Food Policy Research Institute.

Aguilar Zambrano, R. and Haro Haro, X. 2008. *La revolución ciudadana: hacia una sociedad participativa y del conocimiento*. Quito: Hojas y Signos.

Agustín, L.M. 2007. *Sex at the Margins: Migration, Labour Markets and the Rescue Industry*. London: Zed Books.

Alvarez, S. 1998. The 'NGO-ization' of Latin American Feminisms. In S. Alvarez, E. Dagnino and A. Escobar (eds) *Cultures of Politics/Politics of Culture*. Boulder, CO: Westview Press, pp. 306–324.

Alvarez, S. 2009. Beyond NGO-ization? Reflections from Latin America. *Development* 52(2): 175–184.

Angel-Ajani, A. 2008. Expert Witness: Notes toward Revisiting the Politics of Listening. In V. Sanford and A. Angel-Ajani (eds) *Engaged Observer: Anthropology, Advocacy and Activism*. New Brunswick, NJ: Rutgers University Press, pp. 76–89.

Araújo, J.Z. 2008. *Cinderellas, Wolves and one Enchanted Prince* [Original in Portuguese, *Cinderelas, lobos e um príncipe encantado*]. Documentary 107 min. Brazil: Pipa Produções.

Araújo, M. 2006. Instaladas câmeras de combate à prostituição. *Correio da Tarde*, 13 September. Available at: http://www.correiodatarde.com.br/editorias/correio_natal-6873 (accessed April 2009).

Avritzer, L. 2002. *Democracy and the Public Space in Latin America*. Princeton, NJ: Princeton University Press.

Avritzer, L. 2009. *Participatory Institutions in Democratic Brazil*. Baltimore, MD: Johns Hopkins University Press.

Azevedo, S. de. 2005a. 'Não quisemos offender o cidadão natalense' / Entrevista: Fernando Bessa. *Diário de Natal*, 20 September: 6.

Azevedo, S. de. 2005b. ONG e UFRN criticam vereadores. *Diário de Natal*, 9 September: 4.

Azevedo, S. de. 2005c. Sexo: por grana e por um príncipe. *Diário de Natal*, 4 September: 1

Baiocchi, G. 2005. *Militants and Citizens: The Politics of Participatory Democracy in Porto Alegre*. Stanford, CA: Stanford University Press.

Barlett, P. 2011. Campus Sustainable Food Projects: Critique and Engagement. *American Anthropologist* 113(1): 101–115.

Batista, J. 2007. Violência sexual contra crianças e adolescentes no RN: uma questão social e cultural. *Entre Bairros* 10: 2.

Beaman, L. 2012. The Status of Women: The Report from a Civilized Society. *Canadian Criminal Law Review* 16(2): 121–144.

Behar, R. and Gordon, D. (eds) 1995. *Women Writing Culture*. Berkeley: University of California Press.

Benería, L. and Roldán, M. 1987. *The Crossroads of Gender and Class: Industrial Homework, Subcontracting and Household Dynamics*. Chicago: Chicago University Press.

Berglund, E. 2006. Generating Non-trivial Knowledge in Awkward Situations: Anthropology in the United Kingdom. In G. Lins Ribeiro and A. Escobar (eds) *World Anthropologies: Disciplinary Transformations with Systems of Power*. Oxford: Berg, pp. 181–199.

Bernal, V. 2006. Diaspora, Cyberspace and Political Imagination: The Eritrea Diaspora Online. *Global Networks* 6(2): 161–179.

Bezerra, A.C. 2006. PF faz nova operação policial na praia de Ponta Negra. *Tribuna do Norte*, 2 April. Available at: http://www.tribunadonorte.com.br/noticia/pf-faz-nova-operação-policial-na-praia-de-ponta-negra/6336 (accessed August 2010).

Bezerra, A.C. and Lopes, W. 2006. Ofensiva policial fecha bares em Ponta Negra. *Tribuna do Norte*, 6 April. Available at: http://tribunadonorte.com.br/noticia. php?id=6798 (accessed April 2009).

Bickham Mendez, J. 2008. Globalizing Scholar Activism: Opportunities and Dilemmas through a Feminist Lens. In C. Hale (ed.) *Engaging Contradictions: Theory, Politics, and Methods of Activist Scholarship*. Berkeley: University of California Press, pp. 136–163.

Blanksten, G. 1951. *Ecuador: Constitutions and Caudillos*. Berkeley: University of California Press.

Bonorandi, G.D. 2006. Uma resposta para o turismo sexual. *Tribuna do Norte*, 28 March. Available at: http://tribunadonorte.com.br/noticia/uma-resposta-para-o-turismo-sexual/6039 (accessed September 2010).

Branco, A. de Melo. 2000. *Mulheres de seca: luta e visibilidade numa situação de desastre*. João Pessoa: Editor Universitária.

Bridgman, R., Cole, S. and Howard-Bobiwash, H. (eds) 1999. *Feminist Fields: Ethnographic Insights*. Peterborough: Broadview.

Brown, W. 2005. *Edgework: Critical Essays on Knowledge and Politics*. Princeton, NJ: Princeton University Press.

Brown, W. 2006. *Regulating Aversion: Tolerance in the Age of Identity and Empire*. Princeton, NJ: Princeton University Press.

Brown, W. 2009. Whose Secularism? Feminist Theory Workshop, Duke University, 26 May.

Caldeira, T. 2000. *City of Walls: Crime, Segregation, and Citizenship in São Paulo*. Berkeley: University of California Press.

Caldwell, K. 2007. *Negras in Brazil: Re-envisioning Black Women, Citizenship, and the Politics of Identity*. New Brunswick, NJ: Rutgers University Press.

Calhoun, C. (ed.) 1992. *Habermas and the Public Sphere*. Cambridge, MA: MIT Press.

Cameron, J. 2010. *Struggles for Local Democracy in the Andes*. Boulder, CO: First Forum Press.

Cañete, M.F. (ed.) 2006. *Reflexiones sobre mujer y política*. Quito: Ediciones Abya Yala/CEDIME.

Carrier-Moisan, M.-E. 2012. *Of Marriage, Mobility, and Money: Ambiguous Intimacies in the Context of Sex Tourism in the Northeast of Brazil*. PhD Thesis, Department of Anthropology, University of British Columbia.

Chen, N. 1992. 'Speaking Nearby': A Conversation with Trinh T. Minh-ha. *Visual Anthropology Review* 8(1): 82–91.

Chinchilla, N.S. 1992. Marxism, Feminism and the Struggle for Democracy in Latin America. In A. Escobar and S. Alvarez (eds) *The Making of Social Movements in Latin America: Identity, Strategy andDemocracy*. Boulder, CO: Westview Press.

Church, E. 2011. SlutWalk Sparks Worldwide Movement. *Globe and Mail*, 20 May: A10.

Clark, K. 1998. *The Redemptive Work: Railway and Nation in Ecuador, 1895–1930*. Wilmington, DE: Scholarly Resources Books.

Cole, S. 1995. Taming the Shrew in Anthropology: Is Feminist Ethnography 'New' Ethnography? In S. Cole and L. Phillips (eds) *Ethnographic Feminisms: Essays in Anthropology*. Montreal: Carleton/McGill-Queen's University Press, pp. 185–205.

Cole, S. 2003. *Ruth Landes: A Life in Anthropology*. Lincoln: University of Nebraska Press.

Cole, S. 2009. *Rainy River Lives: Stories told by Maggie Wilson*. Lincoln: University of Nebraska Press.

Cole, S. and Carrier-Moisan, M.-E. 2005. Household Responses to Export-led Industrialization in Northeast Brazil. Unpublished paper presented to the Team for Advanced Research in Globalization, Education and Technology, University of British Columbia, Vancouver.

Cole, S. and Phillips, L. (eds) 1995. *Ethnographic Feminisms: Essays in Anthropology*. Montreal: Carleton/McGill-Queen's University Press.

Cole, S. and Phillips, L. 2008. The Violence Against Women Campaigns in Latin America: New Feminist Alliances. *Feminist Criminology* 3(2): 145–168.

Cole, S. and Phillips, L. 2009. Inviting Spaces: Feminisms' Publics and Deepening Democracy. Paper presented at Latin American Studies Association Meetings (LASA), Rio de Janeiro, 10–14 June.

Coletivo Mulher Vida. 2003. *Turismo sexual, tráfico, e imigração: o que nós temos a ver com isso?* Recife: Coletivo Mulher Vida.

El Comercio. 2008. Los Indígenas no creemos en Correa. *El Comercio*, 26 May: 7.

Conaghan, C. 2005. *Fujimori's Peru: Deception in the Public Sphere*. Pittsburgh: University of Pittsburgh Press.

CONAIE. 2010. Resolución de la Asamblea Extraordinaria. Ambato, 25–26 February.

CONAMU, INEC and UNIFEM. 2006. *Encuesta del uso del tiempo en Ecuador 2005*. Serie Información Estratégica II. Quito: CONAMU.

Cooper, J. and Sharp, R. 2007. Engendering Accountability in Government Budgets in Mexico. In M. Griffin Cohen and J. Brodie (eds) *Remapping Gender in the New Global Order*. London: Routledge, pp. 205–222.

Cornwall, A. 2004. Introduction: New Democratic Spaces? The Politics and Dynamics of Institutionalized Participation. *IDS Bulletin* 35(2): 1–10.

Cornwall, A. and Coelho, V.S. (eds) 2007. *Spaces for Change? The Politics of Citizen Participation in New Democratic Arenas*. London: Zed.

Correa, R. 2008. Speech at the closing ceremony of the Asamblea Constituyente. 25 July, Ciudad Alfaro, Press room.

Cox, A. 2009. The BlackLight Project and Public Scholarship: Young Black Women Perform Against and Through the Boundaries of Anthropology. *Transforming Anthropology* 17(1): 51–64.

Culhane, D. 2011. Introduction: New Directions in Experimental and Engaged Ethnography. *Anthropologica* 53(2): 201–206.

Davis, K. 2007. *The Making of* Our Bodies, Ourselves: *How Feminism Travels across Borders*. Durham, NC: Duke University Press.

Day, R. 2005. *Gramsci is Dead – Anarchist Currents in the Newest Social Movements*. Toronto: Between the Lines.

Deere, C.D. and León, M. 2001. *Empowering Women: Land and Property Rights in Latin America*. Pittsburgh: University of Pittsburgh Press.

Degler, C. 1971. *Neither Black nor White: Slavery and Race Relations in Brazil and the United States*. New York: Macmillan.

De la Dehesa, R. 2007. Global Communities and Hybrid Cultures: Early Gay and Lesbian Electoral Activism in Brazil and Mexico. *Latin American Research Review* 42(1): 29–51.

De la Dehesa, R. 2010. *Queering the Public Sphere in Mexico and Brazil*. Durham, NC: Duke University Press.

De la Rocha, M.G. 2000. Private Adjustments: Household Responses to the Erosion of Work. UNDP Working Paper.

De la Torre, C. 2006. Ethnic Movements and Citizenship in Ecuador. *Latin American Research Review* 41(2): 247–259.

De la Torre, C. 2007. Comentario. In L. Verdesoto Custode, *Procesos constituyentes y reforma institucional: Nociones para comprender y actuar en el caso ecuatotriano*. Quito: Abya-Yala and FLACSO, pp. 17–22.

Desmarais, A. 2007. *La vía campesina*. Halifax: Fernwood.

Dewey, S. 2009. 'Dear Dr. Kothari …': Sexuality, Violence against Women, and the Parallel Public Sphere in India. *American Anthropologist* 36(1): 124–139.

Diário de Natal. 2006. Em Ponta Negra, ato contra o turismo sexual. *Diário de Natal*, 10 November: 8.

Dickson, R. 2006. Câmara discute o turismo-sexual em audiência pública. *Tribuna do Norte*, 14 March. Available at: http://www.tribunadonorte.com.br/noticia/camara-discute-o-turismo-sexual-em-audiencia-publica/4619 (accessed August 2010).

Doerr, N. 2007. Is Another Public Sphere Actually Possible? The Case of 'Women Without' in the European Social Forum Process as a Critical Test for Deliberative Democracy. *Journal of International Women's Studies* 8(3): 71–87.

Douglas, M. 1966. *Purity and Danger: An Analysis of the Concepts of Pollution and Taboo*. London: Routledge and Kegan Paul.

Dryzek, J. 2000. *Deliberative Democracy and Beyond: Liberals, Critics, Contestations*. New York: Oxford University Press.

Dufour, P., Masson, D. and Caouette, D. (eds) 2010. *Solidarities beyond Borders: Transnationalizing Women's Movements*. Vancouver: UBC Press.

Dyck, N. 2000. Home Field Advantage? Exploring the Social Construction of Children's Sports. In V. Amit (ed.) *Constructing the Field – Ethnographic Fieldwork in the Contemporary World*. New York: Routledge.

Edelman, M. 2009. Synergies and Tensions between Rural Social Movements and Professional Researchers. *Journal of Peasant Studies* 36(1): 245–265.

Eley, G. 1992. Nations, Publics, and Political Cultures: Placing Habermas in the Nineteenth Century. In C. Calhoun (ed.) *Habermas and the Public Sphere*. Cambridge, MA: MIT Press, pp. 289–339.

Elias, N. 1978. *The Civilizing Process*. New York: Urizen Books.

Enke, A. 2007. *Finding the Movement: Sexuality, Contested Space, and Feminist Activism*. Durham, NC: Duke University Press.

Eschle, C. 2001. *Global Democracy, Social Movements, and Feminism*. Boulder, CO: Westview Press.

Faria, N. (ed.) 2003. *Construir la igualdad: debates feministas en el Foro Social Mundial*. Lima: REMTE; Montreal: MMM; São Paulo: SOF.

Faria, N. and Nobre, M. (eds) 2003. *A produção do viver*. São Paulo: Sempreviva Organização Feminista.

Faria, N. and Nobre, M. 2005. *Feminismo e luta das mulheres: analises e debates*. São Paulo: Sempreviva Organização Feminista.

Farmer, P. 2003. *Pathologies of Power: Health, Human Rights, and the New War on the Poor*. Berkeley: University of California Press.

Federici, S. 2004. *Caliban and the Witch – Women, the Body and Primitive Accumulation*. New York: Autonomedia.

Feinberg, R., Waisman, C. and Zamosc, L. (eds) 2006. *Civil Society and Democracy in Latin America*. New York: Palgrave.

Ferree, M.M. and Tripp, A.M. (eds) 2006. *Global Feminism: Transnational Women's Activism, Organizing, and Human Rights*. New York: New York University Press.

Field, L. and Fox, R. (eds) 2007. *Anthropology Put to Work*. New York: Berg.

Fonseca, C. 2003. Philanderers, Cuckolds, and Wily Women: Re-examining Gender Relations in a Brazilian Working-class Neighborhood. In M.C. Gutmann (ed.) *Changing Men and Masculinities in Latin America*. Durham, NC: Duke University Press.

Fortun, K. 2001. *Advocacy after Bhopal: Environmentalism, Disaster, New Global Orders*. Chicago: University of Chicago Press.

Franceschet, S. 2003. 'State Feminism' and Women's Movements: The Impact of Chile's Servicio Nacional de la Mujer on Women's Activism. *Latin American Research Review* 38(1): 9–40.

Fraser, N. 1990. Rethinking the Public Sphere: A Contribution to the Critique of Actually Existing Democracy. *Social Text* 25/26: 56–80.

Fraser, N. 2007. Transnationalizing the Public Sphere: On the Legitimacy and Efficacy of Public Opinion in a Post-Westphalian World. *Theory, Culture & Society* 24: 7–30.

Freedman, J. (ed.) 1977. *Applied Anthropology in Canada*. Canadian Ethnology Society Proceedings No. 4. Ottawa: National Museum of Man.

Fregoso, R.-L. and Bejarano, C. (eds) 2010. *Terrorizing Women: Feminicide in the Américas*. Durham, NC: Duke University Press.

Freire, S. 2006. Operação contra turismo sexual detém nove estrangeiros no RN. *Folha Online*, 1 April, available at: http://www1.folha.uol.com.br/folha/cotidiano/ult95u119979.shtml (accessed December 2009).

Fung, A. and Wright, E.O. (eds) 2003. *Deepening Democracy: Institutional Innovations in Empowered Participatory Governance*. London: Verso.

Gal, S. 2003. Movements of Feminism: The Circulation of Discourses about Women. In B. Hobson (ed.) *Recognition Struggles and Social Movements: Contested Identities, Agency and Power*. Cambridge: Cambridge University Press, pp. 93–118.

Gibson-Graham, J.K. 2006. *A Postcapitalist Politics*. Minneapolis: University of Minnesota.

Gill, L. 2005. Empire, Ethnography, and Engagement. *Anthropology News* 46(1): 12.

Goetschel, A.M., Pequeño, A., Prieto, M. and Herrera, G. 2007. *De memorias: imágenes públicas de las mujeres ecuatorianas de Comienzos y Fines del siglo veinte*. Quito: FONSAL, FLACSO.

Goldstein, D. 2003. *Laughter Out of Place: Race, Class, Violence, and Sexuality in a Rio Shantytown*. Berkeley: University of California Press.

Goodale, M. 2009. *Surrendering to Utopia: An Anthropology of Human Rights*. Stanford, CA: Stanford University Press.

Gordon, D. 1993. Worlds of Consequences: Feminist Ethnography as Social Action. *Critique of Anthropology* 13(4): 429–443.

Governo do Estado do Ceará. 1980. Levantamento básico dos municípios: Cascavel. Secretaria do planejamento e coordenação. Fortaleza: Edições IPLANCE (Fundação Instituto de Pesquisa e Informação do Ceará).

—— 2000. Perfil básico municipal: Cascavel. Secretaria do planejamento e coordenação (SEPLAN). Fortaleza: Edições IPLANCE (Fundação Instituto de Pesquisa e Informação do Ceará).

—— 2002. Perfil básico municipal: Cascavel. Secretaria do planejamento e coordenação (SEPLAN). Fortaleza: Edições IPLANCE (Fundação Instituto de Pesquisa e Informação do Ceará).

—— 2004a. Ceará em números – 2003. Fortaleza: Instituto de Pesquisa e Estratégia Econômica do Ceará (IPECE).

—— 2004b. Anuário estatística do Ceará – 2004. Fortaleza: Instituto de Pesquisa e Estratégia Econômica do Ceará (IPECE).

—— 2004c. Perfil básico municipal: Cascavel. Secretaria do planejamento e coordenação (SEPLAN). Fortaleza: Edições IPLANCE (Fundação Instituto de Pesquisa e Informação do Ceará).

Governo do Estado do Rio Grande do Norte. 2010 Turismo. *Governo do Estado do Rio Grande do Norte*. Available at: http://www.rn.gov.br/conheca-o-rn/turismo/ (accessed September 2010).

Graeber, D. 2004. *Fragments of an Anarchist Anthropology*. Chicago: Prickly Paradigm Press.

—— 2009. *An Ethnography of Direct Action*. New York: AK Press.

Grasmuck, S. and Espinal, R. 2000. Market Success or Female Autonomy? Income, Ideology, and Empowerment among Microentrepreneurs in the Dominican Republic. *Gender & Society* 14(2): 231–255.

Gregg, J.L. 2003. *Virtually Virgins: Sexual Strategies and Cervical Cancer in Recife, Brazil*. Stanford, CA: Stanford University Press.

Greenwood, D. and Levin, M. 2001. Re-organizing Universities and 'Knowing How': University Restructuring and Knowledge Creation for the 21st Century. *Organization* 8(2): 433–440.

Grewal, I. 2005. *Transnational America: Feminisms, Diasporas, Neoliberalisms*. Durham, NC: Duke University Press.

Grewal, I. and Kaplan, C. (eds) 1994. *Scattered Hegemonies: Postmodernity and Transnational Feminist Practices*. Minneapolis: University of Minnesota Press.

Grupo Edson Queiroz. 1986. *Um homem e seu tempo*. São Paulo: CL-A Comunicações S/C Ltda.

Guidry, J.A. 2003. The Struggle to be Seen: Social Movements and the Public Sphere in Brazil. *International Journal of Politics, Culture and Society* 16(4): 493–524.

Guimarães, T. 2005. Câmara de Natal dá título de 'persona non grata' a anthropólogos. *Folha Online*, 9 September. Available at: http://www1.folha.uol. com.br/folha/cotidiano/ult95u112917.shtml (accessed February 2009).

Gutmann, M. 2007. *Fixing Men: Sex, Birth Control, and AIDS in Mexico*. Berkeley: University of California Press.

Guyer, J. 1997. Endowments and Assets: The Anthropology of Wealth and the Economics of Intrahousehold Allocation. In L. Haddad, J. Hoddinitt and H. Alderman (eds) *Intrahousehold Resource Allocation in Developing Countries: Models, Methods and Policy*. Baltimore, MD: Johns Hopkins University Press, pp. 112–125.

Habermas, J. 1989 [1962]. *The Structural Transformation of the Public Sphere: An Inquiry into a Category of Bourgeois Society*. Cambridge, MA: MIT Press.

Habermas, J. 1992. Further Reflections on the Public Sphere. In C. Calhoun (ed.) *Habermas and the Public Sphere*. Cambridge, MA: MIT Press, pp. 421–461.

Hale, C. 2006. *More than an Indian: Racial Ambivalence and Neoliberal Multiculturalism in Guatemala*. Santa Fe: School of American Research Press.

Hale, C. 2007. In Praise of 'Reckless Minds': Making a Case for Activist Anthropology. In L. Field and R. Fox (eds) *Anthropology Put to Work*. Oxford: Berg, pp. 103–127.

Hale, C. (ed.) 2008. *Engaging Contradictions: Theory, Politics, and Methods of Activist Scholarship*. Berkeley: University of California Press.

Haraway, D. 1988. Situated Knowledges: The Science Question in Feminism and the Privilege of Partial Perspective. *Feminist Studies* 14(3): 575–599.

Harding, S. (ed.) 1986. *Feminism and Methodology*. Bloomington: Indiana University Press.

Harris, O. 1981. Households as Natural Units. In K. Young, C. Wolkowitz and R. McCullagh (eds) *Of Marriage and the Market*. London: CSE Books, pp. 49–68.

Harrison, F. (ed.) 1991. *Decolonizing Anthropology: Moving Further toward an Anthropology for Liberation*. Arlington, VA: Association of Black Anthropologists and American Anthropological Association.

Harvey, D. 2003. *Paris, Capital of Modernity*. New York: Routledge.

Hawkesworth, M. 2006. *Globalization and Feminist Activism*. Lanham, MD: Rowman and Littlefield.

Hertel, S. 2006. *Unexpected Power: Conflict and Change among Transnational Activists*. Ithaca, NY: Cornell University Press.

Holloway, J. 2005. *Change the World without Taking Power*. London: Pluto.

Holston, J. 2008. *Insurgent Citizenship: Disjunctions of Democracy and Modernity in Brazil*. Princeton, NJ: Princeton University Press.

Hoodfar, H. 1996. Survival Strategies and the Political Economy of Low-income Households in Cairo. In D. Singerman and H. Hoodfar (eds) *Development, Change and Gender in Cairo*. Bloomington: Indiana University Press, pp. 1–26.

La Hora. 2008. CONAIE hará oposición al gobierno. *La Hora*, 14 May: B3.

Howard, H. 2011. *Aboriginal Peoples in Canadian Cities: Transformations and Continuities*. Waterloo: Wilfred Laurier Press.

Hymes, D. (ed.) 1972. *Reinventing Anthropology*. New York: Vintage.

IBGE. 2010. *Natal-RN Dados Básicos*. IBGE (Instituto Brasileiro de Geografia e Estatística). Available at: http://www.ibge.gov.br/cidadesat/painel/painel. php?codmun=240810.

Infraero. 2010. Aeroporto Internacional Augusto Severo/Natal: histórico. Available at: http://www.infraero.gov.br/aero_prev_hist.php?ai=88&PHPSESSID=fokbkjn 3p9jqb63uvsqdbvmun1 (accessed February 2010).

Jaggar, A. 2007. *Just Methods: An Interdisciplinary Feminist Reader*. Boulder, CO: Paradigm Publishers.

Jimeno, M. 2008. Colombia: Citizens and Anthropologists. In D. Poole (ed.) *A Companion to Latin American Anthropology*. Malden, MA: Blackwell, pp. 72–89.

Jornal da Globo. 2006a. Aqui se vende sexo. *Jornal da Globo*, 6 March. Available at: http://g1.globo.com/jornaldaglobo/0,,MUL890637–16021,00–AQUI+SE+VENDE+SEXO.html (accessed April 2007).

Jornal da Globo. 2006b. Estrutura para o turismo sexual. *O Globo. Jornal da Globo*, 8 March. http://g1.globo.com/jornaldaglobo/0,,MUL890622–16021,00–ESTRUTURA+PARA+O+TURISMO+SEXUAL.html (accessed April 2007).

Jornal da Globo. 2006c. O triste destino das menores prostitutas no Nordeste. *Jornal da Globo*, 9 March. Available at: http://g1.globo.com/jornaldaglobo/0, ,MUL890618–16021,00–O+TRISTE+DESTINO+DAS+MENORES+PROSTIT UTAS+NO+NORDESTE.html (accessed April 2007).

Jornal da Globo. 2006d. Para acabar com o turismo sexual no Nordeste. *Jornal da Globo*, 10 March. Available at: http://g1.globo.com/jornaldaglobo/0,, MUL890611–16021,00–PARA+ACABAR+COM+O+TURISMO+SEXUAL+N O+NORDESTE.html (accessed April 2007).

Jornal da Globo. 2006e. Troca-se sexo por esperança. *Jornal da Globo*, 7 March. Available at: http://g1.globo.com/jornaldaglobo/0,,MUL890630–16021,00–TROCASE+SEXO+POR+ESPERANCA.html (accessed April 2007).

Juris, J. 2008. *Networking Futures – The Movements against Corporate Globalization*. Durham, NC: Duke University Press.

Kabeer, N. 2005. *Inclusive Citizenship: Meanings and Expression*s. London: Zed.

Kandiyoti, D. 1988. Bargaining with Patriarchy. *Gender & Society* 2: 274–290.

Kapur, R. 2012. Pink Chaddis and SlutWalk Couture: The Postcolonial Politics of Feminism Lite. *Feminist Legal Studies* 20(1): 1–20.

Katsiaficas, G. 2001. The Necessity of Autonomy. *New Political Science* 23(4): 547–555.

Khasnabish, A. 2008. *Zapatismo beyond Borders – New Imaginations of Political Possibility*. Toronto: University of Toronto Press.

Klein, C. 2002. 'Making a Scene': Travestis and the Gendered Politics of Space in Porto Alegre, Brazil. In R. Montoya, L.J. Frasier and J. Hurtig (eds) *Gender's Place: Feminist Anthropologies of Latin America*. New York: Palgrave, pp. 217–235.

Kulick, D. and Wilson, M. (eds) 1995. *Taboo – Sex, Identity and Erotic Subjectivity in Anthropological Fieldwork*. New York: Routledge.

Labrecque, M.-F. 2000. D'une certaine anthropologie et de quelques anthropologues. *Anthropologica* 42(2): 147–156.

Lagalisse, E. 2010. The Limits of 'Radical Democracy': A Gender Analysis of 'Anarchist' Activist Collectives in Montreal. *Altérités – Journal d'anthropologie du contemporain* 7(1): 19–38.

—— 2011. 'Marginalizing Magdalena': Intersections of Gender and the Secular in Anarchoindigenist Solidarity Activism. *Signs* 36(3): 653–678.

Lamoureux, D. 2004. Le Féminisme et l'altermondialisation. *Recherches féministes* 17(2): 171–194.

Lamphere, L. 2004. The Convergence of Applied, Practicing, and Public Anthropology in the 21st Century. *Human Organization* 63(4): 431–443.

Landes, J. 1988. *Women and the Public Sphere in the Age of the French Revolution*. Ithaca, NY: Cornell University Press.

Lara, M.P. 1998. *Moral Textures: Feminist Narratives in the Public Sphere*. Berkeley: University of California Press.

Lara, M.P. 2003. Globalizing Women's Rights: Building a Global Public Sphere. In R. Fiore and H.L. Nelson (eds) *Recognition, Responsibility and Rights: Feminist Ethics and Social Theory*. Lanham, MD: Rowman and Littlefield, pp. 181–194.

Lassiter, L. 2005. *The Chicago Guide to Collaborative Ethnography*. Chicago: University of Chicago Press.

Laurie, N. and Bondi, L. (eds) 2005. *Working the Spaces of Neoliberalism*. Chichester: Wiley.

Lebon, N. and Maier, E. (eds) 2006. *De lo privado a lo público: 30 años de lucha ciudadana de las mujeres en América Latina*. Mexico City: Siglo xxi, UNIFEM, LASA.

Leite, J. de Souza. 2003. A exploração das mulheres na dinâmica do turismo sexual. In S. Camurça (ed.) *Dimensões da desigualdade no desenvolvimento do turismo no Nordeste*. Recife: SOS CORPO: Gênero e Cidadania, pp. 65–69.

León, M. (ed.) 2000. *Sexual and Reproductive Rights: Constitutional Achievements and Prospects in Ecuador*. Quito: FEDAEPS and IEE.

León, I. and León, M. (eds) 2002. *Mujeres contra el ALCA: razones y alternativas*. Quito: ALAI (Agencia Latinoamericana de Información).

Lévi-Strauss, C. 1962. *La Pensée sauvage*. Paris: Librarie.

Lins Ribeiro, G. and Escobar, A. (eds) 2006. *World Anthropologies: Disciplinary Transformations within Systems of Power*. Oxford: Berg.

Lofland, L. 1998. *The Public Realm: Exploring the City's Quintessential Social Territory*. New York: Aldine de Gruyter.

Lopes Júnior, E. 2000. *A construção social da Cidade do Prazer: Natal*. Natal: EDUFRN.

Lopes Júnior, E. 2005. Amor, sexo e dinheiro: uma interpretação sociológica do mercado de serviços sexuais. *Política e Sociedade* 6: 165–193.

Lopez, R. 2004. Intervención de Rosa Lopez. In M.F. Cañete (ed.) *Reflexiones sobre mujer y política*. Quito: Ediciones Abya Yala/CEDIME.

Low, B. 2011. *Slam School: Learning through Conflict in the Hip Hop and Spoken Word Classroom*. Palo Alto, CA: Stanford University Press.

Low, S. and Smith, N. (eds) 2006. *The Politics of Public Space*. London: Routledge.

Lozada, E.P. Jr. 2003. Computers, Scientism and Cyborg Subjectivity in Post-socialist China. *Asian Anthropology* 2: 109–135.

Luxton, M. 1980. *More than a Labour of Love: Three Generations of Women's Work in the Home*. Toronto: The Women's Press.

MacClancy, J. (ed.) 2002, *Exotic No More: Anthropology on the Frontlines*. Chicago: University of Chicago Press.

Maeckelbergh, M. 2009. *The Will of the Many – How the Alterglobalization Movement is Changing the Face of Democracy*. London: Pluto.

Maguire, P. 2008. Feminist Participatory Research. In A. Jaggar (ed.) *Just Methods – An Interdisciplinary Reader*. Boulder, CO: Paradigm Publishers.

Maier, E. and Lebon, N. (eds) 2010. *Women's Activism in Latin America and the Caribbean: Engendering Social Justice, Democratizing Citizenship*. New Brunswick, NJ: Rutgers University Press.

Marcus, G. 1998. *Ethnography through Thick and Thin*. Princeton, NJ: Princeton University Press.

McClintock, A. 1993. Sex Workers and Sex Work: An Introduction. *Social Text*. 11(4): 1–10.

McLaughlin, L. 2004. Feminism and the Political Economy of Transnational Public Space. *Sociological Review* 52(1): 156–175.

M'Closkey, K. 2002. *Swept under the Rug: A Hidden History of Navajo Weaving*. Albuquerque: University of New Mexico.

M'Closkey, K. 2010. New Insights from the Archives: Historicizing the Political Economy of Navajo Wool Growing and Weaving. Paper presented at the Textile Society of America, 12th Biennial Symposium, Lincoln, Nebraska, 6–9 October.

McRobbie, A. 2008. *The Aftermath of Feminism: Gender, Culture and Social Change*. London: Sage.

Melo, H.P. de. 1998. De criadas a trabalhadoras. *Estudos feministas* 6(2): 323–357.

Miraftab, F. 2004. Invited and Invented Spaces of Participation: Neoliberal Citizenship and Feminist' Expanded Notion of Politics. *Wagadu* 1: 1–7.

Mitchell, T. 2006 [1999]. Society, Economy, and the State Effect. In A. Sharma and A. Gupta (eds) *The Anthropology of the State: A Reader*. Malden, MA: Blackwell, pp. 168–186.

Moghadam, V. 2005. *Globalizing Women: Transnational Feminist Networks*. Baltimore, MD: Johns Hopkins University Press.

Moraña, M. 2008. Negotiating the Local: The Latin American 'Pink Tide', or What's Left for the Left? *Canadian Journal of Latin American and Caribbean Studies* 33(66): 31–41.

Moya, J. 2002. Italians in Buenos Aires' Anarchist Movement: Gender Ideology and Women's Participation, 1890–1910. In D.R. Gabaccia (ed.) *Women, Gender and Transnational Lives: Italian Workers of the World*. Toronto: University of Toronto Press.

Naples, N. 2003. *Feminism and Method: Ethnography, Discourse Analysis, and Activist Research*. London: Routledge.

Nelson, L. 2003. Decentering the Movement: Collective Action, Place, and the 'Sedimentation' of Radical Political Discourses. *Environment and Planning D: Society and Space* 21: 559–581.

Oakley, A. 1981. Interviewing Women: A Contradiction in Terms? In H. Roberts (ed.) *Doing Feminist Research*. London: Routledge and Kegan Paul, pp. 30–61.

Oliveira, E. Vládia. 2006. Promotora sugere fechamento de bares e lei seca. *Jornal de Hoje* 21 March.

Ondetti, G. 2006. Repression, Opportunity, and Protest: Explaining the Takeoff of Brazil's Landless Movement. *Latin American Politics and Society* 48(2): 61–94.

O POTI–Diário de Natal. 2006. Todos contra o sexo-turismo. *O POTI–Diário de Natal* 31 December.

Osterweil, M. 2004. De-centering the Forum: Is Another Critique of the Forum Possible? In J. Sen, A. Anand, A. Escobar and P. Waterman (eds) *World Social Forum: Challenging Empires*. New Delhi: Viveka Foundation, pp. 183–190.

Ostrom, E. 1990. *Governing the Commons: The Evolution of Institutions for Collective Action*. Cambridge: Cambridge University Press.

Oxhorn, P. 1995. *Organizing Civil Society*. University Park: Pennsylvania State University Press.

Oxhorn, P. 2009. Citizenship as Consumption or Citizenship as Agency? The Challenge for Civil Society in Latin America. Paper prepared for presentation at the annual meeting of the American Political Science Association, Toronto.

Paine, R. (eds) 1985. *Advocacy and Anthropology: First Encounters*. St John's: Memorial University, ISER.

Pfeiffer, J., Gloyd, S. and Ramirez Li, L. 2001. Intrahousehold resource allocation and child growth in Mozambique: an ethnographic case-control study. *Social Sciences & Medicine* 53: 83–97.

Pheterson G. 1993. The Whore Stigma: Female Desire and Male Unworthiness. *Social Text* 37: 39–64.

Phillips, A. 1996. Dealing with Difference: A Politics of Ideas, or a Politics of Presence? In S. Benhabib (ed.) *Democracy and Difference: Contesting the Boundaries of the Political*. Princeton, NJ: Princeton University Press, pp. 139–152.

Phillips, L. 1995. Difference, Indifference and Making a Difference: Reflexivity in the Time of Cholera. In S. Cole and L. Phillips (eds) *Ethnographic Feminisms: Essays in Anthropology*. Montreal: Carleton/McGill Queen's University Press, pp. 21–36.

Phillips, L. 1996. Toward Postcolonial Methodologies. In P. Ghorayshi and C. Belanger (eds) *Women, Work and Gender Relations in Developing Countries: A Global Perspective*. Westport, CT: Greenwood Press, pp. 15–29.

Phillips, L. 2004. Health Moralities in the Tropics: Ethics and the Other. In B. Gabriel and S. Ilcan (eds) *Postmodernism and the Ethical Subject*, Montreal: McGill-Queen's University Press, pp. 254–270.

Phillips, L. 2011. Eating Cars: Food, Pedagogy, and Politics in a City 'in Crisis'. Paper presented at the Canadian Anthropology Society/Societé Canadienne d'Anthropologie Annual Meetings. Fredericton, NB, 11 May.

Phillips, L. and Cole, S. 2009. Feminist Flows, Feminist Fault Lines: Women's Machineries and Women's Movements in Latin America. *Signs*, 35(1): 185–210.

Pinto, C. 2007. Brazil's National Conferences: A 'Medium-range' Public? Paper presented at the Latin American Studies Association (LASA) Conference, Montreal, 5–8 September.

Piscitelli, A. 1996. 'Sexo tropical': comentários sobre gênero e 'raça' em alguns textos da mídia Brasileira. *Cadernos Pagu* 6–7: 9–34.

Piscitelli, A. 2004a. Entre a praia de Iracema e a União Européia: turismo sexual internacional e migração feminina. In A. Piscitelli, M.F. Gregori and S. Carrara (eds) *Sexualidade e saberes: convenções e fronteiras*. Rio de Janeiro: Garamond, pp. 283–318.

Piscitelli, A. 2004b. On 'Gringos' and 'Natives': Gender and Sexuality in the Context of International Sex Tourism. *Vibrant – Virtual Brazilian Anthropology* 1: 87–114.

Piscitelli, A. 2007. Shifting Boundaries: Sex and Money in the North-east of Brazil. *Sexualities* 10: 489–500.

Prieto, M. 2004. *Liberalismo y temor: imaginado de los sujetos indígenas en Ecuador poscolonial, 1895–1950*. Quito: Abya Yala/FLACSO.

Pruth, C. 2007. Sun, Sea, Sex and Swedes: A Study of Campaigns to Prevent Sex Tourism in Natal/Brazil and Stockholm/Sweden. MA Thesis, School of Arts and Communication, Malmö University.

Rabinow, P. and Marcus, G., with Faubion, J. and Rees, T. 2008. *Designs for an Anthropology of the Contemporary*. Durham, NC: Duke University Press.

Radcliffe, S. and Westwood, S. 1996. *Remaking the Nation: Place, Identity and Politics in Latin America*. London: Routledge.

Radice, M, Canning, T. and Robbins, T. 2011. Urban Libraries as Public Space and Public Sphere. Paper presented at the Canadian Anthropology Society Association/ Société Canadienne d'Anthropologie Annual meetings, Fredericton, NB, 11 May.

Rakowski, C. and Espina, G. 2006. Institucionalización de la lucha feminista/ femenina en Venezuela: solidaridad y fragmentación, opportunidades y desafíos. In N. Lebon and E. Maier (eds) *De lo privado a lo público: 30 años de lucha ciudadana de las mujeres en América Latina.* Mexico: Siglo XXI/UNIFEM/LASA.

Rappaport, J. 2005. *Intercultural Utopias: Public Intellectuals, Cultural Experimentation, and Ethnic Dialogue in Colombia.* Durham, NC: Duke University Press.

Rappaport, J. 2007. Anthropological Collaborations in Colombia. In L. Field and R. Fox (eds) *Anthropology Put to Work.* New York: Berg, pp. 21–43.

Rebhun, L.A. 1999. *The Heart is Unknown Country: Love in the Changing Economy of Northeast Brazil.* Stanford, CA: Stanford University Press.

Régis, A. 2006. Sexo-turismo é debatido em audiência pública. *Tribuna do Norte,* 15 March. Available at: http://www.tribunadonorte.com.br/noticia/sexo-turismo-e-debatido-em-audiencia-publica/4632 (accessed August 2010).

Resposta. 2012. Code of Conduct for the Tourism Industry against Sexual Exploitation of Children. Available at: http://www.resposta.org.br (accessed August 2012).

Ribeiro, F.B. and Sacramento, O. 2006. A ilusão da conquista: sexo, amor e interesse entre gringos e garotas em Natal. *Cronos* 7(1): 161–172.

Robertson, L. and Culhane, D. (eds) 2005. *In Plain Sight: Reflections on Life in Downtown Eastside Vancouver.* Vancouver: Talonbooks.

Rodgers, D. 2007. Subverting the Spaces of Invitation? Local Politics and Participatory Budgeting in Post-crisis Buenos Aires. In A. Cornwall and V.S. Coelho (eds) *Spaces for Change? The Politics of Citizen Participation in New Democratic Arenas.* London: Zed, pp. 180–201.

Rohter, L. 2006. She Who Controls Her Body Can Upset Her Countrymen. *New York Times,* 27 April. Accessed August 28, 2010 http://www.nytimes.com/2006/04/27/world/americas/27letter.html (accessed May 2006).

Rosero Garcés, R., Vela, M. P. and Reyes Ávila, A. 2000. *De las demandas a los derechos: las mujeres in la Constitución de 1998.* Quito: Foro Nacional Permanente de la Mujer Ecuatoriana, CONAMU y Embajada Real de los Países Bajos.

Rudra, N. 2008. *Globalization and the Race to the Bottom in Developing Countries.* Cambridge: Cambridge University Press.

Ruiz, M.C. 2000. The Constitutional Amendments: Visions of the Protagonists. In M. Leon (ed.) *Sexual and Reproductive Rights: Constitutional Achievements and Prospects in Ecuador.* Quito: FEDAEPS and IEE.

Ryan, M. 1998. *Civic Wars: Democracy and Public Life in the American City during the Nineteenth Century.* Berkeley: University of California Press.

Rysman, A. 1977. How the 'Gossip' Became a Woman. *Journal of Communication* 27: 176–180.

Sánchez, S. de Castro. 2008. *Más allá de la insurrección: crónica de un movimiento de movimientos (2006–2007).* Spain: Ediciones ¡Basta!

Sanford, V. and Angel-Ajani, A. (eds) 2008. *Engaged Observer: Anthropology, Advocacy, and Activism.* New Brunswick, NJ: Rutgers University Press.

Satterfield, T. 2009. Reflections on Chasing the Elusive: Hope, Intention and Disruption in the Anticipation of Social Response to Nanotechnologies. Paper presented at the American Anthropological Association meetings, Philadelphia, 4 December.

Scheper-Hughes, N. and Bourgois, P. (eds) 2004. *Violence in War and Peace: An Anthology*. Malden, MA: Wiley-Blackwell.

Schild, V. 2002. Engendering the New Social Citizenship in Chile: NGOs and Social Provisioning under Neoliberalism. In M. Molyneux and S. Razavi (eds) *Gender Justice, Development and Rights*. Oxford: Oxford University Press.

Schirmer, J. 2009. Habits of Mind, Deliberative Democracy, and Peace: *Conversatorios* among Military Officers, Civil Society and Ex-guerrilleros in Colombia. In J. Paley, (ed.) *Democracy: Anthropological Approaches*. Santa Fe: School for Advanced Research, pp. 219–230.

Scott, J. 2009. *The Art of Not Being Governed: An Anarchist History of Upland Southeast Asia*. New Haven, CT: Yale University Press.

Segato, R.L. 2010. Territory, Sovereignty, and Crimes of the Second State. In L. Fregoso and C. Bejarno (eds) *Terrorizing Women: Feminicide in the Américas*. Durham, NC: Duke University Press, pp. 70–92.

Sharma, A. and Gupta, A. 2006. Introduction: Rethinking Theories of the State in an Age of Globalization. In A. Sharma and A. Gupta (eds) *The Anthropology of the State: A Reader*. Malden, MA: Blackwell, pp. 1–41.

Sheller, M. and Urry, J. 2003. Mobile Transformations of 'Public' and 'Private' Life. *Theory, Culture & Society* 20(3): 107–125.

Silber, I.C. 2008. It's a Hard Place to be a Revolutionary Woman: Finding Peace and Justice in Postwar El Salvador. In V. Sanford and A. Angel-Ajani (eds) *Engaged Observer: Anthropology, Advocacy, and Activism*. New Brunswick, NJ: Rutgers University Press, pp. 189–210.

Silva, N. 2004. *Aloha Betrayed: Native Hawaiian Resistance to American Colonialism*. Durham, NC: Duke University Press.

Smith, T.L. 1999. *Decolonizing Methodologies: Research and Indigenous Peoples*. Dunedin, NZ: University of Otago Press.

Smith-Nonini, S. 2009. Inventing a Public Anthropology with Latino Farm Labor Organizers in North Carolina. *NAPA Bulletin* 31: 114–128.

Sousa Filho, A. de. 2005 Atraso e Provincianismo. *Diário de Natal*, 25 September: 14.

Sousa Santos, B. de. 2006. *The Rise of the Global Left: The World Social Forum and beyond*. London: Zed.

Souza, L. de. 2007. Em ação 'as garotas de Ponta Negra'. *Correio da Tarde*, April 13: 12.

Speed, S. 2006. At the Crossroads of Human Rights and Anthropology: Toward a Critically Engaged Activist Research. *American Anthropologist* 108(1): 66–76.

Spronk, S. 2008. Pink Tide? Neoliberalism and its Alternatives in Latin America. *Canadian Journal of Latin American and Caribbean Studies* 33(65): 173–186.

Stephen, L. 2005. *Zapotec Women: Gender, Class and Ethnicity in Globalized Oaxaca*, 2nd edn. Durham, NC: Duke University Press.

Stephen, L. 2007. 'We Are Brown, We Are Short, We Are Fat ... We Are the Face of Oaxaca': Women Leaders in the Oaxaca Rebellion. *Socialism and Democracy* 21(2): 97–112.

Strathern, M. 2004. *Partial Connections*. New York: Altamira.

Sundar, N. 2007. The Dilemmas of 'Working' Anthropology in 21st-century India. In L. Field and R. Fox (eds) *Anthropology Put to Work*. New York: Berg, pp. 181–199.

Taussig, M. 1992 [1989]. *The Nervous System*. London: Routledge.

Tedlock, B. 2007. The Observation of Participation and the Emergence of Public Ethnography. In N. Denzin and Y. Lincoln (eds) *Qualitative Research*. London: Sage, pp. 151–171.

Teixeira, A. Brazão and Batista, J. 2002. Itinerários do prazer: sexismo e publicidade turística em Natal. Coletivo Leila Diniz: Natal. Available at: http://www.rizoma. ufsc.br/pdfs/1041–of1-st1.pdf (accessed October 2007).

Thayer, M. 2010. *Making Transnational Feminism: Rural Women, NGO activists and Northern Donors in Brazil*. London: Routledge.

Tornquist, C. and Resende Fleischer, S. 2012. Sobre a Marcha Mundial das Mulheres: entrevista com Nalu Faria. *Estudos Feministas* 20(1): 291–312.

Tribuna do Norte. 2006a. Campanha publicitária está pronta. *Tribuna do Norte*, 27 April. Available at: http://www.tribunadonorte.com.br/noticia/campanha-publicitaria-esta-pronta/8368 (accessed April 2009).

Tribuna do Norte. 2006b. PF prepara nova operacao contra turismo sexual no estado. *Tribuna do Norte*, 4 April. Available at: http://www.tribunadonorte. com.br/noticia/pf-prepara-nova-operacao-contra-turismo-sexual-no-estado/6541 (accessed August 2010).

Trigueiro, G. 2005. Ame Ponta Negra vai lutar por um novo bairro. *Diário de Natal*. 18 November: 2.

Trinh, M. 1992. *Framer Framed*. New York: Routledge.

Tsing, A.L. 2005. *Friction: An Ethnography of Global Connections*. Princeton, NJ: Princeton University Press.

Turcato, D. 2007. Italian Anarchism as a Transnational Movement, 1885–1915. *Internationaal Instituut voor Sociale Geschiedenis* 52: 407–444.

Twine, F.W. 1997. *Racism in a Racial Democracy: The Maintenance of White Supremacy in Brazil*. New Brunswick, NJ: Rutgers University Press.

UNIFEM. 2002. *Gender Budget Initiatives: Strategies, Concepts and Experiences*. New York: UNIFEM.

UNIFEM. 2004. *Toward Transparency and Governance with Equity: Gender-sensitive Budgets in the Andean Region*. Quito: UNIFEM-Andean Region.

Valenzuela, A. 2004. Latin American Presidencies Interrupted. *Journal of Democracy* 15(4): 5–19.

Van Esterik, P. 1989. *Beyond the Breast–Bottle Controversy*. New Brunswick, NJ: Rutgers University Press.

Vásquez, V.R. Martínez. 2007. *Autoritarismo, movimiento popular y crisis política: Oaxaca 2006*. Oaxaca: Diálogo.

Walby, S. 2002. Feminism in a Global Era. *Economy and Society* 31(4): 533–557.

Waldram, J. 2010. Engaging Engagement: Critical Reflections on a Canadian Tradition. *Anthropologica* 52(2): 225–232.

Warner, M. 2002. *Publics and Counterpublics*. New York: Zone Books.

Warren, K. 2007. Perils and Promises of Engaged Anthropology: Historical Transitions and Ethnographic Dilemmas. In V. Sanford and A. Angel-Ajani (eds) *Engaged Observer: Anthropology, Advocacy, and Activism*. New Brunswick, NJ: Rutgers University Press, pp. 213–227.

Watson, P. 1997. Civil Society and the Politics of Difference in Eastern Europe. In J. Scott, C. Kaplan and D. Keates (eds) *Transitions, Environments, Translations: Feminisms in International Politics*. New York: Routledge, pp. 21–29.

Wells, S. 2010. *Our Bodies, Ourselves and the Work of Writing*. Stanford, CA: Stanford University Press.

Williams, E.L. 2010. *Anxious Pleasures: Race and the Sexual Economies of Transnational Tourism in Salvador, Brazil.* PhD Thesis, Department of Anthropology, Stanford University.

Wilson, S. 2008. *Research is Ceremony: Indigenous Research Methods.* Winnipeg: Fernwood Publishing.

Wolf, D. 1992. *Factory Daughters: Gender, Household Dynamics and Rural Industrialization in Java.* Berkeley: University of California Press.

Wolford, W. 2010. *This Land is Ours Now: Social Mobilization and the Meanings of Land in Brazil.* Durham, NC: Duke University Press.

Wright, M. 2010. Paradoxes, Protests, and the Mujeres de Negro of Northern Mexico. In L. Fregoso and C. Bejarno (eds) *Terrorizing Women: Feminicide in the Américas.* Durham, NC: Duke University Press, pp. 312–330.

Young, I. 1996. Communication and the Other: Beyond Deliberative Democracy. In S. Benhabib (ed.) *Democracy and Difference: Contesting the Boundaries of the Political.* Princeton, NJ: Princeton University Press.

Young, K., Wolkowitz, C. and McCullagh, R. (eds) 1981. *Of Marriage and the Market: Women's Subordination in International Perspective.* London: CSE Books.

Zamosc, L. 2007. The Indian Movement in Ecuador. *Latin American Politics and Society* 49(3): 1–34.

Index